Barry Farm-Hillsdale
in *Anacostia*

A Historic African American Community

ALCIONE M. AMOS

THE
History
PRESS

Published by The History Press
Charleston, SC
www.historypress.com

Copyright © 2021 by the Smithsonian Institution

First published 2021

Manufactured in the United States

ISBN 9781467147699

Library of Congress Control Number: 2020944168

I dedicate this book to my son, Sandy M. Amos,
who always makes me feel like I can do anything!

Contents

CONTENTS

Foreword

I began to research and work on physical historic preservation of Black settlements in 1975. The story of Barry Farm came to my attention in 1980 while conducting archival research in the National Archives and field investigations in the Washington, D.C., area. I had the opportunity to visit both the Freedmen's Village and Barry Farm–Hillsdale sites firsthand. Over the years, I often referenced these communities as nationally significant examples—unique not simply because they were inhabited by African Americans, but because of the federal involvement in planning and implementation, as well as the ways they were used as models for the rest of America. I believe that Barry Farm–Hillsdale is especially unique because of the amount of physical, cultural and human content that remains.

Postbellum African American settlements served many roles as former slaves moved into lives as free Americans. The communities became the sources and incubators of some of America's most authentic history and culture. They provided opportunities for Blacks to own, work and govern land. The settlements developed in a variety of forms, ranging from urban neighborhood enclaves to separate autonomous Black towns. Others were centers of education and agricultural markets, and some even functioned as resorts.

Despite the cultural and physical significance of Black settlements, scholarly research has generally been narrowly focused over the years. Black communities have been severely underrepresented, oversimplified and marginalized in almost every discipline. There are relatively few historians who engage fine-grained research of historic African American places and landmarks. I met Alcione Amos in 2017 when I was invited to deliver presentations of my Black Settlements in America™ work at the Smithsonian Anacostia Museum and Dumbarton Oaks Landscape Fellows Program. I was immediately impressed with her depth and compassionate interpretation as she spread some of her research documents across tables in the museum. Alcione Amos's book shows the results of patient research and broad-based interpretation of the origins and evolution of Barry Farm–Hillsdale over a century in time.

Ms. Amos's methodology uses a variety of sources, including oral history, photographs, private collection documents, municipal records, federal records, military records and print media. The use of multiple sources produces more detail about the multidimensional relationships between people, places and events in the community. The interdisciplinary approach allows Ms. Amos to easily address multiethnic presence and participation in community life. The broad range of cultural research is extremely helpful in understanding the human layers and complexities of a community that existed in the shadow of the national capital. Ms. Amos includes an extensive community genealogy as well as individual and family relationships in her research process and interpretations. The inclusion of genealogical details and information provides an excellent base for cross-reference research to extended families and other geographic locations.

The roles of women add dimensions that are marginalized too often. Examples of women-owned business such as beauty shops, dressmakers and merchants expand the story. Exposure of women's suffrage and the campaign for voting rights adds important civic dimensions to life in Barry Farm–Hillsdale. The role of religion is presented in a way that is more extensive than usual when studying Black communities. The accounts of churches include the names of ministers, names of leading congregants and specific incidents of community service. Other denominations—such as Black Catholics, Methodists and Episcopalians—are also noted. Examination of the diverse composition of the residents helps us understand the complexity and rich qualities of life and culture.

A contextual account of the evolution of the region is provided from the time of native occupation, which illuminates the cross-cultural and vernacular physical form of the community. Ms. Amos provides examples of physical environmental issues, such as flooding events and property layout across hilly terrain. By including natural features, she helps us understand the effects of landscape that are unique to this particular site. Her reference to architectural landmarks makes it clear that Black communities had many types of physical dimensions.

The book provides authentic, and tangible, documentation of the pervasive, persistent and perennial challenges of survival of Black communities. The wide-ranging impacts and contradictions of segregation are discussed. Struggles with physical, political and economic isolation are described through multiple examples. Long-term efforts by organizations, such as the Barry Farm Civic Association, to acquire basic utility infrastructure and municipal services are carefully presented. Even the absence of reliable mail delivery is noted. The latter sections of the community history describe the dramatic impacts of gentrification and displacement, which are still national problems. The initial promise of Black land wealth is contrasted with devastating loss through destructive development by outside speculators and taking of property by eminent domain. The description of the Macedonia Cemetery displacement is particularly moving and has currency relative to the 2019 federal African American Burial Grounds Network Act.

Alcione Amos has produced an exemplary account of one of America's signature Black settlements. Her research will inspire others to take on much-needed study of other Black settlements. This book and case study serve as both academic and practical models for community history and preservation. Ms. Amos clearly reaches her goals to honor the Barry Farm community pride and tell an entire community history.

EVERETT L. FLY
Landscape Architect, FASLA
2014 National Humanities Medalist
San Antonio, Texas
February 15, 2020

Preface

I conceived the idea of writing the history of Barry Farm–Hillsdale when I curated the exhibit "How the Civil War Changed Washington" in 2015. I knew about the existence of the community, but I had not grasped at its significance. In doing the research for the Civil War exhibit, I had the chance to learn about the waves of African American refugees coming into Washington, D.C., during the Civil War. Between forty thousand and fifty thousand of them came into Washington, D.C., fleeing slavery. After the war, they were mostly housed in dilapidated government-created "barracks" or in shacks they had built of discarded materials. I then understood the importance of the creation of the settlement. To have come out of bondage and to have the chance to buy land and build their houses was eagerly grasped by the new arrivals. From that moment on, the idea of writing this book seized my imagination.

A further incentive to do the research and publish this amazing story was the existence of several collections of oral histories and videos that were compiled in the 1970s, 1980s, 1990s and early 2000s. The Smithsonian Anacostia Community Museum Archives holds a collection of oral histories done in the early 1970s with octogenarians and septuagenarians who had been born and lived their lives at the end of the nineteenth century and the beginning of the twentieth century. They had observed the community, heard stories told by their elders and also lived through the changes, many of them negative, that had happened over the decades in the twentieth century. In 1989, the Neighborhood Oral History Project interviewed other residents of Barry Farm–Hillsdale who also told their stories and added to the trove of information from the oral histories of the 1970s. This material is housed at the Historical Society of Washington, D.C. Finally, in 2002, community historian Dianne Dale interviewed ten residents of Barry Farm–Hillsdale and Anacostia as part of the Mark the Place project. Transcriptions of these interviews are also housed in the Dale/Patterson family collection at the Anacostia Community Museum Archives.

The information from the oral histories was complemented by the records of the Freedmen's Bureau, the colloquial name of the Bureau of Refugees, Freedmen, and Abandoned Lands office of Washington, D.C., conveniently posted online by Familysearch.org in conjunction with the Smithsonian Museum of African American History and Culture. I also used genealogical databases online such as Ancestry.com, Familysearch.org and Fold3, as well as online newspaper databases. Other documentation came from the National Archives and Records Administration. This allowed for the collection of an extensive body of research materials that made it possible to reconstruct the history of this postbellum African American community in detail.

I decided to write the history of the community for its first one hundred years, from 1867 to 1970, because that was a period when it still had an identity separate from that of the wider area now known as Anacostia. By the 1970s, with the advent of desegregation (but not integration, as one of the interviewees I quote in the book stated) and the so-called White Flight to the suburbs, boundaries between White Anacostia and African American Barry Farm–Hillsdale were gone, and the whole area quickly became majority African American.

This work would not have been written if not for all the incentive I received at the Smithsonian Institution. I am particularly grateful to the late Portia James, my first boss and mentor, who agreed that this idea was excellent and gave me support to conceptualize it. Her loss in December of 2015 was a significant blow and setback. I am thankful to Sharon Reickens, former assistant director at the museum, who told me that this was a history that had to be written as it pertained to the very community in which the museum had been created more than fifty years ago. Sharon also obtained financial support for the task and was always willing to give moral support when I needed it. Lori Yarrish, the director of the museum for a short period before her untimely passing, enthusiastically agreed that this was a good idea and gave me the go-ahead. Samir Meghelli, my supervisor in later years, gave me invaluable support and spent hours revising the manuscript and discussing its content with me. I am very appreciative of his help. Melanie

Adams, who came to the museum as director in 2019, also gave me support for this project. My interns—Al Vanegas, Sarah Clarkson, Anjelyque Easley and Amanda Hergenrather—are also to be thanked and commended for all the work they did finding material for me. Trish Savage, who collaborated with me in a related project, volunteered to do research for the book and also provided the very important photograph of the last existing original house of Barry Farm–Hillsdale. Located on Elvans Road, this historic house was demolished in 2009.

Overall, I have to thank the Smithsonian Anacostia Community Museum. The opportunity to work there, the support received for my projects and the ready access to its historical collections are what made this book possible.

PART I

History of Place

Chapter 1

Mrs. Barry's Farm

T he St. Elizabeths tract, the area where the postbellum settlement of
Barry Farm was built in the nineteenth century, was ancient land once
occupied by the Nacotchtank indigenous people, who lived in villages
and towns along the Eastern Branch. The river was later renamed Anacostia
River (a corruption of the name of the original native inhabitants).
European explorers first contacted them in the early 1600s. At that point,
their villages stretched from Giesborough Point, today within the Joint Base
Anacostia-Bolling, to a place near Bladensburg, Maryland. By the end of the
seventeenth century, the Nacotchtanks had lost most of their holdings and
were forced to move away from the shores of the river.[1]

Captain Henry Fleet, an early European visitor to the area, wrote in
glowing terms about the Anacostia area, which he visited in June 1632:

> *This place without all question is the most pleasant and healthful place
> in all this country, and most convenient for habitation, the air temperate
> in summer and not violent in winter. It aboundeth with all manner of
> fish. The Indians in one night commonly will catch thirty sturgeons in a
> place where the river is not above twelve fathom broad. And as for deer,
> buffaloes, bears, turkeys, the woods do swarm with them, and the soil is
> exceedingly fertile.[2]*

By 1663, the St. Elizabeths tract had been patented and was owned by
John Charman, who arrived in Maryland in 1648. A century and a half

Archaeological artifacts excavated in the early 1980s from the Howard Road area, before the building of the Anacostia Metro Station. The uncovered artifacts identified the site as being a prehistoric habitation area as well as a workshop to produce lithic tools. *Courtesy Anacostia Community Museum, Smithsonian Institution.*

later, in 1802, after passing through many hands, the land belonged to Stanislaus Hoxton, who sold it to James Barry on January 2.[3] James Barry and his wife, Joanna, who were originally from Ireland, came from Lisbon, Portugal, to Baltimore, Maryland, in 1793. In Baltimore, he was a merchant, a director of the Baltimore Office of Discount and Deposits and a consular representative for Portugal. In 1806, he moved to Washington, where he again exercised the office of director at the local Office of Discount and Deposits. These were the local offices of the Bank of the United States. His new property, on the shore of the Eastern Branch, was described by a nineteenth-century visitor, who had explored the land as a child, as full of "stately trees…luxuriant laurel…[and a] rippling stream." So, two centuries after Captain Henry Fleet described the beauty and abundance existing in the area that would become known as Anacostia, there were still some remnants of it.[4]

James Barry passed away on January 9, 1808. He was deeply indebted, and his property was sold to pay these debts. Eventually, the north half of the tract was purchased by James David Barry, a nephew of James Barry, who built a mansion on Poplar Point. The south portion of the

James Barry came from Ireland in 1793. He brought the St. Elizabeths tract in 1802.
Upon his death in 1808, the land was sold to pay his debts. In 1867, the African American
settlement of Barry Farm was built on that property. *James Barry, Gilbert Stuart, American,
1755–1828, oil on canvas, 28¾ x 24 in., frame: 39¾ x 35¹/₁₆ x 4⁷/₁₆ in. Bequest of Aileen Osborn
Webb (Mrs. Vanderbilt Webb) y1979–52. Courtesy Princeton University Art Museum.*

property, which was then owned by Thomas Blagden, was sold in 1852 to
the U.S. government for the creation of a mental hospital, the Government
Hospital for the Insane. The hospital's name was changed to St. Elizabeths
Hospital in 1916.[5]

James David Barry and his wife, Juliana, owned enslaved people. In 1840,
they owned eight people under bondage, and possibly some of them worked

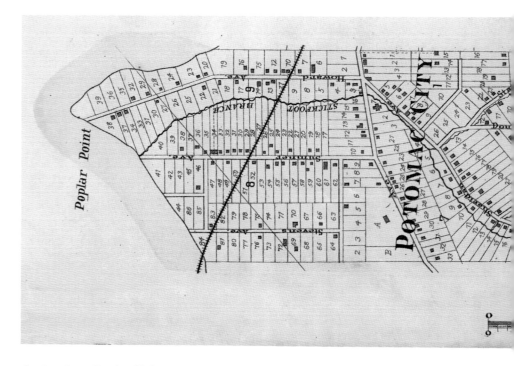

the land on Poplar Point around their residence. Barry died on August 15, 1849, leaving Juliana and four children. The 1850 Census lists Juliana as the owner of five enslaved people. In 1862, she received compensation for— and gave freedom to—three enslaved people under the District of Columbia Emancipation Act.[6]

Five years later, the April 26, 1867 edition of the *Evening Star* reported that Mrs. Juliana Barry sold to John R. Elvans "the large farm…adjoining the insane Asylum, and next to Uniontown, 375 acres," for $52,000. Elvans, a Washington, D.C., entrepreneur, was buying the property in trust for General O.O. Howard, commissioner of the Freedmen's Bureau. The land was going to be divided into lots to be sold to the African American refugees who had poured into Washington, D.C., during the Civil War. According to the news piece, using the condescending tone of the time, the lots were to be sold "to deserving freedmen…in order to test the capability of colored farmers to be self-sustaining, when offered the incentive of ultimate land-ownership." Thus began the creation of Barry Farm, a nineteenth-century settlement for newly freed African Americans.

From early on, the community's given name caused discomfort among the newly freed settlers because the Barry family had owned enslaved people.

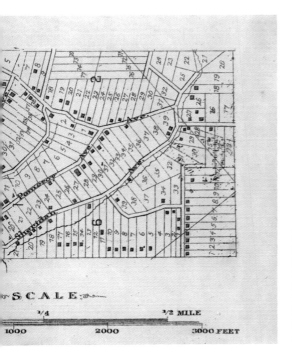

Map of Potomac City, from the *Atlas of Fifteen Miles around Washington, Including the County of Montgomery, Maryland,* 1879. This is the only map in which the name "Potomac City" appears. In 1867, residents of Barry Farm asked for the area to be known as Potomac City. *Courtesy Geography and Map Division, Library of Congress.*

In December 1867, the agent of the bureau in charge of Barry Farm, J.B. Johnson, reported, "The inhabitants are anxious to have the settlement called Potomac City." Indeed, an early map of the area used that name.[7]

In 1873, at the request of prominent residents of the settlement, including Solomon G. Brown, the District of Columbia Legislative Assembly approved on June 5 an official act to change the name to Hillsdale, for the many hills and dales in the area. Interestingly enough, the new name was not officially adopted and never appeared on the official maps of the area. Even to this day, the name Barry Farm is still used. Deeds issued to house buyers in the area give Barry Farm as the location. Because of this complex history, we have chosen to refer to the settlement as "Barry Farm–Hillsdale" in this work.[8]

PART II

The First Decades

Chapter 2

The Creation of a Nineteenth-Century African American Community

Between forty thousand and fifty thousand African American refugees came to Washington during the Civil War. As the Union army swept into Virginia, the enslaved people immediately took off in the direction of Washington using any means they could—walking, riding horses and piling into carts taken from the plantations where they had been enslaved. From the Maryland side, enslaved people also took to the roads to reach Washington. They were destitute when they arrived, and while some had connections around the city, the majority of them had to settle first on the streets and later in temporary housing built from discarded materials.[1]

Even before the refugees could try to settle somewhere, they were being thrown into jail by the authorities who were grappling with what to do with them. The *Evening Star* edition of June 1, 1861, informed that seventy-one African American refugees who came from Virginia and Maryland were sent to the public jail during the previous month. Sixty-four had already been returned to their owners. When asked why they were coming to Washington, the refugees answered, "They thought they would be free if they could get into Washington." The jail, in this case, was a filthy construction in the lot where today the pristine Supreme Court building stands on Capitol Hill. It was dubbed the "Black Hole of Washington"—not because some of the inmates were fugitive slaves but because of the horrible conditions prevalent on the premises.[2]

General O.O. Howard, in his autobiography written in 1907, explained how he decided to set apart in April 1867 a sum of money to deal with the

Makeshift housing settlement occupied by African Americans in Washington, D.C., after the Civil War, date unknown. *Courtesy General Photograph Collection, Historical Society of Washington, D.C. (CHS 07363).*

housing problems facing the post–Civil War African American community in Washington, D.C. Earlier, he had been face to face with the conditions in which the refugee African Americans were living in Washington, D.C. He was approached by "one of the largest owners of land, or rather city lots, situated between Fourteenth and Seventeenth streets and north of K Street" in downtown Washington; this land had been requisitioned by the federal government during the Civil War to build temporary military structures. These structures, once abandoned by the army, were now occupied by African Americans. Some of them were already cultivating small gardens on vacant lots. The owner wanted these squatters removed from his land, by then worth a considerable amount of money.[3]

General Howard decided to take a carriage ride to the settlement to take stock of the situation. There he told an assembled group of men that they could not stay on land that was not theirs. They responded, according to the general, "very pertinently…'Where shall we go, and what shall we do?'" Howard retorted with a question of his own: "What would make you self-supporting?" He heard an almost unanimous answer: "Land! Give us Land!"

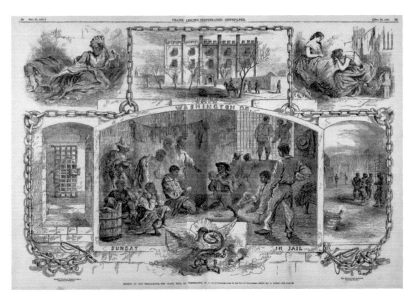

The District of Columbia jail, 1861. Located on Capitol Hill where today is the Supreme Court, the building of the District of Columbia jail was called the "Black Hole of Washington" because of its precarious conditions. It served as a jail for fugitive African Americans coming to Washington at the beginning of the Civil War. *Illustration from* Frank Leslie's Illustrated Newspaper, *December 1861.*

General O.O. (Oliver Otis) Howard, 1860. General Howard conceived and implemented the idea of creating the settlement of Barry Farm to provide land for African American refugees in Washington, D.C., after the Civil War. *Courtesy Library of Congress, Prints and Photographs Division (LC-DIG-cwpb-06986).*

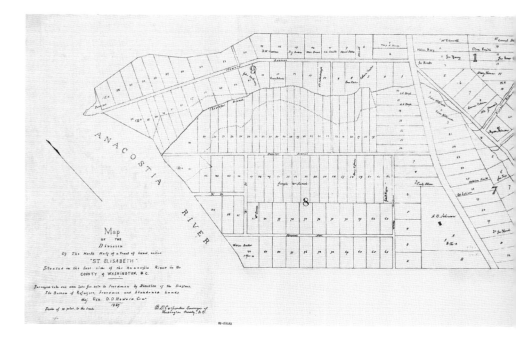

Thus began the idea of creating a settlement near Washington, D.C., that would make available for purchase by newly freed African Americans one-acre lots and enough lumber to build a small house.[4]

With $52,000 provided by the Freedmen's Bureau, 375 acres of land were acquired from the Barry family, across from the Eastern Branch, an area of Washington, D.C., then known as Washington County. The area was quickly surveyed into lots that "were taken with avidity" because the prospect of owning land was a significant opportunity for the newly freed African Americans. General Howard ended his narration of the creation of Barry Farm–Hillsdale with the following statement: "Everyone who visited the Barry Farm and saw the new hopefulness with which most of the dwellers there were inspired, could not fail to regard the entire enterprise as judicious and beneficent."[5]

The area chosen by Howard was particularly hilly and cut by streams. Although the hills could be a challenge for the layout of the settlement, the streams were a boon because they provided readily available water for the settlers. Soon the District of Columbia surveyor, B.D. Carpenter, surveyed the land and produced a map. The map detailed 356 lots divided over nine sections, with the street grid laid out following the contours of the hilly landscape. The most significant body of water running through the

Original map of Barry Farm–Hillsdale, created in 1867 by surveyor B.D. Carpenter. Carpenter planned the streets, which were named avenues until 1873, when the denomination changed to road, according to the hilly terrain. Sheridan Avenue followed the course of Stickfoot Branch, a creek that flowed from east to west before its confluence with the Eastern Branch (Anacostia River.) *Courtesy Geography and Map Division, Library of Congress.*

neighborhood was Stickfoot Branch, which crossed the settlement from east to west until its confluence with the Eastern Branch of the Potomac River, later renamed the Anacostia River.

Nichols Avenue bisected the surveyed area. The road was an old route, perhaps first used by the native peoples who lived in the area and later as the principal artery connecting it to Piscataway in Southern Maryland. It once was known as "Asylum Avenue" because it ran past what was then called the Government Hospital for the Insane (or just the "Asylum"). Asylum Avenue was eventually renamed Nichols Avenue, after Charles H. Nichols, who served as superintendent of the hospital from 1855 to 1872.[6]

The first buyers put down their payments on June 27, 1867. Reverend Richard A. Hall was the first in line. He was pastor of Union Bethel Church at 1518 M Street NW. This church would later merge with Israel Bethel Church to form Metropolitan AME, which still stands today in that same M Street location. Reverend Hall was a man of means, with $5,000 in assets in 1870, and was the head of a large family with seven children. He bought lot 5, section 2 in Barry Farm–Hillsdale on Stanton Avenue with a down payment of $15. He did not reside there long since in 1880 he was already living and pastoring in Atlanta, Georgia.[7] That Reverend Hall was the first buyer fit well with General Howard's desire "to have a few among the purchasers who were reasonably educated, and of well-known good character and repute… encouraged such to settle alongside the more destitute."[8]

The second buyer was Reverend William H. Hunter. He also fit the profile of the kind of settler General Howard wanted to bring to Barry Farm–Hillsdale as good examples for the community. Born enslaved in Raleigh, North Carolina, on June 21, 1831, he became free at an early age when his father bought the family's freedom and moved them to Brooklyn, New York. Hunter attended elementary school in New York and went to Wilberforce University, where he studied for three years and was ordained an AME minister.[9]

Hunter enlisted as chaplain of the Fourth United States Colored Troop on October 1, 1863. He served in that capacity until May 4, 1866. Reverend Hunter was one of only fourteen African American chaplains to serve in the Civil War.[10] After being discharged from the army, he became pastor at the Israel Church in Washington,

Reverend William H. Hunter, circa 1916. Reverend Hunter was one of the first buyers of lots in Barry Farm–Hillsdale. He was the kind of settler General Howard wanted to attract to the new settlement. A Civil War chaplain and college graduate, Reverend Hunter was pastoring at an African American church in Washington, D.C., at the time he purchased his lot. *From* Centennial Encyclopaedia of the African Methodist Episcopal Church, *1916.*

D.C. The church had a large active congregation with a Sabbath School with an attendance of forty-five to fifty children and six teachers. It also offered a library with five hundred books for the use of the congregation. Later, he became the longtime editor of the *Christian Recorder*, the newspaper of the AME Church. He married his wife, Henrietta, in the 1870s.

Reverend Hunter served as a pastor in Wilmington, North Carolina, and Pittsburgh, Pennsylvania; for several years, he was in Boston, where he was in charge of the Book Concern of the AME Church, the publishing arm of the church. Then he returned to live in Barry Farm–Hillsdale, where he had extensive holdings off Morris Road and where he built a beautiful house. The house and the lands surrounding it were called Hunter's Heights. Reverend Hunter last pastored at St. Paul's AME Church in Washington, D.C. He died on October 16, 1908, and was buried at a cemetery in Barry Farm–Hillsdale. Eventually, his remains were transferred to Arlington

Cemetery and reburied along with those of his wife, Henrietta, who passed away on July 9, 1912.[11]

By December 1867, the Freedmen's Bureau had made available for sale lumber for the construction of more permanent dwellings; the settlers began the construction of small fourteen-by-twenty-four-foot houses, called "A-frame" because of the format of their roof, to replace the temporary housing. Although settlers could pay for the lots in installments for up to two years from the date of purchase, the lumber was paid in cash, and the sale had to be authorized by the bureau. Located at the junction of Sheridan Road and Nichols Avenue, the lumber yard was perhaps the very first business operating in Barry Farm–Hillsdale.[12]

Technical assistance and training were an integral part of the provisions made by the Freedmen's Bureau. The bureau hired skilled laborers to supervise the construction of the houses. Fred (Frederick) Smith was remembered as being the "boss carpenter" for the work. At least in the beginning, there were strict standards for the building of the houses. General Howard himself sent a letter to J.B. Johnson, the agent in charge of Barry Farm–Hillsdale, on October 7, 1867, complaining that Peter Williams's house, on lot 12, section 6 was "a disfigurement to the grounds" and that the problem had to be corrected. Howard's letter implies that he took the time to come to the settlement to inspect its development.[13]

Once the community was physically established, the means to build its social and economic fabric were also present. From the beginning, there were incentives and resources for community action. The community provided the funds to buy a lot where the first school was built and started operating in 1868, and the Freedmen's Bureau paid the workers to erect the structure and also provided the materials.[14]

The large one-acre lots in Barry Farm–Hillsdale offered significant economic advantage, such as the possibility of building additional houses

"A-frame" house built by William Fractious, a carpenter, on lot 7, section 4 of Barry Farm–Hillsdale. The original house is to the left. The addition on the right was built to house a bathroom and an extra bedroom after piped water and sewage arrived at Elvans Road in the 1940s. The Fractious family would occupy the house for several generations until it was abandoned and eventually dismantled around 2009. *Courtesy Anacostia Community Museum Archives, photo by Patricia Savage.*

to rent or to shelter family members who married and constituted their families. Ella Pearis, the descendant of first settler James Howard, told the story of how her family's large lot, fronting both Elvans and Sheridan Roads, was subdivided by her great-grandmother into six "to give each child enough to build…a home."[15]

Although Barry Farm–Hillsdale would maintain its rural character well into the twentieth century, the proximity to Washington, D.C., provided the opportunity to find employment for its inhabitants. The "Asylum" was a significant provider of jobs from the very beginning. In 1877, Esquire Harrod, one of the settlement's early residents, and another early resident, Isaac Diggs, worked there handling the horses. Henrietta Holliday and her future husband, Frank Luckett, also worked and lived at St. Elizabeths Hospital in 1880. She was a laundress, and he worked on the hospital's farm. The navy yard, Bolling Air Field and federal agencies provided jobs for residents of the community. In the twentieth century, women living in Barry Farm–Hillsdale worked as domestics at the houses of the White residents of nearby Uniontown and later took in washing and ironing for the officers at Bolling Air Field.[16]

The importance of Barry Farm–Hillsdale for its settlers was very well described by J.B. Johnson, the agent of the Freedmen's Bureau at the site, when he reported on the progress of the project on November 30, 1867: "Men who until within five years had not even owned their hands…now not only had in their possession an acre of land, [but had erected] houses they were to call their own."[17]

Chapter 3

New Beginnings for the Newly Freed People

W hile enslaved, African Americans had no right to enter into contracts, including the right to marry. After emancipation, the Civil Rights Act of 1866, enacted on April 9, established "That all persons born in the United States…and such citizens, of every race and color, without regard to any previous condition of slavery or involuntary servitude…shall have the same right, in every State and Territory in the United States, to make and enforce contracts." This law meant that the newly freed African Americans had the right to get married. Being able to marry was considered one of the most important rights coming out of emancipation. In many cases, marriage became the first civil right exercised by the formerly enslaved African Americans.[1]

On May 30, 1865, General Howard issued orders to his assistant commissioners setting up the conditions to regularize the marriages of formerly enslaved people under their jurisdiction. The District of Columbia Freedmen's Bureau was one of the field offices that established an office of the superintendent of marriages. Part of its duties was to explain to the newly freed people that an act of Congress dated July 25, 1866, stipulated that those living in Washington, D.C., who recognized each other as man and wife before the law were now legally married and their children legitimate. Additionally, they now could register their marriages with the bureau. In many cases, the registrations were sanctioning relationships that were longstanding and stable. Several of the early settlers took advantage of the opportunity provided by the Freedmen's Bureau to legalize their unions.[2]

One such case was that of Abraham Scott and Anne Jackson. Born around 1810, they had been together since 1837 in Prince George's County, Maryland. They had two children from their union. Thirty years later, in April 1867, Reverend M.V. Wright, the bureau's superintendent of marriages, sanctified their union. The couple bought a lot and built a house on Elvans Road in Barry Farm–Hillsdale. Their son John W. Scott, who was a laborer, purchased the lot next door. In 1870, Abraham, Anne and John were living together in the house that the father had built. By 1880, the elderly couple was still living on Elvans Road next to their son John, who had by then constituted a family and had three children. John had built his house since the households were listed separately by the census taker. John and his family were still living on the family homestead in 1920, more than sixty years after he and his parents had bought the property.[3]

One of the most poignant stories among those of early settlers of Barry Farm–Hillsdale was that of Edgar Banks and his wife, Melvinia (also spelled Melvina). The Bankses had been enslaved in Spotsylvania County, Virginia. In 1862, they fled to Washington in search of freedom as part of the African American refugees who fled to the capital city during the Civil War. The Banks family were fortunate in organizing a new life and obtaining land to farm in Maryland before acquiring a lot in Barry Farm–Hillsdale and building their house on Sumner Road. They had brought with them, out of slavery, two children, Amanda and Delia. After they had arrived in Washington, they had two more girls, Fanny and Melvinia, but all was not well.[4]

Edgar Banks asked on November 9, 1867, for the help to write what probably was the most important letter of his life up to that point. When the Banks family fled Spotsylvania County, they were missing their oldest daughter, Winnie. She had been taken to Kentucky at the young age of six by her master, John T. Seay, a wealthy farmer in Graves County. Banks stated, "I am very comfortably situated…and amply able to provide for my child." He then requested that the Freedmen's Bureau return his child to his care. The bureau immediately gave orders that agents in Kentucky find the girl and provide transportation for her to come to Washington. One can only imagine the happiness of the reunion. By 1870, Winnie was a sixteen-year-old teenager living with her family and attending school.[5]

Winnie went on to live a full life, getting married to a man named Jeremiah Lawrence and moving to Providence, Rhode Island, where she passed away on September 1, 1895. She was memorialized at a service at Macedonia Baptist Church in Barry Farm–Hillsdale, where her father had been a pastor, on September 5, 1895.[6]

Letter from Edgar Banks to Freedmen's Bureau, November 9, 1867. Mr. Banks asked for help to get his daughter Winnie back from Kentucky, where her master had taken her as a child. She was returned to her family and went on to live a full life. *Courtesy National Archives and Records Administration, Washington, D.C.*

An interesting characteristic of the settlement's early settlers was that forty-six women had purchased lots and built their houses at the new settlement by 1871. Some of them bought lots together or side by side with their husbands, but others were single women who decided to take a chance on a new life. One such case was that of Elizabeth Chase, a neighbor of the Scott family, whom we have mentioned before. Chase bought a corner lot facing both Elvans and Stanton Roads. She was a free African American who appeared under her mother, Caroline Chase, as a young child in the

1840 Census. In 1860, on the eve of the Civil War, Caroline, Elizabeth and two brothers in their twenties were still living in Ward 2. Caroline and Elizabeth worked as washerwomen, and the young men were laborers. Caroline had been able to acquire a personal estate of seventy-five dollars.[7]

Although Caroline and Elizabeth still appeared in the 1870 Census as residing in Ward 2, by then Elizabeth had already purchased the lumber to build her house in Barry Farm–Hillsdale on June 2, 1868. Perhaps Elizabeth did not have the means to build her house immediately and was still living with her mother in 1870. By 1873, Chase had moved to Barry Farm–Hillsdale and had opened an account with the Freedmen's Bureau Bank. She also had established a restaurant in Uniontown, the White neighborhood adjacent to Barry Farm–Hillsdale. Chase maintained this restaurant until at least 1884, when she was listed as a caterer operating out of her house on Elvans Avenue. Ever the entrepreneur, by 1887 she was running a "notions" store from her home.[8]

Besides being very industrious, Elizabeth Chase was also an early suffragette. In 1877, she and her mother, Caroline, signed a petition to Congress requesting that the "Honorable Body...adopt measures for so amending the Constitution as to prohibit the several States from Disfranchising [sic] United States Citizens on account of Sex." The petition drive was part of a countrywide movement spearheaded by the National Woman Suffrage Association led by Susan B. Anthony. Signed by eighteen men and fifteen women of Barry Farm–Hillsdale, the petition drive seemed to have been spearheaded by Frederick Douglass Jr., who was a resident of the settlement and whose signature was at the top. Solomon G. Brown, a neighbor of the Chase family on Elvans Road, was also one of the signers. It became part of a much larger petition that included ten thousand signatures collected all over the United States and was delivered to Congress later that year.[9]

Elizabeth Chase's life began to unravel around 1895, when her house caught fire and was destroyed. The newspaper report on the event stated that the house was vacant at the time, but still, it must have been a shock for Chase to lose the house she had built at the beginning of the establishment of the settlement. Nine years later, she was declared of "unsound mind" and was committed to St. Elizabeths Hospital for the Insane. Elizabeth Chase, by then in her mid-sixties, had dementia. She would remain an inmate at the hospital for eleven years, passing away on April 9, 1915.[10]

Another early female settler was Eliza Frye Spottswood. Born in Culpeper County, Virginia, around 1849, she came to Washington, D.C., most likely in the wave of African American refugees fleeing enslavement.

"Petition for Woman Suffrage." In 1877, Elizabeth Chase and her mother, Caroline, early settlers of Barry Farm–Hillsdale, signed this petition requesting an amendment to the Constitution to allow women to vote. *Courtesy National Archives and Records Administration, Washington, D.C.*

She bought a lot on Nichols Avenue with money provided by her father. He was a cobbler, and his owner allowed him to save part of the money he earned. Spottswood, in her late teens, was very young when she bought the land. In the 1870 Census, she appeared living with her mother, Susan, in a household headed by a man named Louis Bryan. Most likely Bryan was a lodger and the census taker would not believe that young Miss Spottswood was the owner of the house.[11]

Eliza Spottswood married John M. Shippen on September 30, 1874, at Shiloh Baptist Church. He was born in Hayfield, Caroline County, in Virginia around 1848. John M. Shippen had a diploma from Howard University and a degree in divinity. He taught at the District of Columbia schools and was a principal in the Reno School, the African American school in the Reno neighborhood in upper Northwest.[12]

John and Eliza Shippen had twelve children, but many died in early childhood. The Shippens moved for the first year of their marriage to Alabama, where their first daughter, Clara, was born, and then returned to Washington, D.C., for several years until they moved to the Shinnecock Indian Reservation in Long Island, New York, in 1888. There John M. Shippen taught first to eighth grades at the reservation's one-room school and served as pastor. The family left their three older children in Washington living with family members at Barry Farm–Hillsdale to attend school. Five of the other children attended the reservation's one-room school where their father taught.[13]

John and Eliza Shippen were eager that their children should attend college. Elder daughter Eliza graduated from Oberlin College in 1897. Cyrus graduated from Yale in 1899. Henry graduated from Oberlin Academy but did not complete his college coursework at Howard University. He was working as a golf instructor in 1900. Later on, he ran the family grocery store on Nichols Avenue. Bessie, Eliza and Carrie graduated from the Normal School in Washington, D.C., and went on to teach. Susie died while in high school. Eliza achieved the highest level of education, graduating from Howard University in 1912 and then obtaining a master's degree from Columbia University in 1928 and a PhD from the University of Pennsylvania in 1944.[14]

The three older children always came from Washington, D.C., to join the family on Long Island for the summer. During those summers, Cyrus, Henry and John worked as caddies at the Shinnecock Hills Golf Club. John became very proficient in playing golf, and when the family came back to Barry Farm–Hillsdale, he did not join them. In 1896, Shippen became the first African American player to compete in the U.S. Open. He along with Oscar Bunn, a member of the Shinnecock Nation, had their fees paid by members of the club. Some of the White players threatened not to participate in the tournament, but the U.S. Golf Association president, Theodore Havemeyer, refused the blackmail—John and Oscar went on to play. John Shippen finished the 1896 tournament in fifth place and went on to participate five more times in the U.S. Open. He eventually became the club professional at Shady Rest Golf Course, an African American golf course in New Jersey, from 1924 to 1960. John also manufactured and sold golf clubs. He passed away in Newark in 1968.[15]

John Shippen, date unknown. Shippen's parents were early settlers of Barry Farm–Hillsdale. He became a proficient golfer, and in 1896, he was the first African American player to compete in the U.S. Open. *Courtesy United States Golf Association.*

The Shippen family returned to Washington, D.C., in October 1898. Three years later, on December 26, 1901, John M. Shippen was found dead in the stable at the rear of the family house on Nichols Avenue. There was speculation that he had been killed, but in fact, he had committed suicide with his razor. According to a newspaper account, the reasons were his ill health and "misfortune in business affairs." It was left to Clara, the eldest daughter and a schoolteacher, to take care of her mother and the five younger siblings, who were still in school. The family eventually moved away from Barry Farm–Hillsdale except for Henry, but they owned property on Nichols Avenue until the 1950s.[16]

Although the Shippen family were struck by tragedy, they also represented the successful history of two people who emerged from enslavement and were able to acquire property and provide their children with the means to obtain higher education, which in turn led them to very successful lives. The Barry Farm–Hillsdale community environment provided the foundation for that achievement.

Chapter 4

Resources for Supporting Community Life

I mmediately after the first settlers at Barry Farm–Hillsdale began building their houses, the community felt the need for a school and a church. Religion had always been a part of the life of enslaved African Americans, but education had in general been denied to them. There was such a desire to acquire formal education among the newly freed people that in January 1866 John W. Alvord, superintendent of education for the Freedmen's Bureau, declared in awe, "What other people on earth have ever shown, while in their ignorance, such a passion for education?"[1]

Beginning in October 1867, the Freedmen's Bureau hired some of the new residents of the settlement to erect the school building, which was known officially as Howard School and unofficially by the community as Mount Zion School, after the name of the hill where it stood. The bureau also furnished the construction materials. Esquire Harrod described the structure as being a "plain style building about 70 feet long and 25 feet wide, running east and west with an A-roof," like the ones of the first houses built in the community. The first of two classrooms was opened in January 1868 under the guidance of Reverend John S. Dore, who had been in charge of the Freedmen's Bureau school at Good Hope Road near Uniontown. In February, Miss Flora A. Leland, who until then was in charge at the Good Hope School, moved to the newly opened school.[2]

Miss Frances Eliza Hall, a new teacher, joined Miss Leland in April. The Pennsylvania Freedmen's Relief Organization paid Miss Hall's salary. The new teacher came from New York State and boarded at the residence of

Solomon G. Brown, one of the leaders of the community, and his wife, Lucinda, on Elvans Road. The Browns had acquired lots 30 and 31. Hall would soon buy lot 29 on the same block and build the house in which she would live for the next four decades. It is interesting to note that in the 1868–69 period, there were 152 teachers in freedmen's schools in Washington, D.C. Washington received 489 teachers until 1876, and 218 of them were White women such as Leland and Hall.[3]

In her first report, Hall noted that out of her thirty students, eighteen were male, only twenty-five were always in attendance and only three had been free before the Civil War. Nevertheless, there was a ray of hope, as twenty-nine could "spell, and read easy lessons."[4] The number of students in her class increased steadily. By May 1868, forty-six had enrolled; by June, fifty-three were in her class. Hall was very encouraged that "happy results will follow," as she remarked in her monthly report for July 1868. She left for summer vacation in Auburn, probably with the firm belief that she would be back in September for another year, but sad news awaited her.

In September, the Pennsylvania Freedmen's Relief Organization withdrew its assistance, and the Freedmen's Bureau decided not to assume the expenses to finance Hall's class. Only the class taught by Miss Leland returned for the next school year in October 1868. Leland reported in November that nearly all the students who had left the school had been sent away "for want of room." Undoubtedly, she was referring to the loss of Hall's classroom.[5]

Finally, Reverend John Kimball, Freedmen's Bureau superintendent of education for the District of Columbia, persuaded the Freedmen's Relief Organization to provide twenty dollars per month for the hiring of a teacher, and Hall came back in December 1868 to reopen her classroom. The fact that she took a 50 percent cut in pay shows her dedication to her students. Hall's final report for the Freedmen's Bureau came in June 1869. Her classroom was full to the brim with sixty-six students, and she stated in her remarks, "The rapid influx of people at Barry Farm has filled this school to repletion. The capacity of the building will scarcely accommodate the pupils another school year."[6]

The first public school sponsored by the District of Columbia government opened at Barry Farm–Hillsdale in 1871. Called Hillsdale School, it was located at the corner of Nichols Avenue and Sheridan Road. It was a two-story frame building containing four classrooms. According to a report many years later, the school was "poorly located on the lot which occupies being lower than the road it faces." Former students described how they had to cross a footbridge over Stickfoot Branch to reach the school and how the school

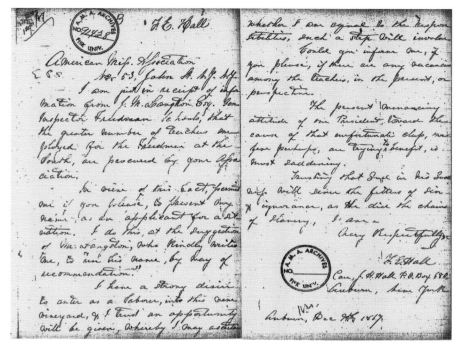

Letter from Frances Eliza Hall to the American Missionary Association requesting a teaching position in a school for newly freed African Americans, April 9, 1867. Miss Hall came in 1868 to teach the Barry Farm–Hillsdale children and ended up living and staying in the neighborhood for most of the rest of her life. *Courtesy Amistad Research Center, Tulane University, New Orleans.*

was just a little frame building that, in later years, became very dilapidated. Nevertheless, in 1871 it doubled the school space for the children of the community, and as such, it must have been very well received.[7]

In 1872, Hillsdale School was staffed by the principal, Mrs. Virginia L. Douglass, wife of Frederick Douglass Jr.; Miss Frances Eliza Hall, who had come from Howard School; and Misses Sarah Shimm and Emma Patterson. It was reported in June that despite the difficulties encountered by the students, who sometimes were taken out of school by the parents to earn money for the household, "advancement was being made." Nevertheless, in 1889, after almost two decades of service, the Hillsdale School building was deemed inadequate for the needs of the growing community. At a meeting of the Hillsdale Civic Association, a report noted that a new school building was very much needed because the fifth- and sixth-grade classes were being held only for half days due to the lack of classroom space.

Hillsdale School building at the intersection of Nichols Avenue and Sheridan Road, circa 1908. The new building doubled the school space for Barry Farm–Hillsdale children in 1871. *From* Report of the Schoolhouse Commission, *1908.*

On June 10, 1889, early settler Mary A. Henson sold a lot on Nichols Avenue to build the new James Gillespie Birney Elementary School. Birney was an abolitionist, hence the choice of his name for a school in the settlement created for freed people after the Civil War. The frame building was located on the east side of Nichols Avenue between Talbert Street and Howard Road. It had only four classrooms, and the rapid development of the community soon demanded the construction of the new Birney Elementary School in 1901. By 1897, the community had already been demanding a new building, stating that the school was "inadequate for the accommodation of the population of school age."[8]

Earlier, after the building of the first Birney School, Hillsdale School did not close. The building continued in use for "industrial arts, home economics, and boys shop classes." By 1895, it was already considered unsafe for the teachers and students but was still being used. In 1897, one speaker at a meeting of school parents discussing the need for school improvements in Barry Farm–Hillsdale declared that the building "was not fit for beasts,"

In the background in this photograph is the first Birney Public School, date unknown. This building was built around 1890. It doubled the number of classrooms available for the Barry Farm–Hillsdale community since the old Hillsdale School continued to be in use. *Courtesy Library of Congress, Prints and Photographs Division (LC-USZ62-4553).*

much less for children. Finally, the building was sold in 1913 and later razed to the ground.[9]

The new Birney Elementary School, described as an elegant building "in the Italian Renaissance style with colonial revival accents" and featuring sixteen classrooms, was inaugurated on Friday, October 18, 1901. Present at the opening were luminaries of the Barry Farm–Hillsdale community such as Solomon G. Brown and Reverend William H. Hunter, both of whom spoke at the assembly. The new building, according to a newspaper account of the event, could accommodate five hundred students from first to eighth grade. The old frame building was not discarded. It was moved to the back of the schoolyard and continued in use until 1914, when it was razed. In that same year, an addition to the original building was constructed containing six rooms and an assembly hall.[10]

The Birney School building was also used as a community center by Barry Farm–Hillsdale residents at night and on weekends. On Thursday, May 16, 1917, for instance, the school hall was the place for an "entertainment for a

Teachers pictured in front of the second Birney School, circa 1910. Today, the Thurgood Marshall Academy, a charter public high school, occupies the building. *Courtesy the Museum of African American History, Boston and Nantucket, Massachusetts.*

stereopticon." This machine, also called magic lantern, combined the use of two images to create a three-dimensional effect and was very popular at the time; it was a precursor to the moving pictures. Also held at the school were adult classes in sewing, cooking and gardening. Civic organizations also met there, and during World War I, the school was used to entertain members of the armed forces.[11]

From the very beginning of the creation of Barry Farm–Hillsdale, churches were an essential and central part of community life. They sponsored literary clubs, social events and educational classes. They also served as community centers, providing meeting space. Most important was the fact that ministers provided leadership and were able to articulate the demands and concerns of the residents of the new settlement. In the beginning, religious affiliation was in general connected with the geographical area from which the new settlers came. An early settler declared that those coming from Virginia were mostly Baptist. Those who came from the southern counties of Maryland mainly were Catholics, but there were also some Methodists and Episcopalians.[12]

Esquire Harrod, the guardian of the earliest history of the settlement, told the story of the creation of the first church in Barry Farm–Hillsdale:

"Mt. Zion AME Church was the first and at the time the only church in our vicinity. It stood on the hill near the…schoolhouse. We worshiped in the school house while it was being erected." Mount Zion AME was connected to Allen Chapel AME Church, located in the village of Good Hope about a mile and a half away. The two congregations shared one pastor. Later on, the church split into two churches named Campbell AME Church and Israel Mission CME Church. Then in 1875, Israel Mission CME Church built a new building at Mount Zion Road. In 1920, the name of the church changed to Hillsdale Station CME Church and then, still later on, to St. John CME Church, the name that stands today.

St. John CME Church is now located at 2801 Stanton Road SE at the corner of Douglass Place. The congregation bought this property in 1925, when the streets in Barry Farm–Hillsdale were widened and realigned and the city condemned the old building. The construction of a new sanctuary started in 1932, and by 1934, a structure that would become the basement of the new church was ready for worship. Finished in 1939, the church building still stands today.[13]

The first Baptist church in Barry Farm, Macedonia Baptist Church, was organized by James Howard, the early settler, who lived on Elvans Road. The church building was located in the 2800 block of Sheridan Road. The date given for the founding of the church was May 1866. This date was before the creation of the Barry Farm settlement. Perhaps the explanation for this discrepancy is that the establishment of the church came "as a result of meetings previously held in private homes," which could have taken place before Barry Farm started being populated in 1867. The lot where the church building was constructed appears in the Barry Farm map of 1867 as being held under trust by Mathias Bartlett.[14]

In 1905, the church building was completely rebuilt, including new pews, a section for the choir and even a new bell. A new cornerstone was laid out. On Sunday, November 26, 1905, the reopening celebrations started with a rally service at 5:00 a.m. Two more services, including one in the evening, completed the festivities. This building would stay on Sheridan Road until the construction of the Suitland Parkway in 1943, at which time it was destroyed.[15]

Catholic settlers faced more difficulties to worship. At first they had to go to Capitol Hill to attend St. Peter's Catholic Church. However, in 1877, Archbishop of Baltimore James Cardinal Gibbons approved the construction of a church in Uniontown, St. Teresa of Avila Roman Catholic Church, dedicated in 1879. Both the White residents of Uniontown, where the church was located, and the African American Catholic residents of Barry Farm–Hillsdale were delighted that they now had a Catholic church in their vicinity.[16]

Nevertheless, African American Catholics were discriminated against in a church that was located in an all-White neighborhood. They "were never ever treated as fellow members and…eventually started a chapel" in the basement of the church. When the church built its school, African American children were not allowed to attend. Finally, the "very nice German priest" who conducted the services for the African American parishioners told them that "they did not have to sit underneath anyone to hear the Word of God," and thus they began looking for a place to build a new church.[17]

This "very nice German priest" was Reverend Franz M.W. Schneeweiss, who led the first meeting of the group that began discussing the creation of an African American parish in Barry Farm–Hillsdale. The lay leaders were Louis Cook and Charles Edelin. The male members of the church began the work of clearing the property that was acquired for the erection of the new church. This land, previously occupied by the Civil War Fort Stanton, belonged to Dr. J.C. Norwood. It occupies one of the highest points in the city, and it affords a panoramic view of Washington, D.C.[18]

On Sunday, June 20, 1920, a procession was formed at the corner of Nichols Avenue and Howard Road and proceeded to the new property. All along the procession route, the parishioners chanted the Litany of the Blessed Virgin and sang hymns. At the site, a cross about twenty-five feet high was erected, and a small shrine housing a statue of Our Lady was placed in it. Father Schneeweiss blessed them, and the life of Our Lady of Perpetual Help Catholic Church parish began. Construction of the church building began in August 1920. A group of faithful men of the parish did the work of digging the foundation and erecting the building. They did this work after a full day at their jobs. The women helped by taking meals to the men working in the construction. Finally, Our Lady of Perpetual Help opened on May 8, 1921. Reverend Schneeweiss was assigned to be its first pastor and stayed on until his passing in 1942. On September 6, 1921, a school to serve the Catholic community started operating in the basement with an initial enrollment of thirty-five students. Thus, Catholic African Americans in Barry Farm–Hillsdale finally had their church and their school.[19]

The community had now all the ingredients to provide a nurturing environment for young generations during the next decades, before the advent of extraordinary events would profoundly change its makeup.

Chapter 5

The Community Takes Root

By 1880, the community was settled, the houses were built and the anchors—the churches and the school—were in place. An examination of the census taken that year in June gives us a snapshot of what was happening within the settlement.

The majority of the men were listed in the census as working as laborers, without specification of what kind of work they did. Married women were listed mostly as "keeping house," while children who were not in school were listed as "at home." There were a few women listed as doing work other than "keeping house." They were dressmakers, washerwomen, a cook, a hairdresser and a woman who worked as a servant at the Insane Asylum. We have previously mentioned Elizabeth Chase, who ran a restaurant. There were also three female teachers living in the community: Sarah Shimm, Emma V. Smith and the White teacher Frances Eliza Hall.

There were many men identified as farmers and gardeners. Those identified as gardeners were probably planting truck gardens. They or their wives sold the produce in the markets across the river. Center Market on Pennsylvania Avenue would have been one of these venues, as well as Eastern Market on Capitol Hill. This activity was a way of earning money at a time when formal employment was hard to come by, especially for African Americans. Ethel G. Greene still vividly remembered in the 1970s that her mother, Mrs. Anna Graham, had a stand at the Center Market in the 1880s, when the family moved to Howard Road and were able to cultivate the large lot. The stand offered honey, fruits, flowers and vegetables.[1]

There was an abundance of male ministers and grocers—five of the first and six of the latter, including two White men who lived at and had a grocery store on Pomeroy Road. There were several waiters and porters, men who had been able to obtain employment in downtown hotels, including Elie E. Adams, who had a coveted spot at the National Hotel.

Jobs in the government were not as prevalent as they would become in later decades. Besides Solomon G. Brown, who worked at the Smithsonian Institution, there were a few men employed as laborers at the navy yard, the Treasury Department, the Capitol and the U.S. Post Office. The Insane Asylum was the other government agency providing a few jobs. Professions catering to the needs of the community were present among the men: shoemakers, blacksmiths, carpenters, house painters, a butcher, a plasterer and a huckster.

Unusual occupations also were present. There were two sailors, brothers John and Elias Harrod, and Alexander Davis was listed as "agent for sewing machine," which we interpreted as being a salesman for the sewing machine company. There were very few men in skilled professions. Frederick Douglass Jr. was a bailiff, and William Stevens worked as a stockbroker. John A. Moss was justice of the peace. Moss and Solomon G. Brown were the leaders of the community.

Most of the younger children, both male and female, were attending Hillsdale School. There was a significant number of grandchildren being raised by the grandparents, as well as adopted children or nephews and nieces living with uncles and aunts. This information demonstrated that in case the need arose, the children of the community would not be left without care.

One of the most striking features of the census was the large numbers of men who were listed as disabled by sickness during the previous year, some of them for the whole year. A report issued some twenty years later recorded malaria as the leading reason for mortality east of the river in Washington, D.C. In the year before June 1899, 20.46 percent of the population in that area had died from that disease. This situation might explain the high proportion of disabled men in 1880, since the characteristic of malaria is a disabling fever occurring at irregular intervals. The other causes of mortality were typhoid fever, diarrhea and tuberculosis.[2]

As the settlement developed, distinctive areas began to appear within it. The lower part, centering on the crossroads of Nichols Avenue and Sheridan Road, was sometimes known as "Central City." The upper area around Elvans and Stanton Roads was known as "The Heights." There was yet another area called "The Bottom," located on Sheridan Road and considered "a slum." The distinctions between these areas became more delineated when two civic associations were organized. Barry Farm Civic Association, under the leadership of James Thomas Howard, centered on Elvans Road and, according to Ella Pearis (perhaps biased because she was the descendant of the founder), was more active than the civic organization that formed around Nichols Avenue, which was called Hillsdale Civic Association.[3]

One of the requests of the people living in "The Heights," through their association, was for a streetcar to come up the hill. They also wanted an overpass connecting dead-end Elvans Road to Nichols Avenue on the other side of Sheridan Road to make for easier access to St. Elizabeths Hospital, as it was an important source of employment for the community. Neither request was ever fulfilled. Transportation did not come up the hill until a bus line started running in 1935.[4]

Eventually, transportation came to Nichols Avenue in 1875, when a White resident of Uniontown, entrepreneur Henry Adams Griswold, brought new energy and vision to a project to build the Anacostia and Potomac Railway Company, first proposed in 1872. Construction of the new line of streetcars began in 1873, and operations started on July 3, 1876, with two cars. A barn and stables were built at the corner of what is today Martin Luther King Jr. Avenue and V Street. Cars ran every twenty minutes until more cars were put in service on July 16, 1878, and the headway was reduced to ten minutes.

The small horse-drawn streetcars might look puny today, but for the residents of Barry Farm–Hillsdale, especially the ones coming down from "The Heights," it must have been a sign of enormous progress. They now could walk down the hills, hop on a streetcar and then alight in front of the navy yard gate on M and 7th Street SE on the other side of the bridge. The trip cut down more than two miles from their hike into town. The *Evening Star* declared, "The citizens of Uniontown and East Washington are delighted and patronize the road so well as to exceed the expectations of the company." With this initial success, several new cars were added, and within a year, the company had extended along M Street SE to the waterfront and connected to the line that went up to 7th Street NW, giving even more access to downtown Washington, D.C.[5]

Another area within Barry Farm–Hillsdale with a distinctive personality, so to speak, was Howard Road. The area was described in 1891 as being "divided up into small truck farms, which are worked with good profit." The road was sadly neglected and was also described as a "mere country lane," but with many residences on either side. Howard Road was well remembered

Anacostia and Potomac River Railway Company, no. 20 streetcar, circa 1890. The arrival of streetcars on Nichols Avenue in 1876 heralded a new epoch for the residents of Barry Farm–Hillsdale, who now had quicker access to Washington, D.C. *Courtesy the Historical Society of Washington, D.C., General Photograph Collection (CHS 06298).*

in the 1970s for the yearly baptism ceremonies held at the foot of the road at the margins of the Anacostia River.[6]

Several well-known families were living on the road, which made its way along the river to Poplar Point, where the Barry family main house had stood once. Two of these families are of particular interest to this story: the Simpsons and the Johnsons. David and Catherine Simpson came from Virginia, most likely as part of the mass exodus of refugee African Americans fleeing enslavement during the Civil War. Their daughter Georgiana was born in Washington, D.C., around 1865. David Simpson was an early settler. He bought a lot on Howard Road. The Stickfoot Branch ran through the back of his land. The presence of an abundance of water was an essential feature for the family since Simpson ran a dairy farm. His business was still remembered in the 1970s as the only dairy farm owned by African Americans in the neighborhood. To supplement the family's income, Simpson also worked as a laborer at the Botanical Garden and later as a hostler. His wife worked as a washerwoman.[7]

51

Georgiana Rose Simpson at graduation, University of Chicago, 1921. She grew up in Barry Farm–Hillsdale, where she went to the local elementary school. She was the second African American woman to receive a PhD. *Courtesy Moorland-Spingarn Research Center, Howard University.*

The Simpson family was keen on education. In 1870, thirteen-year-old Etta Simpson was attending Hillsdale School. The other children, including Georgiana, were still too young to attend. The 1880 Census shows that all six children in the family, including Georgiana, were attending Hillsdale School. After completing the eighth grade at Hillsdale School, Georgiana transferred to the M Street High School. From there she went to teachers' training at Miner Normal School, where Dr. Lucy E. Moten was her mentor. Simpson's career in teaching began in the D.C. school system in 1885. First, she taught elementary school at Hillsdale School, her alma mater. Later, she went to teach at Dunbar High School, the prestigious school for African Americans. By 1911, she had received a bachelor's degree, and in 1921, when the University of Chicago awarded her a PhD, she was the second African American woman to receive a doctorate. Howard University hired her as a professor of German language and literature. Dr. Simpson died in 1944 after a distinguished academic career.[8]

Another prominent family in the Howard Road neighborhood was that of Larkin Johnson. He was married to Emily Edmonson, who was one of those who tried to escape enslavement by running away aboard the schooner *Pearl* from the Washington, D.C., wharf. Emily was part of a group of seventy-seven people. The escape was foiled, and Emily and several of her siblings were sent to New Orleans for sale. Her freedom was eventually paid by money obtained in New York under the auspices of Reverend Henry Ward Beecher, a noted abolitionist.[9]

Emily and Larkin Johnson married in Washington, D.C., on April 5, 1860. Emily had worked as a teacher at the Normal School established in Washington, D.C., by Myrtilla Miner, a White teacher from New York. She also had worked as an activist in the antislavery movement and was a close associate of Frederick Douglass's. Johnson, on the other hand, was an illiterate farmer from Montgomery County, twenty years her senior, who had several children from a previous marriage.[10]

The couple settled in Sandy Springs, Maryland, until the early 1870s, when they bought land on Howard Road backing into the Eastern Branch. Larkin and Emily Johnson had at least four children: Ida, Fannie, Emma and Robert. Johnson worked as a gardener and sold produce at the Center Market on Pennsylvania Avenue. Emily, according to the memories of one of her grandchildren, raised hogs and cows and owned three horses. She also had a carriage with a driver, evidence of her prosperity.[11] Larkin Johnson died in 1885, and Emily passed away in 1895. The family retained the property on Howard Road into the twentieth century.[12]

Mary and Emily Edmonson. It is believed that this picture was taken between 1850 and 1860. Emily Edmonson is sitting to the right of her sister, Mary. Emily moved to Barry Farm–Hillsdale in the early 1870s and remained there until her death in 1895. *Courtesy Library of Congress, Prints and Photographs Division (LC-USZ62-104364).*

It would be interesting to discuss here the grass-roots leadership that grew within the community in its first decades of existence. As mentioned before, Reverend William H. Hunter, who was a Civil War veteran and a religious leader, took the mantle of leadership within the community once he returned to Washington, D.C. Solomon G. Brown, residing on Elvans Road in The Heights, and lawyer John A. Moss, living on Nichols Avenue, are the other two names that were recognized as being influential male leaders in the community in its first decades. Emma V. Smith was one of the most admired female leaders.

Solomon G. Brown was a self-educated man of many talents. He and his wife, as we have seen, bought lots on Elvans Road at the very beginning of its development, erected a house and lived the rest of their lives in the community. Brown built a reputation for being a man of integrity and intellect. He was born on February 14, 1829, the fourth child of free parents Isaac and Rachel Brown in Washington, D.C., near Boundary Avenue and 14th Street (now U and 14th Streets NW). In 1833, his father died, leaving the family in poverty, and Brown was deprived of the possibility of obtaining any formal education. At an early age, he was placed in the household of Lambert Tree, the assistant postmaster at the city's post office. This event would prove extremely valuable for a child whose later life showed that he was intelligent and capable.[13]

In 1844, Lambert secured employment for fifteen-year-old Brown at the post office. Soon afterward, he was detailed to work in the development of the first telegraph system between Washington, D.C., and Baltimore. In later years, Brown stated with great pride that he carried the first telegraph message to the White House. During this period, he worked with Samuel F.B. Morse, the developer of the Morse code, and Joseph Henry, the first secretary of the Smithsonian Institution. It was perhaps because of this early contact that Henry gave Solomon G. Brown a position at the Smithsonian Institution Transportation Department in 1852. He would stay at the Smithsonian for more than fifty years, later becoming an employee of the International Exchange Service. He was the first African American employee of the Smithsonian Institution.[14]

Brown married Lucinda Adams on June 4, 1854. She worked as a dressmaker. They had no children, but as did other couples in their close-knit community, they adopted two girls, Katie and Mary. Their house had two floors and was well appointed, including a library stocked with about three hundred books. Brown went on to participate fully in the life of the Washington, D.C., community as a whole, serving for three years as a member of the House of Delegates under the Territorial Government beginning in 1875. Upon his death on June 24, 1906, the *Afro-American* stated that "he was a power for good in the [Barry Farm–Hillsdale] community, where everything for moral uplift had his earnest support."[15]

John A. Moss was a self-made man who had started life in challenging circumstances. Moss was born enslaved in Upperville, Virginia, around 1845. At the age of fifteen, he was sold to a trader but was able to run away and eventually made his way to Washington, D.C. He worked as a general helper at the Botanical Gardens until the time when he went to work at the Library of Congress in 1870 under the auspices of the abolitionist senator Charles Sumner. There he had the chance to start reading law. He then went to attend the Howard University Law Department and graduated in 1873.[16]

Moss was admitted to the bar in the District of Columbia on March 15, 1873. On the recommendation of Frederick Douglass, among others, he was appointed to the position of justice of the peace consecutively by Presidents Rutherford B. Hayes, James A. Garfield and Grover Cleveland. He was a colorful character and once was thrown in jail by a judge for contempt. Nevertheless, he was known as the "Ajax" by those he defended in court due to his ability. When his clients did not have money to pay for his services, he received payment in kind. An old-timer remembered that "you could always tell when Lawyer Moss had [won] a case…you'd see him coming home from the police court with a goose or chicken or a duck under his arm."[17]

Moss married Ellen Abel on December 11, 1875. The couple had nine children, of whom only six survived into adulthood. He died on May 4, 1921, at age seventy-six of a stroke, and it was reported that he was active in his practice until ten days before his death. A few days later, in a tribute offered at the District Court where he had practiced, the presiding judge stated, "[Moss] was a man out of the ordinary and a man of notable events."[18]

Emma V. Smith was born around 1858 in Maryland. She was the daughter of Frederick and Harriet Smith, both of whom most likely fled enslavement and came to Washington in the influx of African American refugees during the Civil War. Her father was a carpenter and bought a lot on Howard Road fronting the river. Frederick Smith was hired to work in the construction of the settlement and was remembered as the "boss carpenter," as we have previously mentioned.[19]

Emma attended the local schools (Mount Zion and Hillsdale) and then went to Howard University to attend its "Preparatory and Normal Course." She started her teaching career in Prince George's County, Maryland, but by 1876, she was teaching at Hillsdale School along with Frances Eliza Hall,

Solomon G. Brown, date unknown. A Renaissance man, poet and leader of his community, Brown was well remembered by Barry Farm–Hillsdale residents into the twentieth century. *Courtesy Smithsonian Institution Archives (Image # SIA2007-0039).*

her former teacher. Emma would remain a teacher in Barry Farm–Hillsdale, moving over to teach at the Birney School until her retirement on June 30, 1928. Her contributions to the school and the community were celebrated on April 19, 1929, with a testimonial.[20]

Emma V. Smith was a dedicated member of the community who started a program to collect shoes and garments for needy students. She was in charge of the first recreation center, established to serve Barry Farm at Birney School in 1917. She created a public library branch in the school with four hundred volumes. She was a member of the Pioneer Sunday School Institute, led by Solomon G. Brown, and also a founder and a lifetime member of the St. Philip the Evangelist Episcopal Church. After retirement, Smith continued to be active as a member of the Hillsdale Civic Association and the Birney Parent Teacher Association. She left such a positive impression that in the early 1970s she was still remembered as "an exceptional woman…a very strong force in the community."[21]

Under the strong leadership and the watchful eye of the several religious denominations represented in the settlement, Barry Farm–Hillsdale inhabitants formed large, cohesive and aspirational families who in turn created a pleasant community. Over and over again in the 1970s interviews, the word *pleasant* was used to describe Barry Farm–Hillsdale. The citizens of the settlement were unanimous in describing it as "a most delightful place."[22]

The large one-acre lots of the settlement also provided resources to promote the well-being of the community. Being primarily a rural people, the inhabitants took full advantage of the land available to plant truck gardens, raise small animals and establish orchards. Archaeological research at the Howard Road Historic District in Barry Farm–Hillsdale in the 1980s, before the construction of the Anacostia Metro Station, found remains of the consumption of edible animals such as pork, cow, sheep, squirrel, rabbit and chicken. There was also evidence of the butchering of cows and pigs on site. Also recovered were samples that indicated the existence of orchards producing grapes, peaches, plums and cherries, as well as of truck gardens producing squash, pumpkins, watermelons and beans.[23]

These activities not only contributed to the nutritional well-being and the financial security of the families (with the sale of the excess crops) but also allowed for the establishment of a pioneer recycling system well before the practice was widely known. According to longtime resident George J. Trivers, even though there was no trash collection in Barry Farm–Hillsdale, household refuse was not a problem. Those who raised hogs, chickens or owned a horse or a cow would go around to the houses of neighbors and collect their organic

Hog butchering time, the late 1800s, unknown location. Hog raising was a well-established enterprise in the hills of Barry Farm–Hillsdale. Hog butchering time was a community event. The men came together to help and would receive a share of the meat for their efforts. *Courtesy Tulane University, Amistad Research Center.*

trash to feed the animals. Often the organic garbage was made into compost and used for fertilizer. Other refuse was buried or burned.[24]

Another characteristic of the community that made it a pleasant place to live was its cohesiveness. People were willing to share the little they had at the time of need. Edith P. Green of Pomeroy Road described a "pound party" as the way of helping a family in need without offending them. All the neighbors would come together, socialize and bring a pound of food. Other times, anonymously, a basket of food would be left at the front door of a family in need. Another way to share food was at the hog butchering time: those men who helped in the process would take home a share of the meat. Also remembered was that those who owned horses would help to plow and plant their neighbors' land when needed, and residents would help their neighbors build their homes.[25]

58

It is important to note here that hog raising was prohibited by law in the District of Columbia. In 1894, the city government claimed to have dismantled at least one hundred hog raising operations "among the hills back around Hillsdale." Nevertheless, the practice persisted, and in 1895, the District of Columbia's health department was at it again trying to curtail the activity.[26]

Caring for the elderly was another concern of the community. Anita Blake remembered her work visiting older members of the community when she was a teenager. Many people did not have wells from which to take water, the elderly being particularly afflicted by this problem. Blake remembered that she would have to go to the hydrants to fill up their barrels. This volunteer activity was part of community service out of St. Philip the Evangelist Episcopal Church, performed by the young members of the church. Miss Blake, already in her eighties in the 1970s, remembered that the children in the community were raised "to be helpful to other people and to care about their needs."[27]

Within this context of collaboration and helpfulness, twenty-five women of Barry Farm–Hillsdale created the National Sewing Council on April 20, 1900. It was the first recorded benevolent society founded by the women of the community. Mary Watson Webster was the first leader. The council was created out of frustration because the all-White Needle Work Guild of America had rejected the attempt by Mrs. Webster to establish a chapter in Barry Farm–Hillsdale.[28]

To participate in the council, members were asked to donate two new garments per year for distribution for the needy men, women and children in the community. The council was involved in recruiting children to attend Sabbath School in different denominations and distributing provisions and fuel for those in need in the community. Another activity was a sewing school for small girls. An August 1903 newspaper article reported that the council had been able to give clothing and shoes to needy children so that they could continue attending school. The council was still active in 1956 when it promoted a "Home Coming Dinner" at the Webster House at 2328 Pomeroy Road.[29]

Barry Farm–Hillsdale was now ready to enter the new century based on a firm foundation of strong community organizations, dedicated leaders and solidarity among its inhabitants.

PART III

The New Century

───○──────────────────○───

Successes and Challenges

Chapter 6

A Thriving Community

Businesses and Entertainment

A t the dawn of the twentieth century, Barry Farm–Hillsdale was a well-established, thriving community. Two buildings located at the central business intersection at Nichols Avenue and Sheridan and Howard Roads were important to Barry Farm–Hillsdale community life: Douglass Hall and Butler Hall. Mr. George W. Butler built Butler Hall in the middle of the 1890s as a residence for his grandchildren. He planned for them to inherit it upon his death. However, Mr. Butler outlived his grandson, and shortly after Butler's passing, his granddaughter also passed away. In 1900, George Washington Mason bought the building to house Mason's Funeral Home. The business stayed there until 1974, when the funeral home moved out. The solidly built structure, located at 2500 Martin Luther King Avenue, was later occupied by the United Black Fund Inc.[1]

Recently, the ONE DC Black Workers & Wellness Center opened in the location. The center is "a resident-led space that creates and maintains racial and economic justice through popular education, direct action and the creation of world-owned alternatives." After more than 120 years, Butler Hall continues being a landmark at the center of the community.[2]

Sometime in the 1870s, Charles Douglass, son of Frederick Douglass, built the first Douglass Hall. It was a meeting place for civic associations and celebrations, including one honoring Frederick Douglass in 1879. Nevertheless, by the late 1880s, the building was in disrepair, and permits were no longer granted for events to take place there. In 1897, the building

Nichols Avenue looking north toward Uniontown, 1905. On the right side of the photograph, just before Bethlehem Baptist Church, is Butler Hall. On the opposite side of the avenue was Douglass Hall, the building with dormer windows that can be glimpsed on the left. *Courtesy Library of Congress, Prints and Photographs Division (LC-USZ62-69312).*

caught fire and was destroyed. The fire also destroyed or damaged several structures on the corner of Nichols Avenue and Howard Road.[3]

By 1899, a rebuilt Douglass Hall stood three stories high. It would stand as the tallest structure in the community for a long time. The first floor was always rented for businesses. The second floor was a hall used for presentations, church pageants and dances. The third floor was used as living quarters. A reception for Mrs. Mamie Lewis, on September 14, 1899, seems to have marked the return of Douglass Hall as a prime site for entertainment. A description of a formal ball in December of that year encapsulated it all. The evening of December 29, 1899, perhaps to celebrate the incoming century, was the occasion for "the first full dress ball ever given at Douglass Hall." The attendance was large and the "ball floor a scene of ever changing beauty."[4]

Dr. William E. Gales opened a pharmacy on the first floor of Douglass Hall, probably right after it was rebuilt. It is important to note that Douglass Hall Pharmacy was not just a place to buy medicine; it was also a first-aid station for a community that lacked easy access to medical assistance. On a sweltering day in early May 1902, young Walter Queenan "was prostrated by the heat" while playing baseball. He was immediately taken to Dr. Gales's drugstore and given treatment before going home. In 1910, P.M. Marion was wounded while playing in the backyard of his house on Nichols Avenue. Dr. Gales dressed the wound at his pharmacy.[5]

In 1906, Dr. Gales married Frances Dyson, and they had at least three children: Francis, Mildred and Ethel. Dr. Gales kept the Douglass Hall Pharmacy until 1912, when he sold it to Dr. Rezin H. Shipley. Dr. Gales died in 1913. At the time, he was running another pharmacy in Northeast Washington, D.C.[6]

Dr. Gales's pharmacy shared the first floor of Douglass Hall at the turn of the twentieth century with three other businesses: Lewis Barbershop, Armstead Goodlough's grocery store and Henry Sayles's confectionery shop. Sayles's business was well remembered in the 1970s because it sold, in addition to cigars for the adults, the ice cream and confections that the children loved. In 1989, his store was still remembered and characterized as an early version of a fast-food restaurant.[7]

Dr. Rezin H. Shipley, the new pharmacist in the community, was born in Simpsonville, Howard County, Maryland, on October 19, 1865. He enrolled at Howard University in the mid-1890s and graduated from the school of pharmacy in 1899. While in school, he worked as a patrol wagon driver for the D.C. police, Ninth Precinct. Later, he went to work as an assistant for Dr. Gales at the Douglass Hall Pharmacy. Most likely, Dr. Shipley met his future wife, Fannie Beecher Stowe Johnson, the daughter of Larkin and Emily Edmonson Johnson, when she briefly attended Howard University Pharmaceutical School in the 1895–96 school year. Fannie was named after the famous author of the book *Uncle Tom's Cabin*, Harriet Beecher Stowe. They married in 1901 at the Howard Road family house. Georgiana Rose Simpson was one of the bridesmaids. After they returned from their honeymoon, they also went to live on Howard Road near her family.[8]

After Dr. Shipley acquired the drugstore in 1912, he seems to have taken it to a new level. His ad in the 1915 city directory of Washington, D.C., noted that beyond selling medicines, the drugstore also sold toiletries, stationery and cigars. Shipley seems to have mastered the power of marketing and diversifying one's business before the practice was well known. In 1915, he was the only distributor of the famous "Oneida Community Silver Spoons" east of the river. This monopoly put his White neighbors in Anacostia in an interesting position. They either went to buy the silver spoons from the

African American drugstore around the corner or had to cross the river to do so. The same situation developed in 1918 during the First World War, when he was the only representative in the area selling war savings and thrift stamps. Earlier in 1913, he had entered into a contract with the post office to open a postal station in the drugstore with him serving as the postal clerk. All of this must have led to a constant stream of people coming into the drugstore—they might have been tempted by the soda fountain or the trinkets and toiletries even if they did not need medicines.[9]

Dr. Shipley was also a leader of the Barry Farm–Hillsdale community, where he participated actively in the Hillsdale Civic Association, eventually serving as its president. In 1919, he was one of the founders of the District of Columbia Colored Druggists' Association. Dr. Shipley passed away in 1924, the victim of a car accident. His demise must have left a vacuum in the community, as he had served it so well. At the time of his passing, he had already sold his pharmacy to Dr. Lee Andrew Walker.[10]

Fannie Johnson Shipley mothered two children: Cecelia and Earl. She worked as a teacher in the D.C. Public Schools for many years and was an agent for an insurance company. She was also active in the community, participating in women's organizations. In January 1904, for instance, she made a presentation on Harriet Beecher Stowe at the Ladies' Home Literary Circle of Anacostia. Solomon G. Brown was the guest of honor at the meeting. After the death of her husband, perhaps because of the financial strain, Shipley subdivided the second and third floors of Douglass Hall and rented it out to lodgers. She, Earl, Cecelia and her husband, Lucius Gilliard, as well as their daughter, Lucia, also lived at the Hall. Dr. W.E. Hamilton, the community's dentist, was one of the lodgers.[11]

Douglass Hall was well remembered in the 1970s as being a center of recreation and entertainment as well as enlightenment, due to the dances, lectures and debates held on the second floor. Several churches also held their services at Douglass Hall before they were able to build their sanctuaries. The building was razed in the early 1950s.[12]

At the beginning of Barry Farm–Hillsdale in 1867, businesses were scattered throughout the community, but by the turn of the twentieth century, the main center of activity was at Nichols Avenue. The commercial corridor was located between Morris Road, the de facto boundary with the White neighborhood of nearby Anacostia, and went south to the corner of Sheridan and Howard Roads. African Americans from Barry Farm–Hillsdale did not feel comfortable in White establishments and rarely went beyond the boundary of Morris Road to patronize White establishments. It

White-owned businesses on Nichols Avenue, Anacostia, decorated for the Fourth of July, circa 1919. These stores, located on the 2200 block of Nichols Avenue, did not welcome African Americans. African Americans patronized businesses located at Barry Farm–Hillsdale three blocks south on the 2500 block of the same avenue. *Courtesy Library of Congress, Prints and Photographs Division (LC-USZ62-58893).*

can also be safely assumed that not many White patrons ventured south of Morris Road to do their shopping.[13]

The exception was Walter McKenzie, a superb craftsman who had a multiracial, citywide clientele that gladly came to his business in Barry Farm–Hillsdale. McKenzie was the son of Mark (also written as "Mack") McKenzie, a Civil War veteran who served in the Union navy, and his wife, Elizabeth, who were early settlers at Barry Farm–Hillsdale. Mark McKenzie bought a lot on Sheridan Road where Walter was born on October 10, 1876. Both Walter and his father, Mark, were lifelong residents of Barry Farm–Hillsdale.[14]

In his teens, Walter McKenzie drove a grocery wagon, making deliveries around the neighborhood. Family lore suggests that he delivered milk to the home of Frederick Douglass in nearby Anacostia. Mrs. Helen Pitts Douglass noticed his artistic aptitude and, after seeing some of his work, requested that Professor Edmund C. Messer, a noted local artist, give him some lessons. Messer, who also lived in Anacostia, was a friend of Mrs. Douglass's.[15]

Walter McKenzie's first business was located in the back lot of the family house on Nichols Avenue right by Sumner Road, where they had relocated from Sheridan Road. He built carriages and wagon bodies and painted signs in his shop. All the painting and decorative work was carefully done by hand. Later, he expanded to paint advertisement and company trucks. Around 1909, McKenzie moved his shop to Sumner Road, and by 1912, he had bought a new house for his family at 2814 Wade Road. The house was still occupied by his family in 1974.[16]

His sons—Wilfred, Raymond and Lawrence—worked with Walter McKenzie at the business he renamed W. McKenzie and Sons. Among McKenzie's clientele were White merchants in nearby Anacostia. Campbell Hardware Store, a White establishment that had been located near the navy yard at 11th and N Streets SE before moving to the east side of the river, was one of Mackenzie's customers. Another White-owned business that used McKenzie's services was the Mandell Chevrolet car dealership. It was located in Anacostia from 1926 until it moved to Marlow Heights in 1962. McKenzie's shop also painted the lettering for the trucks of another traditional White business in Anacostia, the Curtis Brothers Furniture Company.[17]

Mr. McKenzie, besides bringing business into Barry Farm–Hillsdale, also helped the kids in the community. Both Stanley Anderson and Erma Simon remembered that he paid pennies for empty cans brought in by the neighborhood kids. He used them to mix paint. James Chester Jennings Jr. remembered being inspired by McKenzie's work. He would stop to watch the work at the McKenzie shop and learned a lot from him. Jennings went on to study at Armstrong Technical High School and later worked as art director for a Pentagon magazine, among other jobs in the federal government.[18]

The business continued to thrive until the early 1940s, when techniques changed and Walter McKenzie retired. His son Wilfred went to work for the Government Printing Office. Only Raymond continued carrying on the trade. In the late 1940s, the District of Columbia superintendent of schools bought the land where the McKenzie business was located at the corner of Nichols Avenue and Sumner Road to build the new Birney School, which opened on January 30, 1950.[19]

Another noteworthy aspect of the business community in Barry Farm–Hillsdale was the presence of Jewish store owners, many of whom lived above their stores. We have very little information about the relationships between Jewish merchants and their African American patrons in Barry Farm–Hillsdale. The only account of a personal relationship in the community that we have found is between two young women, Thelma Dale and Bella

Chotin, who befriended each other. They lived next door to each other on Sumner Road and attended separate segregated high schools; the teenagers enjoyed each other's company and even attended events together.[20]

There were at least fourteen Jewish business owners operating in Barry Farm–Hillsdale in the first half of the twentieth century.[21] Louis Miller apparently was the first one to come to Barry Farm–Hillsdale, around 1914. Previously, he had rented a grocery store catering to the African American community in Georgetown located on 37th Street NW. His first grocery store in Barry Farm–Hillsdale was located on Sheridan Road, where he also lived with his wife, Ida, and children, including eldest son Nathan. In 1916, he sold his Sheridan Road store to Nathan Miskin but continued running stores on Nichols Avenue and Stanton Road.

Finally, in the late 1910s, he settled on a large store on the 2500 block of Nichols Avenue at the corner of Sheridan Road, which he called L. Miller's Cash Market. This store was across the street from the family house on Nichols Avenue. The business would be later taken over by his son Nathan. Another son, Max, who was a lawyer, had his law office on the second floor. Housed in a substantial two-story brick building, the store operated in the same location until the 1960s, when Louis Miller passed away. Miller's store was remembered well into the twentieth century and early twenty-first century. In 1989, Jonathan Penn remembered that it was a very large store, and in 2002, Everett McKenzie remembered with pleasure that he used to buy gingerbread there. After the building was demolished, a Texaco gas station took its place until it disappeared as well. The lot is now empty.[22]

Nathan Miskin was another merchant who maintained a business in the community for a long time. According to his obituary, he arrived in Washington, D.C., from Russia in 1916. Around that time, Mr. Miskin bought the Miller grocery store on Sheridan Road. He maintained a store in the neighborhood for forty-three years, until 1959. Mr. Miskin also owned other businesses in Arlington, at Good Hope Road in SE and 3rd and I Streets SE in the neighborhood now known as the Yards. Mr. Miskin was well remembered in oral histories in the 1970s.[23]

Solomon Chotin, Bella Chotin's father, immigrated to the United States around 1915 from Gorodok, Vitebsk, in what was then Russia and today Belarus. In the 1920s and early '30s, he lived in the Bronx, New York, and worked as a house painter. By 1935, he was already settled in Barry Farm–Hillsdale on the 1100 block of Sumner Road and running a grocery store.[24]

In 1944, Solomon Chotin sold his store to Almore Dale. Mr. Dale changed the name of the store to Dale's Market and ran it for the next ten years. By the 1950s, the advent of self-service supermarkets accelerated the decline of the mom and pop grocery stores such as Dale's Market. Almore Dale sold his store to a new owner in 1954. The store then passed to several owners and finally closed for good. The building was eventually razed, and the lot remains empty to this day.[25]

Jewish business owners, although active over the decades, did not have a monopoly on the grocery business in Barry Farm–Hillsdale. Spencer Coleman might have been the first African American grocer in Barry Farm–Hillsdale. He bought lot 8, section 1 on Sheridan Road. Although he appeared as a laborer in the 1870 Census, by 1880, he was listed as a grocer.[26] Isaac B. Ray had a store on Nichols Avenue in the early decades of the twentieth century and was well remembered into the 1970s. In later years, he ran a truck farm and worked for the post office. Also well remembered into the 1970s were the stores of Robert S. Penn and Henrietta Myers, which faced each other on Sheridan Road at the corner of Pomeroy Road.[27]

In 1939, on the eve of the Second World War, which would bring an enormous change to Barry Farm, a collection of ads published in the program celebrating the six decades of St. John CME Church was a portrait of the commercial corridor on Nichols Avenue. Located between the 2300 and 2500 blocks of the main avenue in the community, the variety of the businesses was a testament to its vibrancy.

Martin's Sandwich Shop on the 2400 block of the avenue was also well remembered. On the same block were Mr. and Mrs. John Williams, who started their business in 1917 with an investment of forty-five dollars and sold "Fresh meat, Vegetables, and Groceries." The block was also lined with shops catering to the beauty needs of the women in the community: Lola's Beauty Parlor; Mrs. O.P. Johnson, whose business name was not included in the ad; and the Torsorial Parlor run by Mrs. Lena Stewart. Aiken's Barber Shop took care of the male clientele in the same block. Nichols' Avenue Service Station, run by Mr. W.E. Stevens, located on the 2300 block, competed with the well-established Boyd Fuel and Feed Company, which had been located on the 2500 block for many decades. Three undertakers—Walter E. Hunter, Robert G. Mason and Adams and Smoot—lined the avenue, providing a wide variety of choice for one's final services.[28]

The entertainment business was also well represented over the decades in Barry Farm–Hillsdale with two parks catering to a citywide African American clientele. The parks, Eureka and Green Willow, were the source of cherished memories. Eureka Park was the oldest, already operating in 1896. Eureka Park was described as being more of a pleasure garden since

Dale's Market on Sumner Road, formerly Chotin's Market, date unknown. Solomon Chotin emigrated from Russia in 1915. In the 1930s, he opened a grocery store at Sumner Road in Barry Farm–Hillsdale. He eventually sold his store to Almore Dale. *Courtesy Dale/Patterson Family Collection, Anacostia Community Museum Archives, Smithsonian Institution, gift of Dianne Dale.*

it had lighter amenities such as swings, a merry-go-round, picnic tables, a baseball diamond and a pavilion. A consortium owned the park, and among the owners was Thomas M.W. Green, a resident of Barry Farm–Hillsdale living on Sumner Road. Eureka Park was one of the seven parks catering to African Americans in the city between 1880 and 1925. Built between Sumner and Howard Roads, behind Nichols Avenue, a driveway led from the avenue to the entrance of the park.[29]

People came from all over the city to attend the nightly dances in the summer. Raymond Bumbry remembered, "The street cars could hardly accommodate the people who came over here every night through the week." Those who did not have money to buy a ticket stayed outside and danced near the fence. The favorite dances were the waltz and the two-step. The park was also the place for church picnics, African American political rallies and Fourth of July celebrations.[30]

Although Eureka Park was very popular with the African American population of Washington, D.C., the White neighbors of Barry Farm– Hillsdale were not happy with the goings-on at the park and complained to the district commissioners through the Anacostia Citizens Association. The White residents of Anacostia, apparently, were also not happy with the number of African Americans using the trolleys to come to Barry Farm–Hillsdale to attend both parks. As early as 1908, they were complaining about the park's African American patrons. In April of that year, the Hillsdale Civic Association sent a "strong protest" to the district commissioners regarding the complaints, explaining that the park was located "in a colored settlement" half a mile away from its White neighbors. Nevertheless, in May 1918, the license for Eureka Park was revoked, and its counterpart, Green Willow Park, had to apply for a license on a weekly basis. By 1923, the location where Eureka Park had operated was being used as a summer camp and as a destination for all-day hikes and picnics. In 1926, the National Parks and Planning Commission bought the land to create the Barry Farm Playground.[31]

Green Willow Park opened around 1905, or at least that was the time it started receiving attention. Its owner was Thomas M.W. Green, who had a disagreement with the other owners of Eureka Park and had gone into business on his own. He claimed that the park had begun operation in 1890. The park had its entrance from the 1100 block of Sumner Road in the area, which until recently was part of the Barry Farm Dwellings. It was a popular venue for picnics, held by various organizations such as the Shriners, Odd Fellows and True Reformers. In 1907, a crowd of five thousand people came to Green Willow Park to attend a picnic held by the Cosmopolitan Baptist Church. Major Richard Sylvester, the police superintendent for Washington, D.C., spoke at the event. Besides providing food, sodas, ice cream and watermelon for the attendees, the church also offered a pig race for their entertainment.[32]

Another well-attended event was an annual "hygienic congress" in July 1915, which provided mothers with information on how to improve the health of their babies and promoted a "baby health" contest with six hundred contestants. Dr. Rezin Shipley was present and had a display at the event. Another event held in September 1916 had the goal of raising money to pay the mortgage of Cosmopolitan Baptist Church. Three overweight men named (for the occasion, one assumes) Robert E. Lee, Abraham Lincoln and Stonewall Jackson competed in the race. There was also a pig race, along with a watermelon-eating contest and presentation of "plantation folk songs."[33]

Green Willow Park was restricted to apply for licenses to operate on a weekly basis in 1918. In 1919, it closed during the so-called Red Summer for a few days when there was countrywide violence against African Americans, and the police felt that it was better for it to close down. The park closed its operations for good sometime in 1930, and the property was acquired in the early 1940s to build Barry Farm Dwellings as housing for African American workers in the war effort. In 1926, the District of Columbia government bought Eureka Park's two and a half acres, and in June of that year, it became the Barry Farm Playground, the only one located east of the Anacostia River serving African American children. Its first supervisor and the most noted and best remembered was Mrs. Florence Stokes Matthews.[34]

Mrs. Matthews was born in Washington, D.C., on July 26, 1891, the fifth child of Thomas and Carrie Stokes. She received a diploma from Miner Normal School in 1912 and went to teach in Prince George's County, Maryland. In 1915, Mrs. Matthews received a diploma from the Daniels School of Music upon completion of a teacher's course. Later in life, she studied at Howard University. In 1925, she began her career in the field of recreation when she went to work at the Randall Playground, which was located at the Randall Middle School in SW Washington and was at the time headed by her husband, Samuel D. Matthews. She was then transferred to the Barry Farm Playground, which opened on July 1, 1926. She would remain in that position until 1953, when she was promoted to director of playgrounds in the Southeast and Southwest quadrants of the city. Later on, she was promoted to director of women's sports for the D.C. Recreation Department. She passed away on April 22, 1955.[35]

The idea of creating these playgrounds in Washington, D.C., was based on the belief that "delinquency…[was] closely related to the use of leisure time." Thus, providing activities for the children after school and during vacation was believed to have an "effect on whether they…[were] to be law abiding young citizens or juvenile delinquents." The playground at Barry Farm was open year-round and after school from 3:00 p.m. to 6:00 p.m. during the school year and from 9:00 a.m. to 7:00 p.m. in the summer (including Saturdays). The roster of activities included athletics, physical exercise and quiet story time, as well as handicrafts such as basketry, sewing, crocheting and embroidery for girls. In September 1936, Barry Farm Playground received the third prize in the competition among playgrounds for its display of basketry.[36]

Mildred Raby recalled in a 1989 oral history interview that she had learned sewing and basket weaving at the playground, saying, "It was so good to have something to do in your time that you feel you are accomplishing something." Erma Simon recalled that the baskets and the embroidery that were crafted at the playground were displayed at an exhibit at the end of the season. She also remembered playing tennis, paddle tennis, volleyball, basketball and dodgeball and jumping rope, especially in the summer.[37]

Mrs. Florence Stokes Matthews, the first director of Barry Farm Playground. This portrait was unveiled at the Barry Farm Recreation Center on Sunday, April 24, 1960, at a memorial ceremony to celebrate the life of Mrs. Matthews. *Courtesy Anacostia Community Museum Collection.*

Percy Battles remembered that the playground, later recreation center, was "the home—second home—first home to a lot of people." He pointed out that the parents could be sure that their kids were safe when they were there. He summed up the importance of the center by saying that it was "more than just recreation." He frequented the center from the summer of 1938, when he was thirteen years old, until he was an adult.[38]

Stanley Anderson, who was born in Barry Farm–Hillsdale on Nichols Avenue in 1927, was active in track activities sponsored by the Barry Farm Recreation Center. He later worked at the center as a roving leader and was appointed as a member of the D.C. Council in the late 1960s and early 1970s by President Lyndon B. Johnson to represent Anacostia.[39] Anderson remembered well the Friday night dances at the recreation center. According to him, people would come from all over the city to the dances in the 1930s and early 1940s, and that created problems when the different neighborhood gangs started fighting each other.[40]

Entertainment for the children at Barry Farm–Hillsdale was easy to come by, even before the creation of the Barry Farm Playground. George

Activities Center Building of the Barry Farm Playground (later Barry Farm Recreation Center), 1954. The Barry Farm Playground, which opened in 1926, was the center of recreational activities for the youth of Barry Farm–Hillsdale for many decades. *Courtesy District of Columbia Housing Authority Records, Anacostia Community Museum, Smithsonian Institution.*

J. Trivers, born in 1925, remembered fabricating his toys, chasing rabbits in the woods, catching frogs and tadpoles in the creeks, climbing trees and fishing. During the winter, going down on a sled on the hills of Barry Farm–Hillsdale was a given. During the last decades of the nineteenth century and the first half of the twentieth century, Washington, D.C., saw a fair number of snowstorms, with accumulations averaging almost twenty-five inches between 1870 and 1899 and nearly seventeen inches between 1900 and 1949. Almore Dale remembered that "in the winter…[there was] lots of snow then.…Most any time after Thanksgiving we could depend on these beautiful hills out here having snow." James Chester Jennings Jr. remembered that the area would have at least two significant snowstorms every winter when he was growing up.[41]

Carolyn Taylor Crocker also fondly remembered a sled ride on the west side of the community. She lived on the 2600 block of Nichols Avenue and would go to the slope behind Campbell AME Church and ride down all the way to Sheridan Road before Suitland Parkway was built. She had "wonderful memories" of this period of her life.[42]

Robert Simon Jr. remembered "the best sled ride in the world." The long ride would start at the driveway of Our Lady of Perpetual Help Catholic Church, cross Morris Road, go downhill through Erie Street and Pomeroy Road until reaching Stanton Road and from there go on Suitland Parkway (previously Sheridan Road). Helpful adult neighbors controlled incoming traffic with fire barrels strategically placed in the middle of the street intersections. According to Mr. Simon, the children used to stay out late at night sled riding, and it was "one of the highlights of the winter."[43]

It is important to note that contrary to what happens today, schools did not close in Washington, D.C., when it snowed. Oscar Tyler, born in 1915, remembered that as a child he lived on Stanton Road. One year there was a big snowstorm, and his father improvised a snowplow, tied it to his horse and took the children to Birney School. According to Mr. Tyler, his father did not "care if it's snow, rain or hail. You go to school." Ella Pearis, born and raised on Elvans Road, remembered that she brought home "this big geography [book]," undoubtedly an atlas, to serve as a makeshift sled. She described in an interview in 1986, when she was already eighty years old, how she would go down the snowy hill sitting on the big atlas because you "never stayed out of school."[44]

The Anacostia River, while being a source of entertainment in the winter and summer, was also a source of sorrow. In the winter, Ethel K. Green, born in 1894 and raised on Howard Road, remembered skating on the frozen Anacostia River. Her house on Howard Road backed to the river so she could jump over the fence and go to skate. In the summer, the boys went swimming in the river. More than a few drowned, and the fear of drowning kept Norman E. Dale from going. Stanley Anderson remembered two or three drownings every year. This situation would not be remedied until the 1940s, when the Anacostia Pool was forcefully integrated by the young men of Barry Farm–Hillsdale.[45]

Entertainment at home was also highly cherished. Mrs. Green remembered that in her childhood entertainment was very much at home. Her sisters played in a musical group, and the group performed at "little dances at home." Her parents spent Friday night playing cards and dancing at home or the houses of nearby neighbors, the Shippen and Smith families. She was the daughter of Civil War veteran George D. Graham, who was a federal government employee. Because of their economic security, they had a large house, and during the summer, the family made ice cream with the

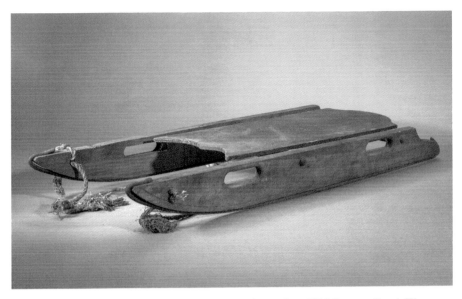

Wooden sled found in the attic of a historic house located on 3038 Stanton Road. The house was built around 1870 and razed in 2015. Sledding down the hills of Barry Farm–Hillsdale was a favorite entertainment for the children in the wintertime. *Courtesy the District of Columbia Historic Preservation Office (DCHPO).*

fruit from their backyard and most likely invited the neighborhood children to partake. Mrs. Green wistfully remembered that all this ended when her father died on January 29, 1904, when she was ten years old.[46]

Perhaps the biggest and best source of entertainment in the Barry Farm–Hillsdale community were the churches. All the churches had activities that could be enjoyed by both adults and the young. There were revivals in the winter, and people would go from church to church attending them. In the summer, there were lawn parties. The church lawns would be decorated with Japanese lanterns, and citronella candles would be lit to keep the mosquitoes away. The churches would organize fundraising dinners serving traditional foods such as fried chicken, chitterlings and pigs' feet. There were spelling bees and oratorical contests in which the youth would present a discourse based on a biblical theme. Easter and Christmas were celebrated with annual programs and pageants. One of the fundraising events that left a mark in the memory of Erma Simon was the "Lemon Squeeze." The lemonade would be prepared individually, and the person buying it would be invited to squeeze the lemons, paying a penny for each seed that was squeezed out.[47]

Chapter 7

Not Everything Was Well

One major event that brought some distress to the life of the Barry Farm–Hillsdale community in the 1930s was the arrival of the Bonus Army marchers. They were protesters camped nearby in the Anacostia Flats who were a source of great concern for the government. For the residents, they were viewed as being mostly "harmless" but still caused a stir.[1]

They were World War I veterans who had been promised a bonus in 1924 that had been deferred until 1945 because of non-agreement on the federal budget. In May 1932, when the country was in the throes of the Great Depression, with unemployment at 25 percent, thousands of veterans came to Washington, the nation's capital, to demand their bonus payment. Some of them settled in the Anacostia Flats beginning on June 6, and eventually 15,000 people—including about 1,100 women and children—were living in the camp.[2]

Conditions in the camp were appalling, and the campers wandered into the African American neighborhood nearby asking for food and, in some cases, shelter from the harsh conditions at the camp. Althea Richardson Smith, a resident of Nichols Avenue who was about five years old at the time, remembered that the "Bonus Men [were] roaming through the neighborhood, and the people would feed them." She also remembered that the men's unkempt appearance frightened the children but that the parents would explain to them that the people at the camp were "under hardship." Charles P. Greene, who was eleven years at the time, remembered that a White Bonus Marcher brought his family to occupy an abandoned house in the neighborhood. It attracted attention because Barry Farm–Hillsdale was an African American neighborhood. The family had two daughters, and the youngest struck up a friendship with Greene's sister; the girls were sorry to part ways when the camp was disbanded.[3]

Indeed, one of the characteristics of the camp that called the attention of the residents of Barry Farm–Hillsdale was the fact that it was integrated, with White and African American veterans living side by side. Accustomed to strict segregation, the nearby residents were surprised at this development. James G. Banks, who was born and raised in Barry Farm–Hillsdale and was twelve years old at the time, declared that the camp was "the first massive integrated effort" that he could remember.[4]

Roy Wilkins, later to be the leader of the National Association for the Advancement of Colored People (NAACP), visited the camp as a young reporter for that organization's magazine, *The Crisis*: "For this army...there was one absentee: James Crow." Wilkins also observed, "They had no time for North, East, South, West black and white divisions. The main problem

Bonus Marchers' camp at the Anacostia Flats in 1932. One of the interesting characteristics of the camp was that it was racially integrated long before integration was seen as a right for African Americans. In this photograph, Bonus Marchers enjoy being entertained by a piano player. *Courtesy Library of Congress, Prints and Photographs Division (LC-USZ62-35302).*

was…to secure relief from the ills which beset them, black and white alike."[5] What Wilkins was not aware of was that many African Americans had already been driven out with the excuse that they were communists. In the eyes of the policemen and undercover agents in the camp, a sure sign of communist tendencies was to be Jewish or African American.[6]

The veterans were camped not only at the Anacostia Flats but also in downtown Washington. The government saw the presence of the Bonus Army marchers as a disturbing symbol of the Great Depression and eventually decided that they had to be removed. July 28, 1932, was the date chosen to start evacuating the camps in downtown Washington. It went very badly, with stiff resistance from the demonstrators and strong reaction from the police in charge of the removal. By the afternoon, troops were called from Fort Myer to evict the demonstrators under the direction of General Douglas MacArthur. There were cavalry and infantry troops, with sabers and tear gas and military vehicles for good measure. After clearing downtown, the military arrived at the 11th Street Bridge with a large searchlight to illuminate the dark camp.[7]

According to Joseph C. Harsch, a *New York Times* journalist who was standing next to General MacArthur, the general gave the order for the camp to be torched. "He summoned a sergeant and gave him the order. The sergeant collected a squad and started down the row of makeshift huts. They wadded newspapers into a corner and set them alight. The row of huts was soon blazing."[8]

Another eyewitness saw the blaze from the river as their boat was returning from a pleasure trip on the Potomac River, "an escape from the sweltering Washington heat." The view as the boat approached the landing on Water Street SW was that "the section on the right side beyond Bowling [*sic*] Air Force Base seemed to be on fire. The whole bank seemed to be burning." The captain's group drove through the Anacostia flats encampment and witnessed its destruction. There were tents, lean-tos, huts built of blankets and quilts all rapidly catching fire. Families, including pregnant women and babies, packed their meager belongings in bundles and swung them over their shoulders so they could run as fast as they could. Ever present were the dust and the tear gas clouds and the stench of uncollected garbage.[9] Thus ended this momentous event that touched the community of Barry Farm–Hillsdale.

If the Bonus Army encampment was an outside problem, there were plenty of problems within the community that persisted for decades. One of the most pressing was the lack of infrastructure and essential services.

Delivery of mail, for instance, was an early demand from the community. There was no electricity, running water, sewage system or paved streets. Crime was not a significant problem in the early decades, but it still existed. Segregation was an unpleasant fact of life and touched everybody, as did the isolation of the community from its White neighbors in Anacostia, Congress Heights and Washington, D.C. In 1918, a writer lamented that the area "south of the Eastern branch" was neglected "in the matter of improvements and facilities, pavements, sewers, water mains, sidewalks and other betterments." Lack of water mains allowed "houses [to] burn to the ground for lack of water to quench the flames." Another recurrent problem for the Barry Farm–Hillsdale community was the loss of property through eminent domain for public projects.[10]

One persistent problem tackled by the Barry Farm–Hillsdale community was the delivery of mail. In 1895, there was already a movement to get mail delivered by "mounted carriers" to Barry Farm–Hillsdale. The community had 2,700 inhabitants, and the post office in Anacostia was two miles away for those who lived in the far reaches of the community. Unspoken, but probably a concern, was the fact that African Americans from Barry Farm–Hillsdale were not welcome by the White residents of Anacostia. It seems that the problem was not solved until Dr. Rezin H. Shipley was given a contract by the post office to open a station in his drugstore in 1913, eighteen years later.[11]

Waiting decades to receive improvements in Barry Farm–Hillsdale was nothing new and would continue into the twentieth century with dire consequences. As one newspaper article noted very colorfully in 1911, "So far as ability to command convenient water facilities is concerned, the residents might almost as well be dropped in the center of the great Sahara Desert." Some families had to get their water from the streams that still ran through the neighborhood in the early twentieth century. Raymond Bumbry, born in 1894, who lived on Stanton Road almost at the corner of Sheridan Road, remembered in 1989 that in the early twentieth century he went to the nearby spring to get water.[12]

Other residents developed creative ways to obtain potable water. Pierre McKinley Taylor remembered that his family's home on Nichols Avenue had what he called "a system" to obtain water for use in the household. The runoff from the roof was channeled through a charcoal filter and then stored in a "big well."[13]

By 1911, the water sources at Barry Farm–Hillsdale, all public and private wells, were believed to be polluted and carrying bacteria that caused typhoid fever. Dr. William K. Scott, the community's doctor, declared that every one of the numerous cases of typhoid fever he had treated was due to the drinking water. He continued, stating that there was only one public well still functioning, as all the others had been closed by the authorities during the last few years due to contamination. Dr. Scott concluded, "Without sewage or piped water of any kind one can hardly expect water from that soil to be free from impurities."[14]

The Sanborn Fire Insurance Map of Washington, D.C., for 1916 depicts that a twenty-inch water main was already installed in Nichols Avenue in 1911. The installation of the water main might have been the beginning of a response from the city to deal with the water supply problem in the area. Eventually, pumps and hydrants were installed in strategic places so the population could have access to clean water. John Dale, who lived on Sumner Road, remembered that his family had to go to a hydrant located on Nichols Avenue to get water for daily needs. Thomas Taylor remembered that the hydrants would freeze in the winter and that the inhabitants had to build fires around them so that the water would flow. The last community hydrant was removed in the 1960s.[15]

According to a survey of the community undertaken in 1944, the "first extensive public improvements made by the District were in 1926." Then streets were widened from thirty-three to fifty feet between 1926 and 1928, and sewers were installed in the Sheridan and Stanton Roads and adjacent streets. Lack of piped water and sanitation was still a problem in the 1940s. Ethel G. Greene wrote a paper titled "My Community—'Barry Farms'" in 1949. Using data from the 1940 Census, she determined that 66 percent of the households in Barry Farm–Hillsdale still lacked some "sanitary facility." This meant that they lacked a private bath, a flush toilet or running water inside the house.[16]

At the beginning of the settlement, the creeks crisscrossing the area, especially Stickfoot Branch (the largest of them), were a source of water and entertainment where the children could swim or wade in the summer. Then, after a few decades, they were polluted and, in the case of Stickfoot Branch, a source of dangerous flooding. The earliest recorded flooding of Stickfoot Branch was also a deadly one. On the night of July 1, 1884, heavy rain fell continuously in Washington, D.C., for two hours, causing widespread flooding. The house of Elizabeth Blue on Sheridan Avenue on the margins of the Stickfoot Branch near Nichols Avenue was completely flooded. The water carried Mrs. Blue away, and she drowned. Her children climbed onto the roof of the house. Police officer Lingan B. (L.B.) Anderson rescued them and took them to safety.[17]

Periodic floods remained a threat. In August 1906, the basement of Bethlehem Baptist Church, located on Nichols Avenue near Sheridan Road, was flooded. Because of the flooding, it was impossible to walk along Sheridan Road, and people had to be transported back and forth in a wagon. A year later, on September 23, 1907, another family faced the danger of death when their house on Sheridan Road between Stanton Avenue and Pomeroy Road was flooded. The household's kitchen, built as an addition to the back of the house, was washed away. The lady of the house, Mrs. Arthur Bradley, and her two daughters barely survived being washed away with the structure while trying to save items from the kitchen. As it was, the stove and the kitchen furniture were lost at the cost of $150.[18]

The flood of 1923 was well remembered by elderly residents of Barry Farm–Hillsdale in the 1970s and documented in the newspapers. Mr. Vivian Herbert Tibbs was one of the two cab drivers who maintained a stand on Nichols Avenue, ready to drive people up the neighborhood's hills. He drove a Model T Ford, and although he did not live in Barry Farm–Hillsdale, he was a member of the Barry Farm Civic Association.[19]

On Saturday, April 28, 1923, Tibbs picked up a passenger on Nichols Avenue, went up Morris Road and then came back down through Sheridan Road carrying three female passengers in his vehicle. The sudden flooding, caused by a cloudburst that raised the water level at the Stickfoot Branch by fifteen feet, swept Tibbs's cab when it approached Nichols Avenue. The driver of another vehicle, which was also overturned and swept by the water, helped the three passengers to safety, but Tibbs did not have the same luck. An eyewitness to the tragedy remembered in the 1970s that Tibbs was screaming for help as he was taken away by the water current, but nobody was able to help him.[20]

After the tragedy, there was a flurry of action asking for money to deal with the drainage problem in Barry Farm–Hillsdale. The *Evening Star* published an article lamenting the small amount dedicated by the city to deal with sewer and drainage in the area that they identified as "suburban Washington," which included Barry Farm–Hillsdale. A delegation from Barry Farm–Hillsdale visited General H.M. Lord, director of the Bureau of the Budget, claiming that the Stickfoot Branch "amounts to nothing more than an open sewer, and sewage and drainage...[were] sadly needed." The delegation presented photos of the area and asked for sufficient appropriation to grant enough money to improve the drainage and sanitary conditions of the neighborhood. Washington, D.C.'s sanitary engineer indicated that nothing could be done until the streets in Barry Farm–Hillsdale were declared public. They were considered private property by the city. A condemnation suit was then filled to transfer ownership of the streets to the city. By the end of the decade, Stickfoot Branch had been covered up to Nichols Avenue—undoubtedly due to the death of Vivian Herbert Tibbs and the intense publicity that it had generated.[21]

Losing land through eminent domain was another problem suffered by the residents of Barry Farm–Hillsdale very early on. Eminent domain is defined as "a right of a government to take private property for public use by virtue of the superior dominion of the sovereign power over all lands within its jurisdiction."[22] It merely means that if the government determines that one's property is needed for public use, it can take it by providing compensation.

The first significant loss of property by Barry Farm–Hillsdale residents happened when the Washington City and Point Look Out Company (later named the Alexandria Branch of the Baltimore and Ohio Railroad) was built in 1873–74. It entered Barry Farm–Hillsdale on the northeast side, cutting through Howard Road, Stickfoot Branch, Sumner and Stevens Roads before coming out right on the margins of the grounds of St. Elizabeths Hospital. Although we have not been able to locate information about the process of eminent domain that took place during the construction of the railroad, one can note from perusing a contemporary map that many owners lost parts of their lots. Then, in the early 1920s, Firth Sterling Avenue bordering the railroad took away more land in the same area.[23]

The second significant loss of property came in the early twentieth century. It had to do with the construction of a sewage outfall and pumping station at Poplar Point, where the Barry family residence had once stood. At first, the government attempted to negotiate the buying of the properties with the owners, but they did not agree on a fair price. Consequently, in November 1903, it was announced that the district government was suing the owners to have the properties condemned. Eventually, the "point lot," the lot at the very edge of Poplar Point, and lots 38 and 39 of section 9 of Barry Farm–Hillsdale were taken in full. Parts of another sixteen lots in sections 8 and 9 were also taken.[24] Other seizures by eminent domain would come in the 1940s, contributing to the decline of the community.

In the late nineteenth century and the early decades of the twentieth century, crime was not a significant issue in Barry Farm–Hillsdale. The newspapers reported petty thefts, con men taking advantage of ignorant persons, raids in illegal "speakeasies" and street brawls in the last decade of the nineteenth century. In the 1920s, four bootleggers operated out of Barry Farm–Hillsdale. The crime that most frightened the community in those early decades was a brutal assassination in late 1902. On Christmas Eve, a woman named Kate Jordan, who worked as a fortuneteller and lived on Howard Road, was assassinated. She had a wide circle of acquaintances because of her profession and was believed to have much money at her home. Her throat was slashed, and she died from hemorrhaging. The bloodhounds the police put on the trail of the perpetrator followed his scent to the edge of the Anacostia River, where they stopped. The belief was that the perpetrator had crossed the river on a boat. His identity was never uncovered.[25] This murder might have been the very first significant crime committed at Barry Farm–Hillsdale since its creation in 1867.

Discrimination and segregation were twin scourges suffered by the Barry Farm–Hillsdale African American community from the very beginning. Coupled with the physical isolation of the area, it created difficulties for the daily lives of the citizens of Barry Farm–Hillsdale. The African American Barry Farm community was squeezed between two White communities: Uniontown (later renamed Anacostia), which was developed in 1854 as the first suburb of Washington, D.C., and Congress Heights, which came into being in 1890 and was adjacent to St. Elizabeths. The only access coming from Washington was the 11th Street Bridge. The sense of isolation was a theme often repeated in the oral interviews. Expressions like "We were like an island," "It was sort of separate," like a "city within a city," "We were sort of in a pocket" and "We were kind of pigeonholed" all expressed the feelings of the Barry Farm–Hillsdale residents. Carolyn Taylor Crocker expressed her thoughts on the subject by stating, "That's no way to live."[26]

African Americans from Barry Farm–Hillsdale were not welcomed at nearby Anacostia, and Whites did not come into the neighborhood unless they were making deliveries. Residents of Anacostia did not appreciate the fact that journalists began conflating Barry Farm–Hillsdale (usually mentioned as "Hillsdale") with their neighborhood as one community. In 1890, a resident of Anacostia wrote to the *Sunday Herald* that "the sluice-gates of…[his] wrath" were open because another newspaper, the *Evening Star*, was publishing a regular column titled "Anacostia Notes" in which news from Hillsdale was also covered. According to the writer, "This tends to impugn the moral status of our community, whereas so near perfection."[27]

Memories of discrimination and disagreeable encounters with White residents of adjacent neighborhoods long lived in the minds of those raised in Barry Farm–Hillsdale. Carolyn Taylor Crocker remembered entering a toy store on Nichols Avenue owned by a White man. The owner had a parrot that repeated the N-word to both White and African American

Bury's Drugstore, circa 1919. Located on Nichols Avenue, this White-owned drugstore did not welcome African Americans. Residents of Barry Farm–Hillsdale did not mind the slight because they could go to the Douglass Hall Drugstore, located three blocks to the south. Today, the Bury's Drugstore building is occupied by Chase Bank. *Courtesy Library of Congress, Prints and Photographs Division (LC-USZ62-67433).*

patrons since the bird naturally could not distinguish the races. Ms. Crocker and her brothers and sisters also knew that they could not go to Bury's—the White drugstore also on Nichols Avenue—but were content to go to the drugstore three blocks away, first run by Dr. Gales and later by Dr. Shipley.[28]

Norman E. Dale, a lifelong resident of Barry Farm–Hillsdale, recalled in 1989, "Well, you could go down…[to Anacostia], but you weren't welcome down there. And, of course, most of us who had any pride wouldn't go down there and face that situation.…[We] had too much pride to go in there and be insulted."[29] Young African American boys growing up in Barry Farm–Hillsdale had memories of fights with White boys. George Patterson, born in 1914 and who lived at Elvans Road as a young child, remembered that when he was attending Birney School, he sometimes did not go straight home. He made a point of detouring by Morris Road, the dividing line between the African American and the White neighborhoods, to go up the hill. Then he would get involved in a big fight with the White kids at the corner of Morris

Road and Maple View Place, and the two groups threw rocks at each other.[30] Almore Dale also remembered scuffles with the White boys. As he told the story, "If we got too far down Nichols Avenue, the white boys would gang up on us and chase us back up to...[our] community." Also, he added, "The same was true when they came over our line—our boundaries."[31]

African Americans were also not welcome in the White neighborhood of Congress Heights, which was located just beyond St. Elizabeths Hospital. John Dale was emphatic when he stated, "They didn't want you to walk through Congress Heights....I can recall that, since I've been a man."[32] Stanley Anderson remembered "being literally run out of Congress Heights as a...boy."[33] James Chester Jennings Jr. remembered decades later that when he rode the bus from a segregated school on the other side of the river into Barry Farm–Hillsdale, White students living in Congress Heights came in the same bus. When he and his colleagues got off at Sumner Road, the White kids would start shouting "'n— this' and 'n— that.'" One time, one of the White boys had his elbow out of the window while screaming the offending words. One of the African American boys picked up a fallen tree limb and hit the elbow protruding out of the window. Mr. Jennings concluded, "I don't think it did that much damage but...."[34]

In 1986, Anita F. Allen, who grew up on Shannon Street in the 1930s and 1940s, remembered another kind of disappointing discrimination. According to her remembrances, "A great experience on Saturdays" was to ride to the end of the line of the streetcar. She and her friends would sometimes ride all the way to Glen Echo but could not get off and go into the park because only Whites were allowed there. After desegregation, Ms. Allen stated, "Even when the law was changed I would never go to the Park because of my resentment of the past."[35]

Despite all of this in the late 1930s, Barry Farm–Hillsdale was a cohesive, thriving African American community. The next decade would be one of the most turbulent of its history and would see the beginning of the dissolution of the original community's identity.

PART IV

The 1940s

○————————————○

And Then Came Change

Chapter 8

World War II, Barry Farm Dwellings and the Military Road

W orld War II brought momentous changes to the Barry Farm–Hillsdale community. In April 1940, when the census takers started making their rounds in the community, the war was already in the air. Hitler had invaded Poland on September 1, 1939. Two days later, France and the United Kingdom declared a state of war with Germany. It would take more than a year for the United States to declare war on Japan after the bombing of Pearl Harbor on December 7, 1941, and for Germany and its Axis partners to declare war on the United States two days later.

In the lead-up to the war, the census takers found a prosperous and stable working-class community. Longtime providers of jobs such as St. Elizabeths Hospital, the gas company and the navy yard still offered positions in nonskilled jobs to residents of the community. New opportunities had opened in downtown Washington, D.C., for laborers, messengers, elevator operators, phone operators, waiters, porters and janitors at hotels, restaurants, department stores and government offices such as the Treasury, Agriculture Department, Bureau of Standards and the Supreme Court and on Capitol Hill. Women, when working outside the home, mostly labored as cleaners, nursemaids, cooks and seamstresses. Some had acquired jobs in the federal government as cleaners and operators of machinery in the Bureau of Engraving producing the country's currency. Another few were teachers in the school system or clerks in the federal government.

A few young men were just beginning their participation in the labor force and found work in reforestation with the Civilian Conservation Corps or as laborers in the Works Progress Administration. Both programs were part of President Roosevelt's New Deal projects to provide employment during the Depression era that preceded the Second World War.[1] Employment prospects also improved for residents of Barry Farm–Hillsdale because of the impending war. According to Erma Simon, it was "good coming out of bad." She remembered that at first African Americans had to take the civil service test to get government jobs, but when the war started, "people were hired because they needed them badly." One of the most significant changes was at the post office. Before the war, African Americans with college degrees were hired only as mail carriers, but with the advent of the war, they got jobs as clerks, with the possibility of promotion to supervisors. In 1989, Miss Simon proudly stated that she rarely saw a White clerk in the post office agencies in Washington, D.C.[2]

Despite the normalcy of everyday life, the threat of the war was hovering over the neighborhood, and with the passing of the Selective and Training Service Act, all males between the ages of twenty-one and thirty-six had to present themselves and register for the draft on October 16, 1940. Thus, Ulysses J. Banks, elder brother of James, was a tall, lanky twenty-one-year-old working for the Welfare and Recreation Association in downtown Washington and came to his old elementary school, Birney, to register. Nathan Joseph Bronstein, the son of the Jewish grocer Benjamin Bronstein, went to register that same day at the Anacostia High School. He was twenty-five years old, single and working for his father in the family grocery store.[3]

Three boys from Barry Farm–Hillsdale did not come back from the war. Minerva and Roland W. Dale had been living in Barry Farm–Hillsdale since at least the 1920s. He was an engraver who worked for private companies until landing a job working with blueprints in the navy yard. Minerva had worked for the federal government but was unemployed in 1940. The couple had two children, Hilda and Roland Jr., both born in Barry Farm–Hillsdale.[4]

Roland Jr. was one of the Barry Farm–Hillsdale young men who went to register at Birney School on October 16, 1940. Almost one year later, he was enlisted in the army as a private in Baltimore and went on duty at Fort Lee, Virginia, as part of Company D of the Ninth Quartermaster Corps. On October 13, 1941, almost a year to the date after he had gone to register for the draft, Roland Jr. was dead. He was tragically killed in a traffic accident while on duty. Four days later, his remains were buried at Arlington National Cemetery.[5]

Milton B. Wright was born in Washington, D.C., in 1918. He was living with his mother, Minnie; brother, Frank; and sister, Novella, on Wade Street and working as a drafter in 1940. On April 8, 1941, Wright enlisted in the army at Baltimore as a private. Three years later, he died while serving as second lieutenant in the Quartermaster Corps in Algeria, North Africa.[6]

The third young man who died in the war was Paul Graham Mitchell, who inherited a rich military background. His maternal grandfather was George D. Graham, who had enlisted as a twenty-year-old in the Union army during the Civil War with the rank of corporal in Company F, 32nd U.S. Colored Infantry, and was promoted to sergeant on September 1, 1864. Three months later, on November 30, 1864, Sergeant Graham was wounded in the Battle of Honey Hill in South Carolina. His wounds were so severe that he was transferred to the New York Harbor Hospital for treatment and mustered out on May 25, 1865. In December of that same year, Sergeant Graham received an invalid pension.[7]

Paul attended Birney School, Cardozo High School and Hampton Institute, where he obtained a Bachelor of Science degree in structural engineering. He then went to work with Albert I. Cassell, who was the director of the Building and Grounds Department at Howard University.[8] Mitchell had been interested in flying since childhood. Even at twelve years old, he made a plane of discarded material with the help of his younger brother, Harold, and friends.[9]

After being drafted, he attended flight school at Tuskegee Army Airfield and graduated on July 3, 1942. His class was the fourth of the Tuskegee Airmen to graduate and the largest until then. He was part of the 99th Fighter Squadron. On April 2, 1943, the squadron departed Tuskegee to New York in preparation to sail overseas. It embarked on April 16, 1943, sailing to Casablanca and then on to the French colony of Morocco. Later, the squadron moved to Tunisia, where the men participated in a victory parade celebrating the liberation of the country. In June 1943, the 99th saw action for the first time while attached to 33rd Fighter Group.[10]

Lieutenant Mitchell wrote home, telling his parents about his first battle. According to him, "We really got our teeth into the battle and it was interesting."[11] Later that month, the 99th Fighter Squadron was attached to the 324th Fighter Group and began flying escort missions between Tunisia and Sicily. The squadron also earned the first of its three World War II Distinguished Unit Citations that month. In July 1943, the squadron moved to Licata, Sicily, and started providing cover for Allied shipping in the Mediterranean Sea and air support for the 7th Army. At the end of the month,

Second Lieutenant Paul Graham Mitchell with his graduating class, July 3, 1942. It was the fourth class to graduate and the largest at the time. Second Lieutenant Mitchell is the seventh from the left. *Courtesy Air Force Historical Research Agency, Maxwell Air Force Base, Alabama.*

the squadron was back in Sicily. On August 11, 1943, Lieutenant Mitchell died when his P-40 Warhawk fighter crashed in midair with another plane in his formation. He was the third pilot of the 99th Fighter Squadron to be lost in action. The pilot in the other plane was able to bail out.[12]

To the dismay of Lieutenant Mitchell's parents, Lucile and Harry Mitchell, the War Department did not immediately inform them of their son's death. Word came through the *Afro-American* newspaper, which had a correspondent embedded with the unit. The official communication from the War Department did not come until the day after the news appeared in the paper. In September 1943, Mitchell was posthumously promoted to first lieutenant. He also posthumously received the Distinguished Flying Cross and had his name given to a war housing project at Tuskegee Army Airfield in 1944.[13]

Civilians left behind at Barry Farm–Hillsdale immediately rose to the challenge to help in the war effort. Already on December 10, 1941, the names of Ulysses J. Banks and Winslow W. Murray, both from Stanton Road; Norman E. Dale, from Wade Road; and Reverend C.B. Ashton, from Morris Road, appeared in a list of Washington, D.C., air raid wardens and leaders of Civilian Defense Committees. Louise Dale was appointed food and house warden on November 1, 1942. In October 1942, a scrap metal drive in the neighborhood to help the war effort was considered highly successful.[14]

As the United States geared up for the war in the early 1940s, it increased its industrial capacity and triggered a significant migration to the cities by those looking for work in the new armaments manufacturing industry. The building of decent and inexpensive housing for defense industry workers became part of the war effort as much as the construction of military facilities, shipyards and armament factories.[15]

In Washington, D.C., a city that was already "dangerously overcrowded" because of the influx of workers for the war effort, the proportion of African Americans moving to the city was underestimated. The National Capital Housing Authority (NCHA) had to request permission to build additional units to try to supply the needs for African American housing. But still, in August 1943, it was being reported that the available housing was "approximating the need, so far as whites are concerned. But it does not meet the need for Negroes." In order to try to close the deficit, Barry Farm, James Creek and Parkside were government housing developments explicitly built to house African Americans and in which workers in defense-related jobs in Washington, D.C., had priority for rental. The three housing developments received residents between 1941 and 1943.[16]

According to the official report by the NCHA relating to the building of Barry Farm Dwellings, they had wanted to build the housing development at another location. Due to the resistance from White residents who lived nearby and from a real estate developer, the NCHA then turned its sights on Barry Farm–Hillsdale. Although not specified in the NCHA report, it seems that the area where they initially wanted to build was in Congress Heights, on Alabama Avenue between 13th and 15th Streets. The Southeast Council of Citizens' Associations expressed its opinion that the construction of the housing development would be "ruining the natural development of Southeast in the post-war era." A later report on segregation in Washington, D.C., stated that "at the height of a critical shortage of housing for Negro war workers...the construction of a project...in the Congress Heights area... had to be abandoned...because of pressure by organized groups which were 'fencing' in the area for whites."[17]

The NCHA report described the new area chosen for the housing development as "a sparsely developed area of approximately 34 acres"

Aerial view of the west side of Barry Farm–Hillsdale, December 1940. The NCHA chose this area to build Barry Farm Dwellings in 1941. To the right of the photograph are Nichols Avenue and Sheridan Road. *Courtesy District of Columbia Housing Authority Records, Anacostia Community Museum, Smithsonian Institution.*

containing thirty-two houses mostly of frame construction and "scattered over the site." The area was part of section 8 of the original plat for Barry Farm in 1867. Eureka Park previously occupied at least two and a half acres of the site. At the time of the building of the Barry Farm Dwellings, the Barry Farm Playground occupied this same area. The thirty-two houses that were destroyed to build the housing development were mostly located on the fronts of those very large one-acre lots created in 1867. The 1931 *Baist* map for Barry Farm–Hillsdale, however, indicates that some lots were empty and that others had been subdivided and had more than one structure built on them.[18]

In the eyes of an urban developer, the site was indeed "sparsely developed," and the houses were "scattered over the site." When surveying the land, there was no accounting by the developer for the "beautiful gardens with all sorts of vegetables," fruit trees, grapevines, nut trees and small livestock that most likely occupied some of the acres. The houses were also described as "substandard" and a "community menace" because they were considered fire hazards and unsanitary. Completely out of consideration was the dignity afforded by the ownership of one's own house.[19]

The main cluster of houses demolished to build Barry Farm Dwellings was located on Sumner Road, described in the report as "one of the principal roads in the picturesque Barry Farm settlement in south east." Indeed, Sumner Road was a significant artery because, before the building of the Suitland Parkway, it was the way that official visitors took when coming from Washington to visit Bolling Airfield. They came from Washington through the 11th Street Bridge, then went up Nichols Avenue, turned right on Sumner Road and left on Firth Sterling Avenue to the gates of the airfield.

Kenneth Chapman, who was a teenager living on Sumner Road at the time, remembered many decades later the names of many of the people displaced by the building of Barry Farm Dwellings. One of them was Cora W. Wilkinson, a widow in her sixties. She was the widow of Richard Ulysses Wilkinson, who was a mail carrier and the brother of Garnet Wilkinson,

Houses on Sumner Road that were demolished (thirty in all) in 1941 to give way to the building of the Barry Farm Dwellings. *District of Columbia Housing Authority Records, Anacostia Community Museum, Smithsonian Institution.*

the assistant superintendent of the segregated school system in Washington, D.C. Cora was the daughter of early settlers John Alfred and Mary Dunmore Green, who had acquired a lot on Sumner Avenue where they built their house and raised Cora and her siblings.[20]

Richard and Cora must have met each other in the neighborhood since he lived with his parents, James and Grace Wilkinson, on Nichols Avenue around the corner from Sumner Road. The couple married on June 26, 1901, and remained living on Nichols Avenue, where their daughters were born. Cora worked as a pioneer kindergarten teacher at Garfield School. Later, she also ran a kindergarten for the children of Barry Farm–Hillsdale in the basement of St. Philip the Evangelist Episcopal Church. She was remembered as a "pleasant sort of individual...[and] community conscious." After her husband's death in 1939, Mrs. Wilkinson moved back to Sumner Road, and she must have been distraught at the events that followed.[21]

On May 2, 1941, NCHA requested the courts to institute condemnation procedures to obtain the houses through eminent domain. In the end, thirty houses were demolished, and twenty-three families were displaced for the building of the complex. Most likely the other seven houses were empty. The authority rehoused eleven of the families displaced in January 1942, but the report does not specify where. The other twelve families were deemed ineligible for help "because of family composition and too high income." Mrs. Wilkinson undoubtedly was included in the last category. Her house in the 1940 Census had received a valuation of $11,000, extremely high for the neighborhood. Thus ended the presence of a family who had settled on their property on Sumner Road seven decades before.[22]

The construction of the 442-unit Barry Farm Dwellings was plagued with delays. There were shortages of manpower and materials such as "hardware, plumbing fixtures, floor coverings." In October 1942, a temporary drainage system failed and isolated the houses that were already built in a sea of mud. A wall separating the site from St. Elizabeths Hospital was endangered because of erosion due to drainage problems.[23]

The first set of houses was finally delivered in November 1942 and the last almost a year later in October 1943. First preference was given to the Housing Authority's tenants who had been living in trailer parks after being displaced because of the expansion of the navy yard, as well as to people employed in the war effort. The new row houses, constructed of concrete blocks, were organized in clusters of three or four row houses. The houses contained two, three or four bedrooms. They had no basements but had small lawns in front and the back.[24]

James Chester Jennings; his wife, Luberta; and their five children moved into Barry Farm Dwellings in 1943 because he was a worker at the navy yard. The family lived on Stevens Road, and her son James Chester Jr. remembered decades later that the development was very clean and pleasant and that everybody knew everybody.[25] Another resident with pleasant memories of the first years of Barry Farm Dwellings was James G. Banks, who would occupy the office of executive director of the National Housing Authority in the 1970s, the successor organization to the one that had created Barry Farm Dwellings three decades earlier. Banks moved to the new housing project with his wife and son in 1945 because he was working at the navy yard. He remembered a neighborhood of mostly two-parent households with well-tended yards and tennis courts for recreation. The housing development manager lent lawnmowers to cut the grass. Most people had come from outside Washington, D.C., to work in the war effort.[26]

Luegene (variously spelled as "Lugene" or "Eugenia") Lee Russell also had good memories about Barry Farm Dwellings. She had resided at Sumner Road since 1921. She witnessed the construction of the housing development from a vantage point. In 1989, she declared, "Barry Farms... was very nice. It was very nice until later years."[27]

With the end of the war, Barry Farm Dwellings entered a new phase as low-cost rental housing and eventually as public housing. The construction of Barry Farm Dwellings represented a disruption of the historic Barry Farm–Hillsdale community. But it was ultimately the construction of the military road connecting Bolling Airfield (today Joint Base Anacostia-Bolling) to Camp Springs Airfield (today Andrews Air Force Base) in Maryland that would mark the beginning of its dissolution. The anti-freeway movement that came into being two decades later might have saved Barry Farm–Hillsdale from being bisected by the military road. In 1943, however, the demands of the war were prevalent, and the needs of the residents were not at all taken into consideration.

Initially designed to provide an easy connection between the two military bases, after the war the road became the route for an easy commute by federal employees living in communities east of the District of Columbia. Now known as Suitland Parkway, it displaced hundreds of Barry Farm–Hillsdale residents, physically divided the community in two and disrupted the standard of living and the social stability that had been cultivated by community members over the previous decades.[28]

Planning for the construction of the road began long before the war. In 1937, the National Capital Park and Planning Commission (NCPPC) had

Barry Farm Dwellings, April 28, 1944. Opened in 1942, Barry Farm Dwellings provided housing at first for African Americans coming to work in the war effort. Later, it became low-rent housing and finally public housing. *Courtesy Library of Congress, Prints and Photographs Division (LC-G613-45237).*

wanted to build a parkway connecting South Capitol Street with Bolling Field and ultimately to Camp Springs Field. The construction did not materialize then for lack of funds. Planning started again in earnest in early 1942, and in February of that year, the preliminary plans for the road were presented to NCPPC. On February 27, the landscape architect in charge of the plans sent a detailed list of the properties that had to be acquired for its construction from South Capitol Street to the district line, about three miles long. Most of them were located on the footprint of Barry Farm–Hillsdale.[29]

Even with all the plans on paper, there were doubts about the project. Who would pay for it? Was the road a real war necessity? The South Capitol Street Bridge had not yet been built—it would not be erected until 1950—so the connection to the city would not be accomplished by building the road. So why build it? Finally, after much prodding, word came down from President Franklin Roosevelt in a letter to Secretary of War Henry L. Stimson dated of August 25, 1942, that the road was indeed a war necessity. The letter read, in part, "In connection with the installation of an army air base at Camp Springs Meadows, you are directed to acquire the necessary land for the proposed installation…including the right of way for a suitable access road…via the contemplated Suitland Parkway route to Bolling Field."[30]

By July 1943, the government was already enforcing the eminent domain order to acquire the properties, and the owners were resisting. Many who owned houses refused to sell them because the construction of the road had not yet started. The NCPPC became concerned with the adverse publicity and also because Congress was resisting the acquisition by the military of land for which there was no immediate military need. Whatever the concerns, the plans went ahead.[31]

Ninety-one houses were in the way of the road—38 percent of them were owner-occupied, 57 percent were rented and only 5 percent were empty. The official statistics did not list how many individual lives were disrupted. Nevertheless, the press was interested in the subject and reported that 112 families comprising 600 people were facing eviction. They had been told on August 21 that they had to vacate their houses within twenty days.[32]

An article in the magazine *Pulse*, published locally in Barry Farm–Hillsdale, stated that the amounts paid for the houses were "pitifully small" and not enough to pay for houses elsewhere in Washington, D.C. Also, many of those residents being displaced were elderly and "too old to start buying all over again, provided they could find some place to move." The article concluded with a truism about urban redevelopment: "[When] progress is made, as in this case, it is often at some one's expense generally those who can ill afford it."[33]

Robert S. Penn and Henrietta Myers, who seemingly had kept grocery stores in a friendly competition for years facing each other on Sheridan Road at the corner of Pomeroy, lost their properties. Penn lost several properties besides his shop and his large house located on the 2700 block of Sheridan, where he had lived for thirty-eight years. He gave an interview declaring that he had been able to move his family to another location but that the new accommodations were "by no means satisfactory."[34]

The Chapman family patriarch, Nathan Chapman, had in the words of his grandson Kenneth come from Piscataway, Maryland, and "planted his foot" on Barry Farm–Hillsdale around 1895. In that year, he married Maude Morse, a girl from Washington, D.C. At first, they lived on Sheridan Road, but pretty soon Nathan bought property on the 1000 block of Sumner Avenue, where he built "an enclave" and where the family would stay for several decades. Nathan Chapman was Catholic and helped build Our

Lady of Perpetual Help Catholic Church. He was also an entrepreneur who worked as a huckster, selling produce and fish door to door. His products were of such good quality that he was well received in White Congress Heights, where African Americans were typically not welcome. His nickname in the neighborhood was "Fish Chapman."[35]

When the order came to vacate, four families were living in the Chapman enclave. Kenneth Chapman, then fifteen years old, remembered that the government said, "Take this and go…you couldn't stay there. You had to go." The price paid for the land and the three houses occupied by the Chapmans was not fair market price. The family members were scattered.[36]

In the end, the NCHA found homes for ninety-nine families; the remaining thirteen had been able to find new housing on their own. The authority resettled people into several public housing developments: Barry Farm Dwellings, Parkside Dwellings, Anthony Bowen Houses and Nichols Avenue Houses. The last two developments were temporary, which meant that those who had moved there had to move again when they were dismantled after the war.

The residents of Barry Farm–Hillsdale on the path of the road were also at the mercy of speculators, who, seeing the opportunity to make easy money, pounced on them. Wilbur L. Gray and his wife, Doris, formed a crafty and devious real estate team. Wilbur was adept at attending the District of Columbia city property tax sales during the Depression to acquire properties that were in arrears. According to an acquaintance, this was a hobby for him. In other cases, he was more stealthy—he would research NCPPC's requests for titles to discover which areas it was interested in. Then he would buy the properties in those areas for very little, especially in the cases when the owners were behind in their real estate taxes. He was well known by the NCPPC staff, who considred him "constant trouble."[37]

Gray and his wife owned at least fourteen properties on the path of the road. One had been acquired by stealth or at least by withrawing information about the real value of the property. Arthur R. Bradley and his wife, Mary, had owned lot 8, section 7 of Barry Farm–Hillsdale since 1910 or earlier. Mary died in 1917, followed by Arthur in 1932. The property then passed to their daughters, Adalena and Sadie. The *Baist* map for the area in 1931 showed a small frame house facing Sheridan Road and backing on Dunbar Road on a steep hill. By 1940, however, both daughters had married and were living in the Northwest quadrant of Washington, D.C.[38]

On April 20, 1943, Doris Gray paid $150 to the Bradley daughters for the parcel. Her husband, Wilbur, notorized the transaction. The Grays were by then well informed on the construction of the upcoming military road. A year earlier, Wilbur had made a call to John Nolen Jr., director of planning of NCPPC, inquiring about the project. His bad reputation had preceeded him, and the memo on file reporting his call contains a terse note: "most unfortunate." A year later, Doris Gray sold the lot to the U.S. government for $1,513, making a hefty gain on her investment.[39]

If the building of the military road displaced six hundred of the living, there is no account of how many dead were displaced and dishonored. Macedonia Cemetery, attached to Macedonia Baptist Church, was also in the way of the road. In a memo dated April 30, 1943, an employee of the NCPPC dismissively stated that there was "no new indication of any new 'plantings'" at the cemetery. There were only a few gravestones, and the suggestion was to remove the graves located within fifty feet from the road. The rest of the area, "on a steep slope," could be entirely planted with trees and shrubs, and in time the presence of the cemetery would disappear.[40]

A study on the history of the cemetery undertaken in 2013 indicated that between 288 and perhaps as many as 380 interments had taken place there. We have not been able to locate any information about the relocation of graves from Macedonia Cemetery, which leads the author to believe that there are many graves still there. On December 17, 1944, the *Washington Times Herald* published a lengthy article about the new road. It dedicated one paragraph to the destruction of Macedonia Baptist Church, which had received $5,000 compensation for its building but was expected to spend almost three times that much to build in a new location. About the Macedonia Cemetery, the reporter wrote, "Its lonely legion of the dead keep silent watch over the splendid highway that passes below."[41]

The building of Barry Farm Dwellings and the Suitland Parkway did not halt the desire of the government to intervene in Barry Farm–Hillsdale, as we will see in the next chapter. Nevertheless, for a little while, there must have been a sense of respite and even elation in the community. The war in Europe ended in May 1945, and the war in the Pacific ended in August of the same year. By the fall of 1945, Barry Farm–Hillsdale's young men were returning home. Mrs. Lucille Dale, in an October 22, 1945 letter to her son, Sergeant Norman E. Dale, wrote, "So many of the…boys are home and discharged….I hope it won't be long before we will be saying the same thing about you." He had been serving in Europe guarding prisoners of war.[42]

A new era was beginning for Barry Farm–Hillsdale, and it would continue to bring momentous changes to the community—not all of them positive.

Chapter 9

Move Them Out!

E ven before World War II started in December 1941, the idea of redeveloping Barry Farm–Hillsdale was already being examined. The first hint of interest was from the Zoning Commission for the District of Columbia, which had concluded in June 1941 that "Barry Farms [*sic*]... warrants, in addition to a thorough zoning study, a comprehensive survey to include all other phases of city planning." A request was sent to the Alley Dwelling Authority to make a study of the Barry Farm area. The authority responded, noting that it was "greatly interested in the future development of this area." From then on, the planning for the future of Barry Farm–Hillsdale as a thriving, close-knit, working-class African American community passed from the hands of its inhabitants and community institutions to those of bureaucrats in downtown Washington, D.C.[1]

The idea to move African Americans out of the central area of Washington, D.C., across the Anacostia River was also being entertained at the very beginning of the war. In early April 1942, Representative Compton I. White, a Democrat from Idaho, was espousing the idea. According to him, Washington was "infiltrated by blacks" and there was fear of this "race infiltration."[2]

In 1944, the NCHA justified plans to redevelop Barry Farm–Hillsdale because the area was a blight and because of the "faulty manner" in which it had been subdivided when planned right after the Civil War. Also, the area was a problem because of its "sparse population, uneconomic building lot lay-out, and uneven topography."[3] In the view of an urban developer, large lots that provided space for the cultivation of food to supplement the family diet and to be sold for additional income, or to be divided to provide space for family members to build homes for their families, was simply "uneconomic." And the "sparse population," which allowed the community relationships to thrive and maintained the environmental and social balance of the community, was also a problem.

The residents of Barry Farm–Hillsdale were becoming aware of the imminent threat to their way of life. When hearings were held by Congress on the NCHA activities between April and June 1944, including the plans to redevelop Barry Farm–Hillsdale, Reverend Millard F. Newman came to testify. He was a resident of Howard Road. His testimony was lengthy and emotional. He mentioned how the community had "struggled through the years to maintain a healthy, wholesome social attitude." Furthermore, it would be rather unfortunate if Barry Farm–Hillsdale was categorized as a blighted area in "some over-all planning that ignored this more profound and deeper thing of people who owned a home they had built."[4]

James C. Mason, who was a long-term resident of Barry Farm–Hillsdale and publisher for many years of a community newspaper and the magazine *Pulse*, addressed the committee regarding his concerns. He stated in a letter that the main reason why many areas of Washington, D.C., occupied by African Americans were categorized as blighted was because "money could not be borrowed from lending institutions for building, rebuilding, or for remodeling properties." A solution would be that "the owners of any properties in areas adjudged blighted, should be given an opportunity and aided financially to conform with city development and planning agencies."[5] Mr. Mason's was a sensible suggestion that remained unaddressed.

Within the context of its planning to redevelop Barry Farm–Hillsdale, the NCPPC conducted a review in 1944 of the three blocks of Nichols Avenue that contained the very active commercial corridor serving the community. It found it thriving. Along the three blocks—from 2400 to 2600—there were fourteen businesses, five churches, two dentists, three doctors and the community's elementary school. The businesses ranged from a grocery store to a restaurant and from barbershops and beauty parlors to shoe repair shops. This was a sign that the neighborhood was vital and thriving even in the tumult of the Second World War. The study also found that just during 1941–42, of the 140 building permits issued for the Barry Farm–Hillsdale area, 139 were for apartment units; only 1 was for a single-family dwelling. This finding was a harbinger of the future explosive development of multi-family unit buildings in the area, which would change its character and eventually contribute to its disintegration.[6]

The report characterized Barry Farm–Hillsdale as a stagnated area, suffering from "'rural' blight and slum conditions." Nevertheless, what seemed to have been one of the main reasons for the desire to redevelop the area was its inability "to pay for municipal services" through the collection of real estate taxes. The conclusion was "that the potentialities of the area can only be realized by its redevelopment as a whole." Furthermore, "The Barry Farm Area offers one of the best opportunities in the District of Columbia for the development of a complete and integrated neighborhood unit."[7] Now, the die was cast for a fight not only between the powers that be in the government and the Barry Farm–Hillsdale community but also between factions within the community's leadership.

The District of Columbia Redevelopment Act of 1945, public law 592, was approved in the 2nd session of the 79th Congress on August 2, 1946. Its main provision was "the replanning and rebuilding of slum, blighted, and other areas of the District of Columbia and the assembly, by purchase or condemnation of real property in such areas and the sale or lease thereof for the redevelopment of such area."[8]

The District of Columbia Redevelopment Land Agency (RLA), which was authorized by public law 592, was to implement redevelopment work in the District of Columbia. By December 1946, it was being reported that three areas had been chosen to be redeveloped. One of the areas was described as a blighted area north of the main business section of Washington, D.C., in Northwest and located east of 14th Street and Florida Avenue, inhabited mostly by African Americans. The other two areas, also with a majority African American population, were located across the Anacostia River in Southeast: Barry Farm–Hillsdale and Marshall Heights. Most revealing was the fact that the contemplated redevelopment in NW would not start until the redevelopment of Barry Farm was completed. That followed the thinking expressed by Congressman White in 1942 that "negroes should be moved…out in the country across the Anacostia river." Furthermore, as it was eventually reported, General Ulysses S. Grant III, chairman of the NCPPC, believed that the African American population dispossesed by the redevelopment near the business district of Washington, D.C., should be relocated to a remote section "in the rear of the Anacostia [River]."[9]

Marshall Heights, a triangular area located in Northeast near the border with Maryland that was also being targeted for redevelopment, was settled by African Americans coming into Washington after the First World War but did not receive a significant influx of residents until the

Ulysses J. Banks, leader of the Barry Farm Civic Association, drawing by Phillip Ratner, date unknown. Mr. Banks, a lifelong resident of Barry Farm–Hillsdale, was the president of the Barry Farm Civic Association in the late 1940s when it fought the plans by the National Capital Park and Planning Commission to redevelop the neighborhood. *Courtesy Anacostia Community Museum, Smithsonian Institution.*

1930s. It had a similar history to that of Barry Farm, with people working during the day in downtown Washington, D.C., and coming home at night to build their houses with their own hands. The residents also cultivated their lots and raised small livestock to feed the families. It had no source of water except for a stream until the mid-1930s, when First Lady Eleanor Roosevelt came to visit and asked that hydrants be installed in the neighborhood. Inhabitants from Barry Farm–Hillsdale and Marshall Heights were against the redevelopment of their neighborhoods.[10]

By early 1947, the Barry Farm–Hillsdale leadership represented by the Barry Farm Civic Association and the Hillsdale Civic Association were mobilizing to present their opinions about the redevelopment of the neighborhood. Unfortunately, they did not present a united front. The Barry Farm Civic Association met on January 14, 1947, under the leadership of its president, Ulysses J. Banks, and passed the following resolution: "[T]hat we, the Citizens of Barry Farms [*sic*], do and hereby register with the Board of Commissioners, District of Columbia, our vigorous protest against the proposed redevelopment of Barry Farms with Projects."

Mr. Banks continued, explaining that the experience of those who had lost their homes to the building of the Suitland Parkway was creating fear among the remaining citizens of the community. They were "much discouraged and disturbed. They will not be able, at the present cost of building materials, to build homes of equal value" with the money provided by the condemnation proceedings. There was a final salvo in the resolution, making a veiled allusion to racial discrimination: "We, the Citizens of Barry Farms, feel that the encouragement and security that this great Democracy provides should be shared alike by all of its Citizens."[11]

In a letter dated December 7, 1946, Miss Althea V. Howard, the corresponding secretary of the Hillsdale Civic Association, stated, "The Hillsdale Civic Association herewith expresses the desire to cooperate fully with the District Commissioners and all designated authorities in the planning for the redevelopment and slum clearance of Barry Farm."[12]

In January, both associations had the chance to send representatives to a meeting with the NCPPC. Both sides maintained their positions. Ulysses J. Banks presented a copy of the resolution against the plan and several photos of nice houses in the community as proof that not all of its housing was derelict. The Hillsdale Civic Association—represented by five members, including Henry D. Wesley, its president—reiterated its support for the redevelopment of the neighborhood. In the absence of further documentation, it is not clear how this disagreement unfolded within the community. But it is safe to assume that it caused stress.[13]

The fight for the redevelopment of Barry Farm–Hillsdale was renewed in 1949. During the hearings for the appropriations "for the Executive Office and sundry independent executive bureaus, boards, commissions, and offices for the fiscal year ending June 30, 1949," architect Howard D. Woodson came to give his statement. Woodson was a famous African American architect who had worked in Washington, D.C., for decades both as an employee of the Office of the Supervising Architect of the Department of Treasury and as a partner at an architectural firm. He was also a community activist who had been engaged in demanding improvements for neighborhoods in the Northeast quadrant of the city. Mr. Woodson's statement clarified that despite the denials of the government, everybody knew that the idea was to clear downtown Washington, D.C., of African Americans—"Negroes" in the parlance of the time—and then to move people out to Barry Farm–Hillsdale and Marshall Heights and establish "ghettos in the southeast."[14]

Next in line to depose was James C. Mason, who had already come before a committee on the same subject in 1944. He now came to present an article he had published in his magazine *Pulse* in June 1947. The title of the article was provocative: "DP's—American Style." The abbreviation DP, of course, referred to the millions of displaced persons in Europe because of the Second World War. He was comparing the African Americans who would be dispossessed by the redevelopment of Barry Farm–Hillsdale and Marshall Heights with those dispossessed by the Second World War. Mason ended his article with an even more provocative statement: "The whole redevelopment plan for Washington as far as Negroes are concerned, is remarkably like a reincarnation of a Hitler-Nazi plan of population shifting, with new ghettos and slums in the making."[15]

The Hitler-Nazi analogy might have been the tipping point, for on January 30, 1948, the House Appropriations Committee rejected the request from the RLA for $3,400 to start operations that would include the redevelopment of Barry Farm–Hillsdale. The threat was averted but not avoided. By March of that same year, John Nolen Jr., director of planning of the NCPPC, had requested a housing survey for Barry Farm–Hillsdale in preparation for future redevelopment. The survey, undertaken by the Bureau of Public Health Engineering of the D.C. Department of Health, included a lot of numbers and percentages but no description of the social fabric of the community that would have presented its full picture. The neighborhood contained 297 structures, of which 12 could not have been inspected because the occupants denied access and 10 were vacant or under construction. Nine White families were living in the neighborhood, most likely Jewish merchants, in addition to four hundred African American families. The population total was 1,537. The surveyor found some lack of piped water and sewage and lack of bath facilities and central heating. Not surprisingly, there was also overcrowding.[16]

Undoubtedly, one of the families visited by the surveyors from the Bureau of Public Health Engineering was that headed by Mrs. Pearl Williams, living at 2849 Sayles Place. Her family consisted of two adults and eight children ranging in age from two to seventeen years of age. Their house was a small four-room frame house, but they owned their home. Mrs. Williams would welcome redevelopment and a chance to move into a larger house, willing to give up her house for a better one. "But where will we go?" she asked the journalist interviewing her. One cannot avoid the comparison with the cry directed at General O.O. Howard, some seventy years earlier, from those displaced African Americans who had come to Washington during the Civil War, when they were told they had to leave the lots they had occupied in downtown Washington: "Where shall we go, and what shall we do?"[17]

The year 1949 was pivotal in the fight of Barry Farm–Hillsdale residents to save their community from redevelopment. Appearing before Congress again were the indefatigable Ulysses J. Banks and the architect Howard D. Woodson. They again brought up the ghetto analogy. Banks also pointed out that in the previous eight years, 250 houses had been built in Barry Farm–Hillsdale by private builders. He finished his statement by pointing out that "a community that is being developed in this fashion…should be given an opportunity to develop by private industry."[18]

Meanwhile, General Ulysses S. Grant III was trying to defend his redevelopment ideas and having a hard time. The previous year, the commission had been denied funds to undertake redevelopment planning for Barry Farm–Hillsdale and Marshall Heights. Representative John Phillips stated that the reason for the denial of funds was that Congress "was not fully convinced that your authority extended quite so far, or that your selection of proper places was what the committee itself thought it should be." Representative Phillips was taken aback when General Grant declared that he had gone ahead and completed the plans for the redevelopment of Marshall Heights and had started the plans for Barry Farm–Hillsdale. Representative Phillips well remembered that spending money to plan the redevelopment of those two areas had been denied the previous year. He inquired of the general, "How did you do that?"[19]

In a last salvo in the hearings on the redevelopment plans held on June 20, 1949, Everett L. Edmond, president of the Marshall Heights Civic Association, declared eloquently, "The solution for slums does not lie in the acquisition of large tracts of developed land by the Government, demolishing the existing buildings, resubdividing the land and running the people out like rats." He concluded, suggesting that the solution should be the enforcement of building regulations, provision of community and educational facilities and the creation of job opportunities.[20]

On July 15, 1949, Congress passed the Housing Act of 1949. It included a prohibition against the redevelopment of Marshall Heights and Barry Farm–Hillsdale. A year later, the NCPPC published a report on the status of

Major General Ulysses S. Grant III (*first from left*), 1949. Major General Grant, as chairman of the National Capital Park and Planning Commission, wanted to redevelop Barry Farm–Hillsdale in the late 1940s. The Barry Farm Civic Association fiercely contested him. *Courtesy National Archives and Records Administration, Washington, D.C.*

its redevelopment plans. The report stated that because the redevelopment of those two areas was forbidden, the commission had to look for other areas to target. Southwest Washington was perfect; it had well-defined boundaries and a high number of African Americans (the latter went unstated but was probably part of the reasoning).[21]

The specter of redevelopment reared its head over and over again in the next few years. In October 1953, the RLA and the Washington Home Builders Association tried to revive the plans to redevelop Barry Farm–Hillsdale. During the process, when the city's Slum Prevention and Rehabilitation Committee requested suggestions from local civic organizations for areas to be rehabilitated around the city, the Hillsdale Civic Association suggested "the 2400 and 2600 blocks of Nichols ave. se. and the 700 block of Howard rd. se." The blocks on Nichols Avenue were the epicenter of the commercial area of Barry Farm–Hillsdale.[22]

In May 1954, it seemed like the time had come when Barry Farm–Hillsdale could not avoid anymore the redevelopment axe. On May 24, the Senate Banking and Currency Committee, which was writing a new housing act, voted to eliminate "the language in the 1949 Housing Act that has blocked redevelopment of Barry Farms and Marshall Heights." Barry Farm–Hillsdale residents immediately expressed their feelings. Those who lived in the "hilly…country town, like it the way it is," stated an article published in the *Washington Daily News*. The residents liked "their large back yards, and wooded hills." They did not want "shiny new apartments and homes." George J. Trivers, the publicity chairman of the Barry Farm Civic Association, put out a press release that was described as a "declaration of war" on the new attempt to redevelop Barry Farm–Hillsdale. The association was incensed that the hearings were closed to the residents. In the end, it was Representative John Phillips, Republican from California, who came through again to help the community. He sponsored a rider written into the appropriations legislation prohibiting the redevelopment of Barry Farm–Hillsdale and Marshall Heights under the District Redevelopment Act.[23]

Even though the possibility of redeveloping Barry Farm–Hillsdale and Marshall Heights was dead and the RLA had turned its eyes directly to Southwest, the idea would crop up again in 1955 in a report that proposed that slums could be eradicated from Washington, D.C., in ten years. But that proposal went nowhere.[24]

The dismissal of the plans to redevelop Barry Farm–Hillsdale was considered a point of great pride by Mrs. Ella Pearis, an activist resident who

Representative John Phillips (CA-R), circa 1953. Representative Phillips protected Barry Farm–Hillsdale from redevelopment by sponsoring a rider into the appropriations legislation of 1954 forbidding the redevelopment of the area. *John Phillips, photographic print b/w (gelatin silver), Tenschert Studio, 1953–54, collection of the U.S. House of Representatives.*

participated in the fight along with Ulysses J. Banks; Levi Brown, secretary of the Barry Farm Civic Association; and George J. Trivers. Brown and Trivers were her neighbors at Elvans Road. She described in an interview in 1974 how many times the plans to redevelop Barry Farm and build public housing in the area had come up in the 1940s and early 1950s and how time and time again the group had gone to Capitol Hill to fight it. She concluded the narrative with the statement, "We defeated them…the idea died out."[25]

Chapter 10

A Prelude of Things to Come

The Integration of the Anacostia Pool, 1949

E ven before the end of the war, there was the beginning of resistance at Barry Farm–Hillsdale to the relentless segregation the community experienced. At one point, Norman E. Dale and other men from Barry Farm–Hillsdale picketed Ball's Liquor Store, a White-owned business on Nichols Avenue, because it did not hire African Americans. He and his group also picketed the Sanitary Grocery Company store on the 2200 block of Nichols Avenue, which later would become Safeway. Subsequently, Dale was drafted into the army and sent to serve in the Second World War at the somewhat old age of thirty-five. Afterward, he always claimed that he had been drafted because he had picketed the White-owned businesses. True or not, the picketing was the first hint of things to come.[1]

At 3:00 p.m. on Tuesday, June 28, 1949, the police broadcast a "trouble call" in Anacostia. This event would have consequences well beyond the streets of Anacostia and those of Barry Farm–Hillsdale. The "trouble call" referred to a "riot" taking place at the Anacostia Park Pool, located in what was then known to the residents as the "Anacostia Flats" and sometimes as "Fairlawn Park." African American young men were trying to desegregate the pool and encountering fierce resistance.[2]

As an aside, it is important to note here the creation of the waterfront park and the use of the Anacostia River by the Barry Farm–Hillsdale community. By the end of the nineteenth century, the mudflats on the margins of the Anacostia River, mixed with accumulated sediment, had created breeding grounds for mosquitoes carrying the malaria parasite.

Sergeant Norman E. Dale, date unknown. Mr. Dale participated in a picket in front of White-owned businesses at Nichols Avenue. He believed that he was drafted to serve in World War II because of that event. The patches in his uniform identify him as being a sergeant and serving in the U.S. Army, Sixth Service Command. *Courtesy Dale/Patterson Family Collection, Anacostia Community Museum Archives, Smithsonian Institution, gift of Dianne Dale.*

The Anacostia River was described then as "this uninviting river, with its miasmatic swamps, whose baneful influence is so seriously felt by a large portion of the citizens of Washington."[3] Later on, it was decided that the mudflats should be filled in and that they should become a public park. Thus was born the park that in 1918 was officially named Anacostia Park and in time would become a source of entertainment and sorrow for the Barry Farm–Hillsdale community.[4]

From the late 1980s to the early 2000s, men who had grown up in Barry Farm–Hillsdale remembered their experiences with the Anacostia Park as children. Robert Simon remembered the call "They are going down to Fairlawn," and he would join the group of friends and cousins going to the park for the egg roll on Easter Monday. Stanley Anderson remembered another entertainment: the kite contests. Kenneth Chapman, however, remembered the pain of segregation. He stated in 2002 that "this side [south side] of the [11th Street] bridge was for the colored and the other side [north side] was for the whites because they had tennis courts and everything [there]."[5]

Swimming in the river was also a source of entertainment but sometimes had dire consequences. Everett McKenzie personally lived the frightful experience of a drowning. He and his eldest brother, Carlton, were swimming in the Anacostia River with a childhood friend who drowned. The McKenzie family lived on Sheridan Road, and the two brothers were so scared that they ran the several blocks home "buck naked." A letter to the editor of the *Washington Post* dated July 5, 1949, stated the grim statistics: 111 persons had drowned in Washington, D.C., between 1945 and 1948, 37 of them being children and 29 of the children being African Americans who had drowned in the Anacostia River or the Kingman Lake, an artificial lake created when the river had been dredged. The writer added, "In all the area east of North Capitol St. there is not a single supervised swimming pool to which colored children may normally go."[6]

In the summer of 1949, the Department of the Interior controlled six public pools located on federally owned land. In theory, these pools were not segregated. Nevertheless, by custom, the Anacostia, East Potomac, McKinley and Takoma pools were used exclusively by Whites, while the Banneker and Francis pools were used exclusively by Blacks. On Thursday, June 23, a group of young African Americans from Barry Farm–Hillsdale and Southeast tried to enter the Anacostia Pool without success. They continued trying for the next three days until June 26, when six "Negro youths from 14 to 21 years old were splashed and booed out" of the pool. According to the newspaper reports, between seven hundred and eight hundred Whites of all ages observed the eviction, with fifty of them being active in evicting the would-be African American swimmers. Richard Robinson, Carl Contee and Richard Cook, friends and neighbors from Bowen Road, were part of the group evicted from the pool.[7]

Not to be dissuaded, the African American kids returned on June 28. Ben Bradlee, then a young reporter at the *Washington Post*, described in his memoirs many years later what happened at the pool. Between 3:00 p.m. and 6:00 p.m., Whites and African Americans battled in the area around the swimming pool. Mounted park police rode their horses, trying to keep the two factions away from each other. Both sides were armed with clubs, and some of these clubs had nails sticking out of them. Bradlee and a colleague covered the event and filed the story, sure that it would appear in the paper the next day. The *Post*, to the disappointment and indignation of the young reporter, did not pick up the story.[8]

The attempt to desegregate the Anacostia Pool continued on June 29, with violent clashes between hundreds of Whites and African Americans. Some of the Whites were members of Henry A. Wallace's Progressive Party and were there to demonstrate against segregation and distribute handbills urging the desegregation of the Washington, D.C., pools. Everett McKenzie also remembered that his younger brother, Eugene (whose nickname was "Mann"), and Clarence "Dusty" Prue were there. James Chester Jennings Jr., also present, remembered that the Anderson brothers—Otis, Thomas and Bill—were part of the crowd. Toussaint Pierce, who had attended the West Virginia State College the previous year, had come to the pool to swim but found that it was already closed. He was then attacked by a White youth who threw a stone at him. Then a park police officer ran him down on a horse. When Pierce picked up a rock to throw back, the police officer grabbed him and took him to the Eleventh Precinct. Pierce was kept for an hour until his father came to pay his five-dollar bail.[9]

At the end of the demonstration, Everett and his brother were so afraid that they decided to head back home by following the railroad tracks that ran in front of the pool and went into the Barry Farm–Hillsdale neighborhood. That was the long way to get home instead of coming out through the usual route of Good Hope Road and Nichols Avenue, which would take them through White Anacostia. Otherwise, they might have been the victims of a car driven by a White man who was accused of trying to run down an African American youth at the entrance to the park.[10] More violence occurred on Nichols Avenue when African American youths taking that route back home

Clarence "Dusty" Prue, date unknown. Prue was one of the young men from Barry Farm–Hillsdale who participated in the integration of the Anacostia pool in June 1949. *Courtesy Wanda Prue.*

jostled and frightened a White girl, who then took shelter at a grocery store located on the 1900 block.[11]

The solution for the rioting was to close the Anacostia Pool. Washington, D.C., organizations divided into two groups: those proposing the reopening of the pool on a desegregated basis and those adamantly against it. Among the groups hoping for the reopening of a desegregated pool were the National Interracial Workshop, the NAACP, Americans for Democratic Action and National Capital Chapter of the American Jewish Congress. Among other measures, they requested that the newspapers not announce the reopening

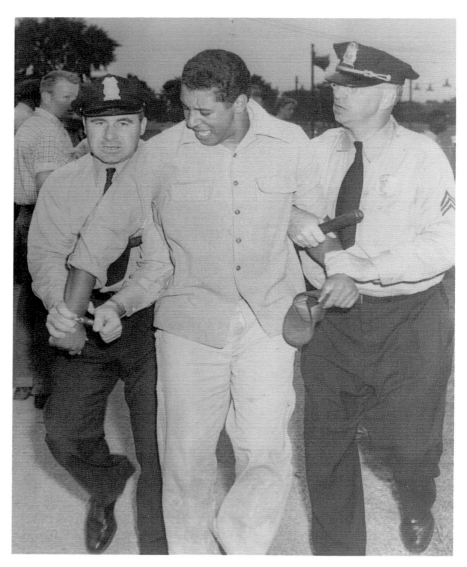

Metropolitan police officers take into custody an African American demonstrator on June 29, 1949, at the Anacostia Pool. Although the caption for this photograph does not identify the young man in custody, it is believed that he was Toussaint Pierce. *Courtesy Associated Press (id. 49062903, neg. 022906).*

Building of the Anacostia Pool with the railroad tracks in the forefront, August 6, 1949. Brothers Everett and Mann McKenzie were so afraid after the attempt to desegregate the pool on June 29, 1949, that they decided to walk back home following the railroad tracks instead of taking the more direct route of Good Hope Road and Nichols Avenue. *Courtesy Historical Society of Washington, D.C., John P. Wymer Collection (WY 3536.29).*

date, that "sanitary precautions" be implemented (it is not clear from the newspaper account what these measures entailed) and, furthermore, that priests and ministers be stationed by the pool.[12]

On the other hand, four White organizations from Southeast Washington—the Eastern Branch of the Kiwanis Club, Anacostia Lions Club, the Fort Davis Citizens' Association and the Fort Dupont Association—requested the reopening of the Anacostia Pool as a segregated facility. According to them, there were no problems when only Whites frequented the pool, and it was wrong to deprive the White children of the use of the pool. Another point was that the pool was in a White neighborhood and near two White schools. This, of course, ignored the existence of Birney School on Nichols Avenue. Another organization incensed with the possibility of integration of the public pools in Washington, D.C., was the Northwest Council of Citizens' Associations. It addressed a letter to the District Recreation Board mentioning the "greater incidence of tuberculosis and syphilis" among the African American population as reasons to maintain the segregation of the pool.[13]

On the other hand, a sensible group of twenty-five White and African American mothers sent a letter to Interior Secretary J.A. Krug stating that they expected "'determined enforcement' of Interior's nonsegregation [*sic*] policy" at the Anacostia Pool, with the provision of adequate policing by White and African American policemen. According to an editorial in the African American newspaper *Chicago Defender*, the closure of the Anacostia Pool promoted an impromptu integration of swimming in the Anacostia River. White kids who had been able to go to the segregated Anacostia Pool while African American children had to swim in the river, with all the attending perils of drowning, now joined in and "all races swim happily there every day." Upon reflection, this might have been the reason behind the letter from the interracial group of twenty-five mothers. They might have been concerned about the peril of their children, White or African American, drowning in the Anacostia River.[14]

The Anacostia Pool remained closed throughout the summer of 1949. In March 1950, the Interior Department decreed that all of its six swimming pools in Washington would reopen "on a non-segregated basis." The Anacostia Pool opened on June 24, 1950, without incident. By October, after the end of the swimming season, integration of the pools was well established, but it was considered both a success and a failure. It was a success because there were no violent incidents. It was a failure because the attendance of Whites dropped considerably. At the Anacostia Pool, the attendance was now 90 percent African American.[15]

Desegregation of the swimming pools did not determine the desegregation of all recreational facilities in the nation's capital. Actually, in White Anacostia, it created so much distress that the Anacostia Citizens Association withdrew its request for the creation of a playground in the neighborhood. The stated reason was that the residents feared that eventually the playground would be integrated and there would be trouble like with what happened at the Anacostia Pool.[16] In 1954, on March 18, the day following the Supreme Court decision on school segregation, the District of Columbia Recreation Board integrated all the recreational facilities in the city. It was almost five years to the date when the fearless youth from Barry Farm–Hillsdale had faced head-on segregation and had integrated the Anacostia Pool by force.[17]

PART V

The 1950s and 1960s

Desegregation (but Not Integration)
and Vibrant Activism

Chapter 11

Desegregation (but Not Integration)
of the Schools

I n June 1956, her peers elected thirteen-year-old Dianne Dale as Miss
Barry Farms to reign over the Fifth Barry Farm Playground Festival.
More than three thousand people, according to a newspaper account,
participated in the festivities. Miss Dale proudly paraded in a convertible
through the streets of the neighborhood where she had lived since she was a
child. Her family had been a pillar of the community; they moved to Barry
Farm–Hillsdale in 1892.[1] Four years earlier, in 1952, a group of White
beauty queens holding dainty umbrellas and riding on a flower-decked car
sponsored by the American Building Association had won the first prize for
the Greater Southeast Seventh Annual Parade and Crab Apple Blossom
Festival in Anacostia Park.

Both parades took place annually a few blocks apart from each other, in
adjacent neighborhoods that had existed since the nineteenth century and
in the same Southeast quadrant of the city. Only one thing separated these
two communities: race. Barry Farm–Hillsdale was African American, and
Anacostia was White. Thus, those White young women who attended all-
White Sousa, Kramer and Hine Junior High Schools in Southeast would not
have met Miss Dianne Dale, who attended all-Black Douglass Junior High
School in Barry Farm–Hillsdale, also located in Southeast.[2]

This state of school segregation in Washington, D.C., had endured for a
century and had been recently shattered in 1954 with *Bolling v. Sharpe*, the
companion case of *Brown v. Board of Education*, the landmark Supreme Court

Dianne Dale, Miss Barry Farms, 1956. Miss Dale reigned over the Fifth Barry Farm Playground Festival, which was attended by three thousand people. *Courtesy Dale/Patterson Family Collection, Anacostia Community Museum Archives, Smithsonian Institution, gift of Dianne Dale.*

case decision that determined that African Americans and Whites should attend school together in Washington, D.C. Mostly as a result of these events, in a few decades the composition of the population of Anacostia changed from all White to mostly Black, and the identity of Barry Farm–Hillsdale as a thriving African American community disappeared.[3]

The segregated school system in Washington, D.C., was organized in 1862 when Congress passed a law specifying that 10 percent of the taxes paid by African American residents of the District of Columbia and Georgetown should be set aside for the creation of schools for African American children. The law also created a separate board of trustees to oversee the segregated schools. In 1864, Congress passed legislation designating that money allotted to the African American schools be paid directly to the Board of Trustees of the Colored Schools. Thus, the existence of two school systems, one White and another African American, became reinforced even though there was no legal demand for separate systems.[4]

One item of the law would have unforeseen negative consequences for African American students in Washington, D.C., for the next nine decades before desegregation in 1954. The Act of 1864 determined that school funds should be allocated based on the percentage of Georgetown and Washington, D.C., African American and White children between the ages of six and seventeen as established by the decennial population census.[5] None of those involved in writing the law could anticipate the large influx of African Americans coming to Washington, D.C., fleeing the harsh conditions in the South. Those children, who migrated to the city between the decennial censuses or who were born to parents who arrived during that period, were not counted. Thus, the funds allocated for the schools remained the same until the next census. On the other hand, the White population of the city grew slowly or decreased, determining that the White schools were better funded.

The next significant change in the educational system of Washington, D.C., came in 1871, when the territorial government was established and created a unified board of education composed of two Black men, one Black woman, two White women and four White men. This racial and gender composition remained constant over the decades. Consequently, African American members of the board had to maneuver to obtain allegiance of White members whenever fighting for improvements in the African American school system.

This system of "separate but equal" schools for African American and White children in Washington, D.C., was bankrupt by 1947. Between 1937 and 1947, there was a significant surge in the African American students in the segregated school system of Washington, D.C. During that period, enrollment of African American students had increased by 18.8 percent, while the enrollment of White students had dropped by 13.9 percent. As a school administrator put it, "White children were rattling around in half-empty schools in some places."[6]

In the administrative sector, there were three officers in charge of the African American schools: one first assistant superintendent and two associate superintendents. By contrast, five administrators managed the White schools. Funds for the African American schools were apportioned in accordance to the 1940 Census, which established that 34.1 percent of inhabitants between the ages of six and seventeen were African American, while in 1947 the African American enrollment in the schools was already 44.8 percent. Furthermore, many of the White children in the city attended private schools, making the statistics taken from the 1940 Census meaningless. In 1947, the District of Columbia was allocating $126.52 for each Black child and $160.21 for each White child.[7]

Nowhere were the discrepancies between what was available to African American and White students in Washington, D.C., more evident than in the school facilities occupied by each group. Sixteen African American elementary schools serving 3,258 students were operating on double shifts. By comparison, only 413 White elementary school students were attending schools that had double shifts. Six of the seven African American middle schools were over capacity; only Shaw Junior High School was under capacity, by 70 students. Randall Junior High School, where most of the students from Barry Farm–Hillsdale went after finishing elementary school, had operated on double shifts since 1942. By comparison, all of the eleven White junior high schools were under capacity.[8]

A report issued in 1949 on the status of schools in Washington, D.C., stated that all the eight White high schools in Washington, D.C., were under capacity except for Anacostia High School. Furthermore, all the White high schools "scored on educational adequacy well above the satisfactory level." By comparison, the three African American high schools (Dunbar, Cardozo and Armstrong) and two vocational schools (Washington and Phelps) were over capacity. All of them were below the satisfactory level of educational adequacy.[9]

Carl F. Hansen, future superintendent of the Washington, D.C., Public Schools, found out in March 1947 when he arrived to assume the position of executive assistant to the school superintendent that "the colored branch of the school system was only a dimly outlined appendage of the white structure."[10] Perhaps the prevailing philosophy was inadvertently noted in a report issued by the school superintendent a few months later on May 21, 1947: "Absolute equality of educational opportunity is impossible. Reasonable equality of educational opportunity is the goal."[11]

Legal challenges to the segregated school system in Washington, D.C., started in 1944, before the end of World War II. In February 1944, John P. Davis, legislative secretary of Representative Vito Anthony Marcantonio of New York, attempted to enroll his five-year-old son, Michael, at the White elementary school in his neighborhood in Brookland. Noyes Elementary School was located at walking distance from Davis's house, located at 3105 14th Street NE. Michael's assigned "colored" school was seventeen blocks away, some six and a half miles by public transportation. Davis stated in an interview with the newspapers that the fact that his child could not attend a school within walking distance from his house constituted "denial of equal protection of law under the Constitution."[12]

It is interesting to note that Mr. Davis was seen as an agent for the cause of desegregation in Washington, D.C., rather than a concerned parent. That was the view of Martha Strayer, a reporter for the *Washington Daily News* and past president of the Washington Press Club, in a letter to First Lady Eleanor Roosevelt in June 1944. She described John P. Davis as "a light-colored Negro" who, she implied, had intentionally bought a house in a section of Brookland where there was no school for African Americans. She stated that Davis was going to try to register his child (whom she misidentified as a girl) in a White school to "simply [make] a demonstration which will create [a] very serious feeling." She then stated in a somewhat ominous tone, "It's all tied up with this attempt to breakdown segregation."[13]

The Washington, D.C., Board of Education ordered the principal at Noyes Elementary School to deny admission to Michael Davis and requested funds to build a nearby school for African American students. The board also stated that Mr. Davis knew that there were no African American elementary schools near the house he bought and, thus, he should not complain about it. Eventually, a temporary school building was erected in front of the location where the Davis family lived. Six African American families were displaced for the construction of this one-room school.[14] Mr. Davis went on to file a suit in the U.S. District Court of Washington, D.C. Judge James W. Morris sided with the board of education in its denial of admission to young Michael to Noyes Elementary School and dismissed the suit. According to Judge Morris, the facts presented in the case "did not show discrimination, but merely alleged an inconvenience to the boy."[15]

Nevertheless, parents of schoolchildren in Washington, D.C., seemed to have already reached a breaking point in their acceptance of the situation as it was. On November 18, 1946, the Dunbar Alumni Association met with the superintendent of schools, Dr. Hobart M. Corning, and the first assistant superintendent in charge of "colored" schools, Dr. Garnet C. Wilkinson, to complain about the situation in the famous school, the flagship for African American high schools in Washington for many decades. Dr. Wilkinson challenged the statements made by the alumni organization asserting that Dunbar was no longer the school with the same very high standards as when they had attended.

Did Dunbar students now have to take entrance examinations in colleges that used to admit them outright? Not because of lower standards, stated Wilkinson, even though the school was overcrowded and did not have enough teachers—Dunbar had forty-five teachers and needed sixty-one. Dunbar students did not receive seven hours of weekly instruction on chemistry? Not true, stated Wilkinson. He then admitted that it was possible that when several classes were in the laboratory at the same time, one teacher would not be able to give all the students enough attention. Were third-year classes for French, German or Spanish not being offered? Not enough students elected to take those courses, responded Wilkinson. Thus, the classes were not provided.[16]

The life and career of Dr. Garnet C. Wilkinson, once the principal of Dunbar High School and later assistant superintendent, had a deep connection to Barry Farm–Hillsdale. Wilkinson was a member of an African American family from Charleston, South Carolina, who had been free at least since 1840.[17] Dr. Wilkinson's father, James William Wilkinson, was born in Charleston on February 11, 1842. He received an education, and in 1871, he was working as a teacher in Darlington County. By 1879, he was living in Summerville, Colleton County, where his son Garnet was born on January 10. We believe that his family had a connection with the White Wilkinson family, who in 1850 had owned a plantation in Colleton County, holding eighty-five enslaved people. This connection would explain the fact that James was working as a farmer there in 1880.[18]

James W. Wilkinson moved his family to Washington, D.C., around 1888 and went to live in Barry Farm–Hillsdale, first on Nichols Avenue and later at Morris Road, where he lived until his death. Sometime in the early 1890s, he obtained a job in the War Department as a clerk, a position he occupied until his death in 1916.[19]

Upon moving to Washington, D.C., nine-year-old Garnet attended classes at Hillsdale School and then went on to study at the M Street High School, the best high school for African Americans in the segregated Washington, D.C., school system at the time. His father's position as a government employee would have placed him within the elite of Washington's African American community at the time, which sent their children to the M Street High School. In 1902, Wilkinson completed his studies at Oberlin College in Ohio and returned to Washington to teach Latin and then history and physics at his alma mater, M Street High School.[20]

His career proceeded apace. In 1912, he was appointed the principal for Armstrong Manual Training High School, the trade high school for the Washington, D.C., "colored" school system, and then became principal of Dunbar High School when it first opened its doors in 1916. Dunbar was the successor of M Street High School.[21] In 1921, Wilkinson was appointed temporarily as assistant superintendent in charge of the "colored" schools. At the time, the *Washington Bee*, an African American newspaper, reported that residents of Barry Farm–Hillsdale were sending the "good will of the entire community…wishing him a successful administration." The

Garnet C. Wilkinson, assistant superintendent of schools in Washington, D.C., in charge of the African American school system. Mr. Wilkinson came to live in Barry Farm–Hillsdale when he was nine years old. He attended Hillsdale School. *Courtesy Scurlock Studio Records, Archives Center, National Museum of American History.*

newspaper pointed out that Wilkinson had been a resident of the "village during his early school days." In September of the next year, he was confirmed in the position. In 1924, he was promoted and received the title of first assistant superintendent. He was still occupying that position when he met with the Dunbar Alumni Association twenty-two years later in 1946 and dismissed its concerns about the situation at the school.[22]

As Washington, D.C.'s parents of school-age children began to ramp up their demands for better and integrated schools, Wilkinson was against it. He believed that "integration posed a direct threat to the progress Black students had experienced under segregation." Wilkinson thought that integration was a threat to the vocational programs offered by the system, which he stated offered African American students a better chance to enter the employment market.[23]

Wilkinson's beliefs were backed up by none other than Dr. W.E.B. DuBois, who in 1935 lauded the segregated school system of Washington, D.C., for offering "efficiency, discipline, and human development" for its pupils. DuBois cast doubt at the time that an integrated system would have offered the necessary "sympathetic touch between teacher and pupil; knowledge on the part of the teacher, not simply of the individual taught, but of his surroundings and background, and the history of his class and group" to African American students.[24] Assistant Superintendent Wilkinson certainly subscribed to this philosophy when he was confronted by the movement to integrate schools in Washington, D.C., in the late 1940s.

Victory in the Second World War brought a sudden acceleration to the troubles faced by the school system in Washington, D.C. On Sunday, September 16, 1945, the *Evening Star* reported that at opening time on Monday, the Washington, D.C., school system would have "more pupils and fewer teachers [than] at any time since 1941." The week before, twelve female elementary school teachers resigned from their positions in the expectation that their husbands would be returning from the war at any moment. Fifteen teachers at the junior high schools and vocational schools left their jobs in the hope that the postwar economy would provide other career opportunities. The resignations were so swift and unexpected that it would have been impossible to start the school year with enough teachers on the payroll.[25]

The newspaper report continued, stating that "due to the increase in students in old buildings already overloaded, officials said about 20 colored elementary schools" would have to operate on double shifts. Only two White elementary schools would have to do the same. Wilkinson tried to downplay the problem by saying that just some of the classes in the African American elementary schools would have to be taught in double shifts. The truth was that the end of the war was increasing the problems of an already overburdened and underfinanced segregated system.[26]

The appalling—and worsening—conditions at Browne Junior High School, located in the Northeast quadrant of the city, were the impetus for the growing school desegregation movement. In March 1947, Agnes E. Meyer, then the wife of the *Washington Post* publisher Eugene Meyer and an advocate for social reform, published an article about it. She described Browne as a "shabby, overcrowded" school but also a place of "hard work and careful guidance" by the teachers, turning out "good human beings and good Americans." The capacity of the school building was for 880 students, but it was attended by 915 students in the morning shift and 812 students during the afternoon. There were forty-minute classes under this system instead of the normal fifty-five minutes. There were no activities periods, and lunch was only twenty-five minutes long. The school had six science teachers but no laboratory. All the teachers did double duty. On the bright side, Browne seemed to be well ahead of its time in applying gender equality. Both female and male students studied sewing, and female students attended carpentry, electricity and metal workshops. According to the teachers, this "variety of experience…helps them decide where their interests and talents lie."[27]

Despite all the efforts of the principal and the teachers and the goodwill of the students, it was impossible to provide an excellent education under those circumstances. The solution offered by the board of education, upon a suggestion from Dr. Garnet C. Wilkinson, was to transfer two old buildings used as elementary schools for White students to house Browne students. Wilkinson characterized this action as a "heroic method" to solve the problem. Browne School parents did not appreciate the "heroic" methods proposed to solve the overcrowding problem in the school.

Reportedly, nearly three hundred people jammed the meeting of the Committee on Buildings and Grounds of the Board of Education when it discussed, among other items, the transfer of the Webb and Blow elementary school buildings from the White division to the segregated African American division to house the overflow of students from Browne. The chairperson of the committee, Mrs. Philip Sidney Smith, was surprised. "We did not anticipate so much opposition," she declared. Twice the issue of school desegregation was brought up, and twice Mrs. Smith pounded the table with her gavel and stated, "That is not the issue."[28] Mrs. Smith was wrong though; desegregation was ever becoming the issue.

Randall Junior High School in Southwest, where most of the African American students from Barry Farm–Hillsdale went after attending Birney Elementary, was the other junior high school operating on a double shift at the time. Randall was the feeder school for nine elementary schools, and in 1949, it enrolled 1,468 students in facilities that had the capacity for only 901 students. Even using the Bowen School annex, it had an overflow of 507 students.[29]

The final approval by the board of education for the transfer of the Blow and Webb school buildings took place on November 19, 1947, and the transfer took place on December 1. Earlier, the Browne PTA had already filed a suit in the District Court. Then a new class action suit was filed under the name *Carr v. Corning*—Marguerite Daisy Carr[30] was the daughter of the Browne PTA president James C. Carr Sr.—and other claimants asking for admission to nearby Eliot Junior High School, which was reserved for White students and was underused. The District Court dismissed the case by a two-to-one decision, and on appeal, the District of Columbia Circuit Court of Appeals affirmed the lower court in February 1950.[31]

Gardner Bishop was one of the parents at Browne Junior High School who was enraged with the school's situation. His daughter, Judine, had enrolled in the school as a ninth grader in 1947 and was subjected to the trials of having to move around two buildings located blocks apart to receive her education. Mr. Bishop, who was a North Carolina native and owned a barbershop on U Street, was skeptical from the very beginning that lawsuits were going to be successful. According to his account years later, he thought that the tactic "wasn't going to work." He wanted immediate relief, not a lawsuit.[32]

At a meeting of a group of Browne parents on November 29, 1947, held at Jones Memorial Methodist Church at Benning Road and 44th Street NE, a new strategy was devised: civil disobedience. The parents agreed with Gardner Bishop; they wanted immediate relief, and they were going to keep their children away from school until a solution was found. On December 3, 1947, a petition was presented at the board of education meeting by Bishop as a spokesperson for the group. Being a business owner, Bishop was not afraid of losing his job due to his actions, and he was self-described as having "more mouth than anyone else."[33]

The strike started on December 4, 1947, and on December 5, the *Washington Post* had on its front page a headline story: "Five Students Attend Classes as Parents Strike Second Day." Parents picketed in front of the Franklin Building in downtown Washington, where the board of education had its offices, and in front of the Blow annex. Interviewed by a reporter, Eulalia C. Mathews—one of the leaders of the strike—stated categorically, "We shall continue to picket and to keep our children out of school until the Board of Education gives us something better than the Blow and Webb buildings."[34]

To try to appease the striking parents, the head of the school board, Mrs. Henry Grattan Doyle, agreed to attend a mass meeting of the Browne parents at the Jones Memorial Church. According to Gardner Bishop, he even liked her as a person, but she was patronizing without knowing it. During the meeting, Mrs. Doyle chastised the parents for keeping their children out of school. Afterward, she stated to Bishop, "These are fine-looking people."[35]

The students' strike at Browne lasted until February 2, 1948. The students returned to attend classes in five school buildings. In addition to the original Browne building and the Blow and Webb annexes, part of Thomas and Merritt Elementary School buildings were also turned over to be used by the junior high school students. The assignment of junior high school students to buildings previously used by elementary school students had put some elementary school classes in half time.[36] The board of education was compounding the problem of school overcrowding instead of dealing with it.

The events around Browne Junior High School in the fall of 1947 led to the emergence of Gardner Bishop as a strong leader and to the creation of the Consolidated Parent Group Inc. With the help of the National Association for the Advancement of Colored People (NAACP), they became the central players in the grass-roots efforts to desegregate schools in Washington, D.C. Article II of the Consolidated Parent Group constitution, written in 1948, stated that the group would work to "abolish racial segregation and other discriminatory practices now imposed upon minority groups in the public schools and recreational areas of the District of Columbia." Their motto was "Give the Child a Fair Chance."[37]

In 1950, the situation of the schools serving Barry Farm–Hillsdale's children was deteriorating. Birney Elementary School, which had opened at the beginning of the twentieth century, moved to a new building at the corner of Nichols Avenue and Sumner Road. Now identified as "Old Birney," the

1901 building was slated to be used for junior high school students at the Barry Farm–Hillsdale area. It would be used for that purpose until the new Frederick Douglass Junior High School building opened on Douglass Road in 1952. The "Old Birney" building was also used to house the overflow of elementary school students coming from the Turner Elementary School, located on Stanton Road and Alabama Avenue, and accordingly was also identified as the "Turner Annex."[38]

Luberta Jennings, who moved to Barry Farm Dwellings in 1943 because her husband, James Chester Jennings, was a worker at the navy yard, remembered years later that five of her children were in school in the late 1940s and early 1950s. The younger ones attended "Old Birney." Some of the Jennings children also had to go to Garnet-Patterson Junior High and Armstrong Senior High in Northwest and Randall Junior High in Southwest. She remembered the expense of paying for the children to go to junior and senior high schools across town in Southwest and Northwest because the schools in Southeast, which her children could have attended, were segregated. Most hurtful to her was that her eldest son, James Jr., had not been able to join the Cadet Corps at Armstrong High because he could not get to school on time. The buses coming from Congress Heights, packed with White students, would not stop at the Barry Farm–Hillsdale bus stop. She recalled that many times in the winter, her children had to trudge in the snow many miles to reach their schools on the other side of town. This situation was longstanding and had been experienced by Kenneth Chapman, who had attended Cardozo High School in the early 1940s. In an interview in 2002, he stated that children from Barry Farm–Hillsdale had "experienced busing" long before the practice had been implemented in the 1970s and 1980s as a tool for integration.[39]

Sarah Bolling, a widow and employee of the federal government, was living at 1732 Stanton Terrace, just outside the footprint of Barry Farm–Hillsdale, with her two children, Spottswood Thomas Jr. and Wanamaker Von. When Spottswood Jr. finished elementary school at Garfield, located at 25th Street and Alabama Avenue SE, he was assigned to attend junior high school at "Old Birney." Mrs. Bolling felt that "Old Birney" was a health hazard and sent her child to Shaw Junior High School in Northwest. Not that Shaw was much better. A report issued in 1949 stated that the "educational adequacy of the [school] plant is so low that no reasonable amount of rehabilitation could correct its deficits." By the late 1950s, the school had become widely known as "Shameful Shaw" for its crumbling physical condition and severe overcrowding. A new school building was not erected until 1971.[40]

While parents in Barry Farm–Hillsdale faced these hurdles to provide decent educational opportunities to their children, a new junior high school for White students was opening nearby. On March 6, 1950, 497 White students entered newly built Sousa Junior High School at 37th Street and Ely Place SE. The *Washington Post* described the new building in glowing terms, including a large library with a "huge circular window…and natural light pouring through it"; special rooms for home economics, art and music classes; print, wood and metal workshops; two gymnasiums; two recreation rooms; a cafeteria; an auditorium; a music room; and twenty-five classrooms, some of which remained empty.[41]

During the summer of 1950, Dr. Garnet C. Wilkinson met with a group of residents from Barry Farm–Hillsdale that identified itself as the "Committee-at-Large" to discuss how to provide "adequate Housing of junior high school pupils" coming from Garfield, Turner and Birney Elementary Schools. The members of the committee represented a cross-section of the established leadership of the community, such as Ulysses S. Banks, president of the Barry Farm Civic Association; Dr. Charles E. Quarles, the community's pharmacist, who was then leading the Coordinating Committee of Anacostia; and Alfred Watson and Althea V. Howard, respectively president and secretary of the Hillsdale Civic Association. Also present was Alice B. Finlayson, the principal at the new Birney Elementary School, and the pastors from St. John's CME and Bethlehem Baptist Church. The group was concerned that in September of that year, almost four hundred children graduating from the elementary schools serving Barry Farm–Hillsdale and adjacent African American communities would be ready to attend seventh grade and there was no place for them to go. The proposed solution was to house the newly minted seventh graders at "Old Birney." The committee requested that "Old Birney" be "physically improved, staffed and equipped for the junior high school program."[42]

The Consolidated Parent Group, under the leadership of Gardner Bishop, opposed the position presented by the committee. The parent group had a chapter at Barry Farm–Hillsdale holding meetings at Campbell AME.[43] They were recruited to join the fight against the segregation of schools in Washington, D.C. It is not clear how the group from Barry Farm–Hillsdale was chosen, although it might have been because the plight of the junior high school students was a familiar one after the Browne case.

On June 23, Gardner Bishop presented a letter to the board of education in which he compared how White junior high schools in Southeast better served their students, especially at the new Sousa Junior High School. The letter specifically mentioned that "Negro junior high school students [from the community] must attend classes in elementary school buildings while white children go to buildings of junior high design."[44]

On August 30, 1950, Gardner Bishop sent another letter to the board of education requesting permission to appear at the September 6 meeting. Melvin Sharpe, the president of the board, asked for more information on the nature of the presentation. The response from the Consolidated Parent Group, which came in a telegram, was very clear: "We would like to discuss conditions at Garfield Turner New and Old Bierney [*sic*] and the parents desire as to a solution to present conditions affecting their children in this area." A note at the bottom of the telegram indicated that the group would have five minutes to present their case at 9:00 a.m. on September 6.[45]

In the letter Bishop delivered on September 6 to the board of education, he specifically requested that the new Sousa Junior High School be used on "an integrated basis." This letter also acknowledged that the idea of using "Old Birney" as a junior high school was sponsored by "self-esteemed" persons in the community who had attended the meeting with the school system leadership, implying that they gave themselves more credit than the community at large gave them, at least on this issue. The petition presented to the board along with the letter was signed by almost four hundred residents of Barry Farm–Hillsdale, the majority of whom were residents of Barry Farm Dwellings. There were also letters from pastors of six of the churches serving the community, including Reverend D.A. Bell from St. John's CME, who might have had a change of heart since the meeting with Wilkinson.[46] All the efforts were in vain, as on October 4, 1950, at a board of education meeting, "Old Birney" was officially designated as Douglass Junior High School. Seventy parents and children sat in silence at the meeting in protest.[47]

The first significant step in the desegregation fight in Washington, D.C., took place on Monday, September 11, 1950, the first day of the new school year. On that day, Gardner Bishop organized a group of parents and students to go to Sousa Junior High School and demand admission. There is a discrepancy in the number of students who went—ten, eleven, twelve, fifteen and twenty-five are reported in different accounts.[48] Reverend S. Everette Guiles from Campbell AME Church, who had allowed the parents' group to meet at the church, accompanied the students. He was transporting some of them in a car lent for that purpose by Mrs. Frances Mason Jones, the owner of Mason Funeral Home, an establishment that had been on Nichols Avenue, the main commercial corridor of Barry Farm–Hillsdale, since the beginning of the twentieth century. The Capital Taxicab Company provided transportation for

Reverend S. Everette Guiles, pastor at Campbell AME Church at Barry Farm–Hillsdale. Reverend Guiles was a strong supporter of the movement to integrate schools in Washington, D.C. He drove one of the cars that took Barry Farm–Hillsdale children to Sousa Junior High School on September 11, 1950. *Courtesy Dale/ Patterson Family Collection, Anacostia Community Museum Archives, Smithsonian Institution, gift of Dianne Dale.*

the rest of the group. They were met at the school door by the principal, Eleanor McAuliffe, who "courteously but firmly" turned them down. That was the beginning of the end for the segregation of schools in Washington, D.C.[49]

In the meantime, the parents of children who had to attend "Old Birney" were tempted to boycott the school, but they were advised by their counsel to keep the children in school and sue the school board. This time, the legal strategy was not going to ask for equalization of facilities between the two segregated school systems—it was going to attack public school segregation in Washington, D.C., as being unconstitutional.[50]

Renowned civil rights lawyer James M. Nabrit Jr., together with George E.C. Hayes,[51] had taken the cause of the Consolidated Parent Group Inc. under the leadership of Gardner Bishop and the parents of the children of Barry Farm–Hillsdale who were denied entrance to Sousa Junior High School. Nabrit's opinion was that the equalization approach to the issue of segregation was "an expensive, circuitous, indecisive, and unsound approach." As Nabrit stated in 1951, African American "[c]itizens of the United States are not required to apologize for insisting with all the power at their command upon the immediate, full and complete enjoyment of all their Civil Rights."[52]

The residents of Barry Farm–Hillsdale believed that they had the right to "full and complete enjoyment" of their civil rights and wholeheartedly supported the effort. Mrs. Frances Mason Jones remembered some twenty years later that they raised money with recitals performed by the students from Maurice Green's studio on Morris Road; with dinners at Campbell AME; and even with an event at a school where $1,000 was raised. Mrs. Jones was particularly proud of the event at the school, which was organized with the assistance of the teachers under the nose, so to speak, of the school administrators. In the same vein, Gardner Bishop had memories of going to "chitlin parties" where people paid $3 to eat and also of running raffles to benefit the effort. He also remembered that Marshall Field & Company, the big department store chain from Chicago, donated money for the cause. Even the Jack and Jill Club's children presented a money tree to support the effort. At least two churches in Barry Farm–Hillsdale, Campbell AME and Mathews Memorial Baptist Church, also donated money. The fundraising was essential for the success of the litigation since, even though Hayes and Nabrit did not charge for their services, money was necessary to pay for all the other expenses related to the legal work. Essential to the success of the enterprise was the unity of purpose and the "ideological clarity" of the group. In later years, Gardner Bishop recalled that the Consolidated Parent Group Inc. had received support from people of all economic levels within the African American community and had crossed racial lines reaching out into the White community.[53]

After all the appeals to the board of education in Washington, D.C., failed, the *Bolling v. Sharpe* case was filed in the District Court for the District of Columbia in November 1950. It sought permanent injunctions that would restrain the principal defendant, board of education superintendent Melvin Sharpe, from excluding African American children from Sousa Junior High School solely on account of race. The names of the Bolling brothers appear at the top of the list because the Consolidated Parent Group had decided to list the children in alphabetical order. The other plaintiffs were Sarah Louise Briscoe, who lived with her parents on Eaton Road at Barry Farm Dwellings, and Adrienne and Barbara Jennings, who lived with their parents on Stevens Road, also at Barry Farm Dwellings.[54]

Because of the decision to alphabetize the names of the plaintiffs, the Bolling case was unusual in the sense that the two top listed plaintiffs were male. Most of the early school desegregation cases that paved the way for the desegregation of schools in 1954 were filed on behalf of girls, as was the case with *Carr v. Corning*. A companion case to *Bolling v. Sharpe* filed on the same day by Nabrit and Hayes listed Valerie Cogdell as the top plaintiff. She lived with her parents, Lillian and Karl Cogdell, on Stevens Road at Barry Farm Dwellings. The other plaintiffs were Wallace Morris, son of Eva Morris, who also lived at Barry Farm Dwellings; Felicia Brown, daughter of Emerson Brown and Evelyn Brown; and Lauretia Parker, daughter of Jessie Parker. This case was abandoned, and *Bolling v. Sharpe* went on to the Supreme Court.[55]

Bolling v. Sharpe was also unusual in another regard. It claimed that the plaintiffs were deprived of their liberty and property without due process of law in violation of the Fifth Amendment to the Constitution of the United States.[56]

The other cases claimed that their plaintiffs were being denied their Fourteenth Amendment rights, which states, "[N]or shall any State… deny to any person within its jurisdiction the equal protection of the laws." Eventually, the *Bolling v. Sharpe* ruling established the reverse incorporation doctrine in legal practice, meaning that just as the "Fourteenth Amendment's Due Process Clause has been held to incorporate provisions of the first eight amendments, the Fifth Amendment's Due Process Clause was construed to incorporate…the equal guarantee of the Fourteenth."[57] This legal maneuver was necessary because the District of Columbia was not a state and, consequently, not directly covered by the Fourteenth Amendment.

Nabrit's approach was bold and reportedly, at least initially, without the support of the NAACP. Nevertheless, he presented his case to the U.S. District Court for the District of Columbia. Judge Walter M. Bastian ruled in April 1951 that since *Bolling v. Sharpe* was not questioning the inequality of the school facilities, the case had no merit because the question of segregation in the Washington, D.C., schools had already been decided by the ruling of *Carr v. Corning* the previous year.[58]

The legal team—now joined by Howard Law professors James A. Washington Jr., Dorsey E. Lane, Herbert O. Reid Sr. and Charles W. Quick— began working on an appeal to the U.S. Court of Appeals. In October 1952, Nabrit received a call from the clerk of the Supreme Court advising that Chief Justice Frederick (Fred) M. Vinson wanted him to petition the court to have the *Bolling* case brought up with the three other cases on school desegregation scheduled to be argued in December. An order of *certiorari* was then issued. *Certiorari* is an order from a higher court (in this case the Supreme Court) to a lower court (in this case the Court of Appeals) to send the records of a legal proceeding for review.[59]

As the 1952 school opening day approached, the District of Columbia continued to grapple with the usual problems of overcrowded schools and scarcity of teachers. In August, School Superintendent Corning was planning to fire White schoolteachers so he would be able to hire African American schoolteachers. There were up to one hundred surplus White teachers in Washington, D.C. Meanwhile, White suburban school systems in Prince George's County, Maryland, and Fairfax, Virginia, offered positions to fifty of those displaced. In October, it was reported that thirty-four elementary schools were overcrowded; twenty-six were African American schools, and of those, two schools were on double shift. On December 17, the board of education voted "to invite the leaders of Washington to give their views on the best ways to prepare for a possible integration of the District school system." Seven days earlier, on December 10, 1952, the Supreme Court had heard the arguments for *Bolling v. Sharpe.*[60]

James M. Nabrit Jr. and George E.C. Hayes delivered a passionate legal argument. Nabrit built his case on the fact that the individual rights of Americans were enshrined in the Bill of Rights, and when these liberties were threatened, "it was up to the Supreme Court to scrutinize such acts with the utmost suspicion." He concluded his argument with what was considered the most eloquent statement in the three days of oral arguments on the cases under the umbrella of *Brown v. Board of Education*:

> *You either have liberty or you do not. When liberty is interfered with by the state, it has to be justified, and you cannot justify it by saying that we only took a little liberty.... We submit that in this case, in the heart of the nation's capital, in the capital of democracy, in the capital of the free world, there is no place for a segregated school system. This country cannot afford it, and the Constitution does not permit it, and the statutes of Congress do not authorize it.*[61]

The Supreme Court decision came on Monday, May 17, 1954. The delivery of the judgment and opinion of the court was announced at 12:52 p.m. The content of the decision for *Brown v. Board of Education*, delivered by Justice Warren Burger, can be summarized in the following statement: "[I]n the field of public education the doctrine of 'separate but equal' has no place. Separate educational facilities are inherently unequal."[62]

The decision in *Bolling v. Sharpe* was next. Pursuing the line of argument that had been advanced by James M. Nabrit in 1952, Justice Burger stated:

> *Liberty under the law extends to the full range of conduct which the individual is free to pursue, and it cannot be restricted except for a proper governmental objective. Segregation in public education is not reasonably related to any proper governmental objective, and thus it imposes on Negro children of the District of Columbia a burden that constitutes an arbitrary deprivation of their liberty in violation of the Due Process Clause.*
>
> *In view of the decision that the Constitution prohibits states from maintaining racially segregated public schools, it would be unthinkable that the same Constitution would impose a lesser duty on the Federal Government.*[63]

By 1:20 p.m. it was done: "The law of the land no longer recognized a separate equality." Ethel Payne, the highly respected African American newspaperwoman who was dubbed "the first lady of the black press," was present at the Supreme Court, reporting for the *Chicago Defender* when the decision was delivered. She later wrote, "The members of the press went completely wacky. There I was—right in the middle of it and almost out of my mind!"[64]

Soon after the decision was rendered, Gardner Bishop gave an interview to the *Afro-American* newspaper in which he expressed his feelings about the seven years of efforts to desegregate the schools in Washington, D.C.: "[It] seemed like a long time ago and sometimes I wondered whether it was worth it." The *Evening Star* heralded, "The first praise went unstintingly to Gardner Bishop and the Consolidated Parents Group, Inc." Sarah Bolling described her reaction to the momentous decision to Ethel Payne: "I'm so happy it's over with….It has been a long hard struggle."[65] Spottswood Bolling, then living with his mother in Northeast Washington and attending Spingarn High School, refused to give an interview. He was more concerned that "[p]eople at school start to tease me."[66]

Luberta Jennings and her family had also moved away from Barry Farm–Hillsdale; they were now living on Irving Street in Southeast. Interviewed by the *Afro-American*, she stated, "The Supreme Court I was sure, would render a favorable decision in the school segregation cases." She still remembered "how much trouble we went through out here in southeast Washington trying to get suitable facilities for our children."[67]

The superintendent of schools, Hobart M. Corning, was ready for action. He submitted to the board of education a proposal for desegregation in the District of Columbia schools on May 25, 1954, and had the full text published in the *Washington Post* the next day. He stated the obvious at the beginning of his proposal, that the Supreme Court opinion "placed upon the Board of Education and the Superintendent of Schools the responsibility for accomplishing the complete desegregation of all public schools in the District of Columbia." He also stated that he would accomplish "the transition in Washington as rapidly and as effectively as possible" and that the desegregation of schools in Washington would be "complete [in] all schools [and be] accomplished with least possible delay."[68]

The Corning plan was approved five to one at the board meeting of June 23. The dissenting member was Dr. Margaret J. Butcher, one of the African American members of the board who did not think the plan would achieve integration fast enough. The all-White Federation of Citizens Associations was against the plan and in a telegram stated, "With shock and regret we note that you are proceeding to consider a

Mrs. Luberta Jennings and her daughters, Adrienne and Barbara Jennings, 1954. The Jennings family were living on Stevens Road at Barry Farm Dwellings when *Bolling v. Sharpe* was filed in 1950. Adrienne and Barbara were plaintiffs in the case. *Reprinted with permission from the D.C. Public Library, Star Collection at* Washington Post.

precipitous and, we believe disastrous program of integrating District public schools." The Federation lawyers filed a suit in District Court on September 7 to "restrain temporarily the District of Columbia School Board from proceeding with integration of the school system." Two days later, Federal Judge Henry A. Schweinhaut served judgment on the suit, refusing to halt school desegregation.[69]

Corning's desegregation plan had built-in flexibility for the White parents who were nervous about desegregation. A map was drawn to determine school boundaries within which children would attend the schools near their house. Nevertheless, the only children to be immediately transferred at the start of the school year in September 1954 were 2,700 African American children who were previously attending severely overcrowded schools. Other transfers were optional, and students would be able to finish their schooling in their current school if so desired.[70]

On opening day in September 1954, the schools serving Barry Farm–Hillsdale were barely integrated. Anacostia High School had 6 African American students out of 1,274 and no African American teachers. Douglass Junior High School, in turn, had no White students out of 1,016 and no White teachers. Sousa Junior High School had 94 African American students out of 873 and 6 African American teachers out of 34. Birney Elementary School had 7 White students out of 1,233 and no White teachers. A perusal of the list of schools appearing in the *Washington Post* edition of September 16, 1954, told the story: schools in White neighborhoods had mostly White students and schools in African American neighborhoods had mostly African American students.[71]

The six students who first integrated Anacostia High School came into their first day of classes under the protection of the police, but not because Whites were attacking them. A rumor had circulated that African Americans were going to come to the school en masse and demand full integration immediately, so the police had decided to cordon off the school and police cars were circulating throughout the neighborhood.[72]

Active resistance to integration at Anacostia High School did not happen until later. On October 4, White students at Anacostia High School started a four-day demonstration against integration. On that date, the number of African American students at Anacostia High School was up to forty-three, as the board of education had previously decided to speed up the integration of the schools and proceeded to allow high school students to attend the schools near their homes.[73]

When those 43 pioneers arrived to attend school that Monday, they were met by a milling crowd of more than 1,200 White students, and the street in front of the school was lined with police. The African American students were let into the school before the bell rang by a sympathetic teacher. When it was time to go in, only 200 White students did so, and they were jeered by the crowd that stayed outside with epithets such as "chicken" and "n***** lovers." In all, about nine schools were involved in the disturbance. Besides students from Anacostia High School, students at McKinley and Eastern High Schools also demonstrated and cut classes. Students at Kramer, Sousa, MacFarland, Hine, Stuart and Taft Junior High Schools were also involved in the protests. The Metropolitan Police Department and the superintendent of schools took the firm position that the desegregation of schools would continue, and eventually the demonstrations fizzled out. By Friday, October 8, the protest had ended.[74]

On the ground, students experienced the shock of integration from different perspectives. African American student Gerald B. Boyd Sr. entered Anacostia High School in 1956. He remembered many years later that the White teachers "didn't really know how to deal with black students....They weren't aware of some of the characteristics and the cultural differences, so it was a tough situation for African-American students." Other teachers, such as the basketball coach Russell Lombardy, who later became principal of the school, were memorable in a positive way. According to Boyd, Coach Lombardy stated on the first day of try-outs for the basketball team, "I don't care if you're white, blue, black, brown, whatever color. If you can play basketball, you're going to make this team."[75]

Dianne Dale, who entered Anacostia High School in 1957 after attending Douglass Junior High School, suffered "the greatest cultural shock." Her White classmates were mainly indifferent, but there was also some open discrimination; some teachers called African American students names. For the first time, she saw how "unequal the systems were and how narrowly proscribed were [her] movements in greater society to that point." She was certain that she was as smart as her White classmates, yet "they knew more than [she] did" because they had had better school facilities and broader experiences. She felt "shortchanged" and sometimes would say during the flag salute "...and liberty and justice for who?" That was her protest.[76]

Sheila Eileen Cogan, who lived in Southeast, graduated from all-White Ann Beers Elementary School in 1954 and entered Sousa Junior High School when the school was desegregated in September. Many years later, she remembered vividly, "There was nothing that prepared us pupils to understand the magnitude of the changes that were occurring. It just happened." She felt lucky that two teachers at Sousa, one White and one African American, tried to encourage communication between the two races.[77]

Sheila entered Anacostia High School in 1956 and remembered that "there were some...cultural issues...and the high school groups were generally... separated, or separated themselves." Her 1960 graduation prom brought to the fore how separate the races were at Anacostia High School. The prom took

Integrated class at Anacostia High School, 1957. After the turmoil of 1954, classes were integrated at Anacostia High School. *Courtesy Library of Congress, Prints and Photographs Division (LC-U9-1033-16).*

place at the gym's basketball court, "and there is a line down the center [of the court]—all the white students danced on [one] side of the line, and all the black students danced on the other side of the line." Cogan also remembered that a White girl burst into tears because an African American boy had asked her to dance. She asked her friends, "Should I accept his invitation?" Her friends did not know what to tell her. Sheila recalled, "We did not know how to handle it. That was part of the issues that we were dealing with."[78]

Once desegregation was a *fait accompli*, many White parents dealt with it by removing their children from public schools or moving out of the District of Columbia to the still segregated nearby suburbs. While the so-called White Flight—the movement of District of Columbia Whites to suburban areas in Maryland and Virginia—had been taking place for a while, the *Bolling* decision accelerated its pace. By 1964, ten years after desegregation, 87.6 percent of the students in the District of Columbia public school system were African American. By 1977, that percentage had risen to almost 95 percent. For all practical purposes, the District of Columbia public school system had become re-segregated three decades after the fight to desegregate it had started. In 1957, Hobart M. Corning, still superintendent of schools, stated that the desegregation of schools in Washington, D.C., was complete, but integration had not been accomplished. "There is a vast amount of difference between desegregation and integration....Desegregation is merely the moving about of people and things....Integration is a much longer process."[79]

Gerald B. Boyd Sr. explained the process most clearly:

> *I realized right away that there is a difference between desegregation and integration. Desegregation was a court decision...you have to obey....*[It] *says that this school shall be opened to black students....Desegregation is physical. Now integration, you see, is...mental. It means that although you can allow these black students in your school, your attitude may not change. So although they* [the black students] *are physically around you, mentally you're not dealing with it....You would go eat in the cafeteria, all black students would be in a section and all the white students would be in...*[another] *section....So that's not integration.*[80]

The situation did not improve with time. Fifty years after the desegregation of schools in Washington, D.C., a study with the suggestive title of "Separate and Unequal: The State of DCPS Fifty Years after *Brown* and *Bolling*" pointed out that "*de facto* re-segregation" had happened in Washington, D.C. By 2005, White children between ages five and seventeen in Washington, D.C., composed 22 percent of their cohort. Only 2 percent of them attended public schools. Gerald B. Boyd Sr. was right when he stated, "That's not integration."[81]

Chapter 12

The 1960s

The Community's Loss of Identity and Vibrant Civil Rights Activism

On Sunday, May 8, 1966, the *Washington Post* featured a lengthy article titled "This Is Anacostia." Nowhere in the article was there mention of Barry Farm–Hillsdale, although there was mention of "the low-income Barry Farm project," referring to Barry Farm Dwellings. The identity of the neighborhood had been subsumed into the identity of Anacostia.

This loss of identity was already becoming apparent in the late 1940s. On October 19, 1949, a group of businessmen from Barry Farm–Hillsdale met at Douglass Hall, in the heart of the community. At the meeting, they decided to form an organization "to better acquaint [themselves]…with problems of [their]…respective businesses and professions." The group met again on December 19, 1949, and elected the first president of the new organization, which they named Anacostia Business and Professional Organization. All of those involved were businesspeople in Barry Farm–Hillsdale, not in the nearby Anacostia, which was still very much segregated. A list of the businesses participating in the organization in 1951 said it all: Dale Market on Sumner Road, C and C Cleaners and Joe's Barbershop in nearby Wade Road, near the Barry Farm Dwellings. No fewer than twelve other businesses were located on the 2400 and 2500 blocks of Nichols Avenue, the commercial center of the community. Beauty salons, barbershops, a pharmacy, a market and an upholsterer were also included in the list.[1]

Another organization created around the same time to represent the community's churches, schools and civic groups before city government bodies took the name Coordinating Committee of Anacostia and Vicinity.

Dr. Charles Qualls, the owner of the Anacostia Pharmacy, located on the 2400 block of Nichols Avenue, was a leader in the creation of both organizations. When a committee was organized to press for the immediate admission of African American students from the neighborhood to Anacostia High School in the aftermath of the May 1954 *Bolling v. Sharpe* decision, it received the name of Anacostia Emergency Educational Committee. Reverend Guiles and Dr. Qualls were members of this committee.[2] In 1967, when the Smithsonian Institution opened a museum on the 2400 block of Nichols Avenue in the heart of Barry Farm–Hillsdale, it named it Anacostia Neighborhood Museum.[3]

The reason why these organizations took the name "Anacostia" instead of Barry Farm or Hillsdale remains somewhat unclear. However, after the construction of the Barry Farm Dwellings, the name "Barry Farm" grew to be inextricably connected to it, while usage of the name "Hillsdale" survived only among a small number of people.

By the mid-1960s, another significant change was remaking the area: rapidly changing demographics. The May 8, 1966 edition of the *Washington Post* mentioned the high number of Whites who had abandoned Anacostia,

Anacostia Neighborhood Museum, September 1967. Members of the Anacostia Historical Society are seen here standing in front of the newly created museum. The museum's location was at the heart of the Barry Farm–Hillsdale community. *Courtesy Smithsonian Institution Archives (image # 94-2464).*

adding that the area was now predominantly African American: "There was…a need for housing for low-income groups…land in Anacostia was plentiful and cheap. Private developers moved in, as did the District of Columbia government, which has built 33 percent of its low-income housing in far Southeast. Negroes needed the housing desperately and thousands moved across the river. Whites moved out."[4]

The growth in population was also astonishing. Far Southeast, as the area was then identified, grew 50 percent between 1950 and 1967, while Washington, D.C., grew only 6 percent. In 1950, 82.4 percent of the population in Far Southeast was White. By 1967, only 37.4 percent of the residents in the area were White. Only the areas north of Good Hope Road and south of Pennsylvania Avenue had remained predominantly White at that time. The area of Southeast near Barry Farm–Hillsdale was predominantly African American.[5]

Barry Farm–Hillsdale was also affected by zoning changes. Between 1962 and 1967, there were six cases of rezoning in the footprint of Barry Farm–Hillsdale. All were from R-1-B zoning for a one-family detached dwelling to R-5-A low-density apartment housing. The immediate impact was a steep decline in homeownership leading to a transient population occupying the private, newly built low-rent and public housing complexes. Given these changes, the living conditions in the neighborhood also were declining.[6]

Private developers were particularly happy with the rezoning since they could place as many as sixty apartments on an acre of land previously occupied by a one-family detached house. Arthur Morrissette, a White businessman and onetime resident of Southeast, declared in an interview in 1972 that he was "very proud that they did rezone" the area. According to him, the Barry Farm–Hillsdale area had been one of the "worst slums in the City" and the rezoning had allowed the construction of countless apartment buildings and improved the neighborhood.[7]

A report from the late 1960s did not have the same view: "The housing profile of the Anacostia area has changed disastrously in the last ten (10) years. An area that was once populated by one family housing has now changed into a conglomeration of apartment houses multiplying as a cancerous growth, devouring all available land and straining the very fiber of the area inorder [sic] to support the growing population inadequately."[8] In 1968, well-known journalist William Raspberry stated in his "Potomac Watch" column in the *Washington Post*, which he bluntly titled "Anacostia: Housing's City Dump," that the neighborhood had turned into "the public-housing dumping ground, not only because it has the cheapest and most underdeveloped land, but because it has the least political clout."[9]

A commensurable increase in services did not accompany the rise in the number of residents. By 1969, four elementary schools were serving the immediate area of Barry Farm–Hillsdale: Birney on the corner of Sumner and Nichols Avenue; Moten on the corner of Morris and Elvans Road; Nichols Avenue Elementary, at the "Old Birney" school building on Nichols Avenue; and Savoy on Shannon Place. All of them except for Nichols Avenue Elementary School were over capacity. Moten, built in 1955, was already 83 percent over capacity.[10]

Older residents who had enjoyed the closeness of the community in the past lamented the overcrowding of the old neighborhood. Ethel G. Greene moved to Howard Road around 1888. In 1975, she gave an oral history interview in which she denounced the creation of the "overcrowded community, without having planned for it." She was adamant that many of the buildings that had contributed to the overcrowding had to be torn down and that one-family detached housing should be built to give people the "chance to indulge in a little home ownership...where you can grow and plant." She had a yearning to go back to a neighborhood with fruit trees and vegetable gardens. Almore Dale, member of a family who had been in the neighborhood since the nineteenth century, declared emphatically, "The influx of people here has been tremendous over the last twenty or thirty years, and things have gotten out of hand." Another cause for the demographic change and the increase in the population density in the neighborhood was the redevelopment of Southwest. By 1960, more than 4,600 families comprising 23,000 people were relocated. At least 42 percent of them moved to Southeast.[11]

Despite all its problems, or perhaps because of them, the residents of Barry Farm–Hillsdale—and in particular those living in the Barry Farm Dwellings—rose once more to the task of trying to improve conditions in the neighborhood and Washington, D.C., as a whole, just as they had in the 1940s and 1950s. This time both the young people and the adults organized themselves under the aegis of the Southeast Neighborhood House (SEH).

The Southeast Neighborhood House had started in Capitol Hill in 1930 as a daycare center for African American children under the name of Southeast House. The organization stayed in Capitol Hill until the late 1950s, when it was displaced from its location at 324 Virginia Avenue Southeast by the construction of the Southeast Freeway.[12] In 1962, Ralph D. Fertig, a civil rights activist, took over the leadership of the organization and relocated its

Sign for the Southeast Neighborhood House, which provided training and support to activists in Barry Farm—Hillsdale and the Anacostia area for many years. *Courtesy Anacostia Community Museum, Smithsonian Institution Collections.*

activities east of the Anacostia River. SEH's first location was an abandoned storefront on 2025 Nichols Avenue lent by W. Ledru Koontz, a longtime White resident and businessman of Anacostia.[13]

At first, SEH was working with a restricted budget and five employees. What it lacked in financial resources it had plenty in creativity and dedication of its staff. Zora Martin (later Zora Martin Felton), who had followed SEH from its location in Capitol Hill, where she had been working since 1958, went to work with the women of Barry Farm Dwellings. After earning their trust, Ms. Martin came up with a creative way of helping them obtain groceries of better quality and at more affordable prices than what was offered by the small stores available in the neighborhood. They would have to trek up the hill to Alabama Avenue to reach the Safeway Supermarket and return juggling the kids and the shopping bags. It was too much effort, they said.

Ms. Martin suggested that they should go as a group and, after shopping, share the cost of a taxicab and send all their groceries down the hill accompanied by one of the group members. Then everybody else could walk home and collect their purchases. They could take turns among themselves on who would ride in the cab. At first, the group was suspicious. Eventually, a core group of collaborative shoppers emerged, and they also began to form a sense of community in what had been previously a fractured neighborhood. This was the first intervention of SEH at Barry Farm Dwellings and would be followed up with more intensive ones a few years later.

The lack of resources and staff at SEH changed in 1965, when the organization received a grant from the United Planning Organization (UPO) under the aegis of the Office of Economic Opportunity. The money was going to be used to hire neighborhood residents as workers to implement the "War on Poverty," as President Lyndon Johnson's 1964 anti-poverty program was known.

The first thirteen neighborhood organizers were hired by February 1965 and began a five-week training course to learn how to steer those in need of assistance to agencies that could help them find jobs, housing, legal aid, medical care and assistance with problems with welfare. The group included two Whites and eleven African Americans, with six men and seven women. The first success of the program in fighting poverty was the hiring of ten people who had been unemployed until then. They all resided in Southeast, and most of them lived in public housing. They graduated on March 5, 1965, at a ceremony attended by Mrs. Hubert H. Humphrey.[14]

Among those first workers was Alberta Johnson, who had left school in the ninth grade and was taking care of seven children. She had lived a life of hardship and knew how to speak the language of the people she was trained to help. Another worker was Lois Wilson, who was also living in poverty when she spoke at the group's graduation. She expressed emphatically that the workers had been trained to "find the needs of the people," but that as a matter of fact, they were the "people." Ms. Wilson had a teaching certificate in elementary education and in the past held jobs as a clerk in the U.S. government and as a housekeeper. She resided at the Knox Dwellings in Southeast, where she was president of the tenant council.[15]

Another graduate from this first group was Mary Kidd, a White Canadian who had moved to Southeast in 1962 when she came to Washington, D.C. When asked why she had come to live in Anacostia, she stated that it was because the rent was cheap. As a Canadian, she was surprised at the fact that she had trouble in the community with both Whites and African Americans. She unwittingly provoked the ire of both groups by trying to organize the parents at the school where her children were enrolled and other activities in which she tried to involve both White and Black community residents. According to her, she was characterized as a "sell out" by the White community and as trying to be a "white leader" by the African Americans.[16]

Another of the members of that first class of neighborhood organizers was John Kinard, who would work as a consumer education aide. Kinard was a minister, had been a community worker with Operations Crossroads Africa in East Africa and worked as a U.S. Department of State escort for African leaders visiting the United States. He would leave his position as an organizer in SEH and go on to be the founder and first director of the Smithsonian Institution's Anacostia Neighborhood Museum, now the Anacostia Community Museum, in September 1967. He kept that position until 1989, when he passed away.[17]

By 1966, there was a feeling at SEH that the program was not as successful as it could be because organizers were spread too thin and there was a need to shift activities from merely giving information to individuals to helping them view "themselves as agents of social change." SEH began a more concerted mobilization effort to get community residents to organize and act together to address their needs. In a memorandum dated July 14, 1966, the leadership at SEH informed the organizers that they should now implement "direct action" and operate primarily to diagnose "the problem rather than the solution to it…[and] engage in a joint exploration of the problems with those" they served. The whole idea of the new engagement style was to give the opportunity for the members of the community to define their problems and find the solutions. Several initiatives followed this shift in emphasis, including the organizational efforts centered at Parkchester Courts, Howard Road Apartments and Barry Farm Dwellings, all located within the footprint of Barry Farm–Hillsdale.[18]

In 1952, Fred Schneider and Melvin Schlosberg built the Parkchester Courts development, comprising ten buildings, occupying approximately 4.5 acres and including 182 one- and two-bedroom apartments on Wade Road across from Barry Farm Dwellings. The builders were beneficiaries of a Federal Housing Administration (FHA) Section 608 loan. FHA Section 608 was the section of the Housing Act of 1949 that financed multi-family unit structures. During its existence, it funded the construction of 711,000 apartments. Most of these apartments were small one-bedroom units unfit for families and in poorly built structures mostly in urban areas.[19]

FHA Section 608 allowed builders to take their profits even before they built the apartments. It was called "mortgaging out"—that is, to borrow more than the construction cost and pocket the difference as a windfall profit. Schneider and Schlosberg took a windfall of $120,000 from Parkchester Courts. This would be the equivalent of more than $1.1 million in today's money.[20] Parkchester Courts went into foreclosure by FHA in December 1966. By then, seventy-eight of the apartments were vacant due to vandalism, and SEH was proposing to help the tenants organize a cooperative. By October 1967, FHA and the residents organized by SEH had reached an agreement and created the Parkchester Cooperative. Eventually, seventy-nine units were renovated and sold to members. The renovations took into consideration the size of the families buying them. Thus, some of the original units were joined to create larger ones with up to four bedrooms and two baths. Former renters received priority to buy the apartments, and sweat equity was applied to down payments.[21]

In March 1966, two SEH organizers went knocking on doors at the Howard Road Apartments. The complex, built around 1942 in the 700 block of Howard Road, included thirty-two two-floor buildings containing four one-bedroom units each. The 1945 *Baist* map for Barry Farm shows the 32 buildings built on four of the original lots of section 9 and arranged around two courtyards. In 1966, about four hundred people occupied the 128 apartments. The building complex was owned by Arthur Morrissette, the entrepreneur who had characterized Barry Farm–Hillsdale as a "slum," and his partner, David Gruber.[22]

The buildings were in an isolated area. That section of Howard Road was cut off from the main Barry Farm–Hillsdale community by the railroad tracks, and it was hemmed in by the D.C. nursery on one side and expressways on the other. By 1966, "the many residences" that had lined the road on the way to the Anacostia River in the late nineteenth century and early twentieth century were long gone. The community organizers from SEH observed that "the physical isolation of Howard Road undoubtedly has serious negative psychological effects on the people living there."[23]

On the other hand, the community organizers from SEH also speculated that perhaps that feeling of isolation gave the residents a strong sense of identity and allowed them to organize very quickly. By May 1966, the Howard Road Tenant Council was already operating under the leadership of Katie Ridley and holding weekly meetings. By the middle of June, the council was ready to present its grievances to the owners and the managing company.[24]

Ms. Ridley, described as "a little woman with a big voice and an understanding of leadership," was working as a teacher's aide with the St. Philip Head Start program when she was appointed president of the Howard Road Apartments Tenant Council. She described many years later how an SEH organizer knocked at her door and asked, "How do you like these conditions you are living in?" Her answer was simple: "I don't." Under the guidance of the SEH workers, she went on to develop her leadership skills. In 1992, she stated that "although I was not a college graduate [I] used common sense. [The] useful skills [I] gained at SEH [helped me] to motivate others."[25]

Until they were organized, she and her neighbors had been afraid "to take their grievances even to the resident manager, [who was African American] much less to take them to the landlord [who was White.]" Threat of an eviction notice was a constant. The conditions of the buildings were appalling. The structures were at least twenty-five years old, but the hallways had never been painted. Vermin overran the apartments. The residents were able to obtain materials, but not labor, to paint their apartments—but even then only every five years.[26]

There were also the problems of lack of security because all the back doors of the apartments could be opened by the same master key, and the locks on the front doors were not strong enough to withstand a burglar. The Howard Road Apartments had the reputation among criminals of being the place to go to get "a free TV." Besides the vermin, the primary health hazard for the tenants was the heating system. It consisted of coal furnaces in each apartment. The furnaces were difficult and dangerous to operate. Most of the tenants did not know how to operate them properly. By their very nature, the furnaces were also very dirty.[27]

Although there were communication problems and infighting among the members of the tenant council and even among the workers from SEH, by October 1966 some improvements had resulted from the organizing. Maintenance improved, with minor repairs being done more promptly. The hallways were painted, and the residents took an active role in policing them so that the newly painted walls would not be marred. There was a communal cleanup effort and food sale day in August, and on that same day a swing set and a slide were installed by the residents. The playground equipment was acquired with donations from the owners and the residents in a rare sign of unity.[28]

The problem of replacing coal furnaces with gas heating was much more difficult to solve because it was expensive. At first, the owners stated that they would not be able to replace the system at all. Then, faced with sit-ins and pickets in front of their rental office, they entered in an agreement with the residents to partially replace the system with an accompanying increase in the rent. By 1967, not all the problems at the Howard Road Apartments had been solved. The back locks, for instance, had not been changed.[29] The activism of the residents of the Howard Road Apartments, with the help of SEH workers, ultimately had beneficial results. In addition to the physical improvements, it gave the residents the knowledge of how to organize and help themselves. As Katie Ridley very aptly stated in December 1966, "I [now] know where to go and how to go about it."[30]

Pharnal Longus was a Washington, D.C., native who as a child had spent time at the Southeast House daycare center in Capitol Hill. He went on to graduate from Dunbar High School and then got a BA degree from West Virginia State College. After working as a social worker while serving in the U.S. Army, he received a master's degree in social work from Howard University and was one of the new community workers hired by SEH.[31]

By the time Longus arrived at Barry Farm Dwellings to work in organizing its residents, the community had suffered severe deterioration, and some of its residents were suffering from the ills caused by neglect and extreme poverty. Longus observed, "One driving through the neighborhood could easily mistake it for a concentration camp or an institutional setting. All the houses have the same architectural structure, the physical deterioration is rampant. Houses needed painting repair, the streets were poorly paved, and decent sidewalks were needed."[32]

An array of social distress came from such conditions: economic powerlessness, family disorganization, ill health, juvenile delinquency, high crime rates, alcoholism, drug addiction and early death. As incredible as it might seem, the neighborhood was also divided by social classes. On top of the social strata were those who had steady employment, usually as low-level civil service employees. They tended to live along the main street of the development, Sumner Road, and were dismissively called "Sumner Roaders" by the other residents. The middle class of Barry Farm Dwellings—those who worked as domestics and hospital aides, for instance—lived on the middle street, Eaton Road. The lower class, so to speak, those who were on welfare, lived mostly on Stevens Road, the third and last street of the development. It was among the latter that "the source of political leadership for change and the force that moved the neighborhood" in Barry Farm Dwellings was identified by the SEH workers.[33]

SEH's *modus operandi* was highly successful. Once a group was organized at the Dwellings by the SEH workers, the members decided which government institution they were going to press seeking a solution for a specific problem. Then the group would request an audience to air their grievances, with the authority in charge of the institution that could deal with the issue. If denied an audience, they would go *en masse* to the office of that person and force a meeting. The authority at the institution would be surprised by the pressure and forced to hear them. Later, the members of the group would feel liberated from their fears of contesting authority and empowered by being supported by their neighbors. The media was always informed of upcoming actions, thus garnering the coverage for the events. By and large, the actions taken by the newly organized groups in Barry Farm Dwellings followed this script.[34]

Ms. Lillian Wright (later Lillian Wright Smith), a mother of four and a resident on Stevens Road, was described as "fearful and shy." She had no fear when she led a "rebellion," as described by the *Washington Post*, in February 1966 against the National Capital Housing Authority (NCHA), then under the leadership of future Washington, D.C., mayor Walter Washington. NCHA planned to undertake an improvement project at Barry

Farm Dwellings focusing on the outside of the units. With the help of the SEH workers, a group of women who lived on Stevens Road organized themselves under the name of Band of Angels.[35]

They called a press conference and announced that they had not been consulted about the plan and that they demanded a meeting with NCHA. The group eventually got not only two meetings but also a promise from Walter Washington that he would "consider shifting the emphasis of an upcoming…repair job from the exterior of the buildings to the interior of the buildings." The residents were afflicted by vermin infestation, leaks, faulty faucets and defective furnaces inside their units. Six months later, the rehabilitation project was being implemented with the help of a residents' working group.[36]

Another member of the Band of Angels was Etta Mae Horn (later Etta Horn-Prather), born Etta Mae Welch in Charlotte, North Carolina, on October 3, 1928. As a young twenty-one-year-old living in Washington, D.C., she had married Joseph Xavier Horne in 1949 and went on to have seven children with him. The marriage did not work out, and by 1966, because of ill health, she could no longer perform domestic work as she had in the past and was receiving welfare.[37] Ms. Horn described herself at the time as being "just a good welfare recipient, a good mother, and being a good community person, that means mind my own business and stay as dumb as I was." She was living on Stevens Road when one of the SEH workers knocked at her door in 1966. On that occasion, she did not answer the knock at her door; she had no time. Later that day, Lillian Wright came to talk to Horn and convinced her to go to a meeting that evening. This was the beginning of lifelong activism for Horn. She went on to be a witness in the halls of power in Washington, D.C., and a nationwide advocate for welfare rights. Later, she was the director of a daycare center for children in her neighborhood.[38]

Within months of their organization, the women of the Band of Angels had been able to articulate "the issues that later became the agenda of [countrywide] welfare rights activists: inadequate income, inferior housing, and health care, and the lack of attention to poor women by public agencies."[39] At the same time that the women were getting organized, the youth of Barry Farm Dwellings were getting together to take on the establishment and get improvements for their lives. In the summer of 1965, an Office of Economic Opportunity Neighborhood Youth Corps project, under the leadership of Leroy Washington, had included twenty-six neighborhood teenagers. The program was disbanded after six months. Now, in February 1966, Leroy, described as "a school dropout, bright but illiterate, unemployed, a father

Etta Mae Horn, 1968. Ms. Horn is the third from the left, front row. She is marching on Mother's Day, May 12, 1968, in Washington, D.C., under the banner of the National Welfare Rights Organization. The march marked the opening of the Poor People's Campaign. *Courtesy the Jack Rottier Photograph Collection, 1953–83, Collection #C0003, Box 28, Folder 23, Special Collections Research Center, George Mason University Libraries.*

of three sons," was looking to organize his friends into a group that would obtain not only employment training but also recreation facilities for the young people of the area. They were also concerned about public services. They named the new group Rebels with a Cause, perhaps inspired by the famous 1955 James Dean movie. William Scott, who was one of the founders of the group, stated that the name of the group came about because at the time they were a "young group that really had a cause." They also believed that they would be given a hard time by the powers that be and, thus, aim to rebel against it.[40]

By mid-February, the group reportedly included three hundred members and had caught the attention of the officials at the National Housing Authority and the United Planning Organization (UPO). The group obtained support from UPO executive director James G. Banks for a special survey of the youth needs in Southeast, after it had threatened a sit-in at the organization's headquarters. Later, when they were unsatisfied with the pace of the survey, the Rebels "politely invaded" Banks's office until he skipped the meeting he was attending at the time and came to talk to them. They were following the playbook devised by the SEH community workers. They first had attempted to make an appointment; when that failed, they had occupied the office, and they were duly covered by the media to give maximum exposure to their demands. Banks was impressed. "Where else do you have teen-agers and young adults talking about improving housing, schools and recreation? Those are basically responsible objectives."[41]

Soon the Rebels found a new backer in a famous entertainer: Eartha Kitt. In March 1966, Ms. Kitt was starring in a play, *The Owl and the Pussycat*, an interracial romantic comedy, at the National Theater in Washington, D.C. The women of Club Twenty, a fundraising group working with SHE, sold tickets for one of her performances as a benefit for the organization. Eartha Kitt then came to SEH to present a check from the benefit performance to Ralph Fertig.[42]

Fertig was thankful but, according to his own words, "told her how so much more was needed, and gave her the story of the Rebels with a Cause." Eartha Kitt agreed to take a tour of Southeast with the Rebels, where she saw "dirt streets that had never been paved…crowded apartment buildings without the luxury of hot running water" and other appalling conditions. Two nights later, Fertig was called for a meeting in Kitt's dressing room at the National Theater. The guest of honor was Representative Roman C. Pucinski, a Democrat from Illinois who chaired the Subcommittee on Juvenile Delinquency and Youth Crime. Ms. Kitt told Fertig, "I want you to tell Puchi what you told me about the Rebels with a Cause."[43]

Ms. Kitt followed up the initial contact by attending a Rebels rally on March 17 at Turner Elementary School after her performance at the National Theater. She brought along Representative Pucinski and UPO director James G. Banks; taking advantage of the audience, the Rebels explained their needs. They talked about how the poverty programs in the area benefited primarily the very young and the old residents, that there was nothing for the youth. There were no jobs and no recreation. Eartha Kitt stated that her purpose in helping the Rebels was to "spark some hope in them, let them know people are caring." At the end of the meeting, she was made an honorary member of the group.[44]

The Rebels were extremely successful in organizing themselves and in involving 1,500 youths in their programs, which included clubs, dances and field trips to museums. They were instrumental in having a recreation center built near Frederick Douglass Dwellings by presenting plans for a 5.5-acre recreation center, including an Olympic-size pool, directly to Joseph H. Cole, the superintendent of the Recreation Department in Washington, D.C. The Rebels also were very proud of being able to work with the District of Columbia Highway and Traffic Department to obtain a traffic light placed at the corner of Nichols Avenue and Sumner Road. At that corner, the children from Birney Elementary School were in constant danger of being run down by the cars driving through the neighborhood.[45]

Ultimately, the Rebels were the model for a citywide anti-poverty and anti-delinquency program to empower teenagers to develop their own educational, employment and recreational activities. As a report at the time stated, "From a band of jobless 'locked out' youths was born a program destined to affect many young lives in the [city]."[46] Despite all this success, in August 1966 the Rebels and SEH community workers were involved in a serious incident with the police. This incident revealed not only the deep frustrations racking the community but also the latent racism of the police in the area. Interestingly enough, it all started in nearby Congress Heights.

Congress Heights had been a solidly White neighborhood, with the air of a small southern town and deep-seated racism, until the 1950s. By that time, large housing developments for African Americans such as Stanton Dwellings on Alabama Avenue had been built in the area. By 1960, White Flight was in full force. Unscrupulous real estate agents started using the technique of block-busting. After selling a house to an African American family, they would go around the neighborhood corroborating the fears of declining property values in the White residents. The residents, in turn, would sell their houses for less than their value to the real estate agents in fear that the houses would be even less valuable in the near future. The agents then would sell the houses at inflated prices to African American buyers anxious to buy property in areas that had been closed off to them in the past. Inevitably, there was racial strife while the change in the ethnic composition of the neighborhood was taking place.[47]

Some entertainment businesses that catered only to Whites remained open in 1966 in Congress Heights. One of them was the 1023 Club, described as "a redneck biker bar" located on Whaler Place SE near the district border with Prince George's County. On August 15, 1966, a series of incidents took place around the bar in which African American youths attacked White patrons, broke windows and cut the power. Police from the Eleventh Precinct on Nichols Avenue arrived, dispersed the crowds and made arrests. The youth, some of them members of the Rebels, stated that they were angry because the bar discriminated against African Americans and because the White bikers endangered the residents, in this case presumably the new African American residents.[48]

Community organizers of SEH called an outdoor meeting at the Congress Heights Community Development Center to discuss the events when police arrived and arrested a young man as being a suspect in the disturbances of August 15. One of the organizers in the meeting, James L. Covington, and a youth participant inquired about the reason for the arrest and were promptly arrested by the police for interfering. All three were taken to the Eleventh Precinct.[49]

Following the arrests, SEH organizers got together about twenty young people with hastily prepared signs stating "Lawful Assembly Denied," "Police Abuse" and "Police Brutality" and took them to picket at the precinct. The demonstration broke up, and the participants went to SEH about a block from the precinct. Soon other demonstrators took their place, and this time they congregated across from the precinct and started throwing bottles and rocks, while another group around SEH was setting off firecrackers and blocking Morris Road. Others pelted cars coming down Nichols Avenue. Reportedly, no damage was caused either to passing cars or to the precinct's building.[50]

The police were not effective in curbing the demonstration and made things even worse when they called on security officers from a nearby building on Good Hope Road to bring their dogs. The appearance of the dogs seemed to inflame the demonstrators even more. One youth stated categorically, "It was those dogs....Nobody threw a rock or bottle until those dogs showed up." There is no doubt that the images from 1964 in Birmingham, Alabama, of the police dogs snarling and attacking African American demonstrators must have flashed in the minds of the demonstrators.[51]

Other violent responses from the police that further inflamed the situation included the use of squad cars to drive menacingly toward groups of demonstrators that had congregated at the corner of Morris Road and Mount View Place in the vicinity of the SEH and later in the evening a charge by policemen to disperse the crowd, which resulted in ten arrests and thirteen injuries.[52]

In response to the disturbance, the police department moved immediately to replace the Eleventh Precinct leadership by appointing two African American policemen. A committee was also organized to investigate the disturbance. The committee included Walter Williams, a twenty-year-old Rebel; Henry K. Willard II, a fourth-generation Washingtonian and the great-grandson of Henry A. Willard, the founder of the city's storied Willard Hotel; and Sterling Tucker, a civil rights organizer and politician who in 1974 became chairman of the first elected D.C. Council in more than a century.[53]

The committee presented its conclusions in October, which noted that there were mistakes on both sides. The committee stated that SEH workers erred in organizing a picket line in the middle of the night at a place where large crowds could assemble quickly. Nevertheless, the committee considered that the police also had made several mistakes that had led to the all-out confrontation and to the injuries and arrests. Two months after the report was issued, it became clear that many of the policemen at the Eleventh Precinct were particularly ill-disposed against the African American residents in the area as well as to SEH.[54]

Mary Kidd, the Canadian who had been in the first group of community workers trained by SEH, was invited to join the Police Advisory Council of the Eleventh Precinct. She was appalled by the attitude of both the White and African American members of the group toward the African American population in the area. According to her, all the White members in the advisory group "were…racists at heart" and the African American members "were just as determined to be hard on black people as the white were [*sic*]."[55]

The advisory council met at the precinct's roll call room, and Kidd noticed that the chairs and desks where the policemen sat were carved with racist imagery and sayings. She was determined to bring that to light. She made rubbings of the carvings and called journalist William Raspberry. After Raspberry was unsuccessful in getting access to the roll call room at the Eleventh Precinct, he went ahead and published a column about the carvings illustrated by three of the least offensive ones. Among swastikas and proclamations of White power, there was one that stated, "F…S.E. Neighborhood House Communists."[56]

These were not the only manifestations of racism in the precinct. Max Robinson, then working as a reporter for WRC-TV, produced a series of programs on Anacostia. In one of them, White policemen appeared with their backs to the camera and with their voices distorted. They told the interviewer how the word "n----- rolled from their lips like water from a dam." African American prisoners were "kicked, doused with water and spat upon" while being held in the cellblock. Another officer ominously stated that "if the white officers were unleashed, there 'wouldn't be a Negro left standing.'" The police admitted that the water dousing incident was being investigated. The carvings were promptly removed from the furniture in the

Police Precinct Building, 1971. In August 1966, the youth of Barry Farm–Hillsdale and Anacostia confronted the Eleventh Precinct policemen. Today, the building is occupied by the Whitman-Walker Health Max Robinson Center. *Courtesy Anacostia Community Museum, Smithsonian Institution Collections.*

roll call room. Raspberry was not assuaged by these actions. He stated that police officials pretended that there were no problems or "paint[ed] them over," thus guaranteeing that there would be no solution.[57]

The summer of 1966 also brought the visit of a controversial figure of the civil rights movement to Barry Farm Dwellings. Stokely Carmichael, recently elected leader of the Student Nonviolent Coordinating Committee (SNCC), came to Washington to discuss President Lyndon Johnson's civil rights bill. He was also interested in discussing local issues, such as lack of local governance in Washington, D.C., and in advocating for the ouster of the district school superintendent, Carl F. Hansen, who was White. Future D.C. mayor Marion Barry's organization, Free DC, arranged Carmichael's visit to Barry Farm Dwellings, and SEH neighborhood workers, including Philip Perkins, rallied the residents to come to hear Carmichael.[58]

At the rally at Barry Farm Dwellings in July 1966, attended by 150 people, Carmichael used the recently coined slogan "Black Power." The slogan had just been used for the first time at a rally in Greenwood, Mississippi, the previous month during the Meredith March Against Fear. Soon the slogan would become a rallying cry for the civil rights movement. Using a bullhorn to address the Barry Farm crowd, Carmichael "announced his intention of creating a broader-based SNCC capable of delivering 'black power' from the grass roots."[59]

Despite its apparent success, at least one resident of Barry Farm–Hillsdale did not believe that the "war on poverty" programs had been beneficial to the youth in the neighborhood. Frederick Saunders, who was raised and went to school in Barry Farm–Hillsdale, attributed more trouble than benefit to the "war on poverty." Saunders had been a roving leader for the Department of Parks and Recreation, and when SEH started organizing the youth in the area, most of the young men who he was working with accepted paid jobs as organizers. According to Saunders, when the money dried up, the young men turned to selling drugs to earn money, and many ended up in jail. He believed that the whole thing had been "a false illusion...[which] had fed [the youth] a bill of goods."[60]

In May 1967, William Raspberry presented a different view. According to him, UPO (and by extension SEH) had been extremely successful in organizing the poor to "exert influence on established city agencies to get things done—just as the nonpoor [*sic*] have always done...[but] people when

Stokely Carmichael at Barry Farm Dwellings, 1966. In July 1966, Carmichael talked at a rally attended by 150 people at Barry Farm Dwellings. Philip Perkins, a neighborhood worker, is standing to his left. *Courtesy Anacostia Community Museum, Smithsonian Institution Collections.*

organized are no longer meek recipients of handouts. They become vocal, insistent and demanding, and this new attitude triggers resentment." Now the president and Congress were being pressed to "stop making concessions, to keep the rebellious poor in their place." So came the cutbacks. According to Raspberry, for the war on poverty to be successful, it would require implementing "a shakeup of the entire social and political system," and that was not done. In the previous September, Pharnal Longus had already noted that the successful organization of the residents of Barry Farm–Hillsdale had been "so revolutionary [that it] threatened the power structure."[61]

By late 1967, newspaper articles were printing headlines stating "Antipoverty Dreams Fade" and "D.C. Youth Corps Faces Slash in Jobs." By the late 1970s, the "Promise of '60s Faded" was another newspaper article headline. The Rebels with a Cause, who had "emerged, confident they knew how to deal with the too familiar poverty," were no more. Now the "untapped resources of the poor, young black men [were] unwanted." Drugs had flooded the city, and the programs geared toward the poor had died under benign neglect while the country was engulfed in the Vietnam War and the political scandal of Watergate.[62]

In April 1968, Barry Farm–Hillsdale was less affected than other areas in the city by the riots that ensued after the assassination of Dr. Martin Luther King Jr. On Friday, April 5, there were afternoon reports of disorderly crowds gathering at Good Hope Road and along Nichols Avenue. More serious disturbances were happening in nearby Congress Heights. In the following days, a few businesses at Good Hope Road were damaged and set on fire. There was also some theft and arson on Nichols Avenue, but not as widespread as in the 14th Street corridor. Mrs. Frances Mason Jones, who managed Robert G. Mason Funeral Home on Nichols Avenue, was told that the young men in the community "gave word not to touch her establishment because of the care she gave to the many families during time of bereavement."[63]

The assassination of Dr. King did bring one lasting change to Barry Farm–Hillsdale: its main street, which began as Monroe Street in honor of the country's fifth president, James Monroe, and then was long known as Nichols Avenue in honor of Dr. Charles Henry Nichols, the first superintendent of St. Elizabeths Hospital, was renamed Dr. Martin Luther King Jr. Avenue on January 15, 1971, the slain leader's birthday.[64]

Conclusion

G iven the history recounted herein, how could the Barry Farm–Hillsdale community survive? Created in 1867 after the Civil War to deal with the housing problem faced by the newly freed people of Washington, D.C., this community's resilience and rich history of activism could not surmount the challenges to its existence coming from governmental actions and wider society. Like many other historic African American communities in cities across the United States, Barry Farm–Hillsdale was essentially planned out of existence.

Barry Farm–Hillsdale was subjected to serial displacement from eminent domain for various government projects during several decades beginning in the late nineteenth century. The construction of an outfall for St. Elizabeths Hospital and of a rail line in the nineteenth century were some of the first projects. In the twentieth century, Barry Farm Dwellings and the Suitland Parkway displaced hundreds of families and frayed the social fabric of the community. Federal government policy also contributed to the destruction of the neighborhood. FHA Section 608 was the section of the Housing Act of 1949 that financed multi-family unit structures. During its existence, it funded the construction of 711,000 apartments. The majority of these apartments were small, one-bedroom units unfit for families and in poorly built buildings mostly in urban areas. The Parkchester complex, built on the footprint of Barry Farm–Hillsdale, was a product of FHA 608.

The local D.C. government also contributed to the destruction of the community by allowing rezoning that led to the building of multi-family units in lots that had been previously occupied by single-family homes. This policy added to the overpopulation of the neighborhood. Despite its impact, there was no provision of additional services to deal with the influx of new residents.

Despite all the obstacles placed in its way, in the mid-1940s and early 1950s, the community successfully came together to fight segregation in swimming pools and schools. The community was also successful in the 1950s in fighting redevelopment plans that would have wiped it out, as was eventually done to the Southwest quadrant of the city. Leaders and citizens alike were indefatigable in fighting for their rights. In the 1960s, again the spirit of activism energized residents, especially of the Barry Farm Dwellings, to challenge the inequities of the welfare system and the lack of opportunities for youth.

Lurking in the background were societal factors that determined the eventual disintegration of what had been a close-knit African American community. Desegregation without real integration led to the flight to the suburbs not only of the White residents of nearby Anacostia but also of those within Barry Farm–Hillsdale who had the economic means to do so. Although the 1968 riots did not affect Barry Farm–Hillsdale as they did other African American communities across the river, they contributed to the acceleration of the movement to the suburbs. The advent of the crack cocaine epidemic in the 1970s and 1980s destroyed the last remnants of the cohesion of the historic community. Subsumed into Anacostia, which so ironically was created as an all-White neighborhood in 1853, Barry Farm– Hillsdale was no more.

There was once more a bright moment in the 1970s. The Smithsonian's Anacostia Neighborhood Museum, which today is the Anacostia Community Museum, went out looking for people who had lived in Barry Farm–Hillsdale to collect their memories. People came from far and wide to tell their histories. They fondly remembered Barry Farm–Hillsdale of the late nineteenth century and early twentieth century. There was pain in the memories of the hardships, but there was also great pride in telling the community's history.[1] This book intends to honor that pride and tell that history in its entirety.

Notes

Abbreviations

AA—Afro-American (Baltimore)
ACM—Anacostia Community Museum, Smithsonian Institution
AOHP—Anacostia Oral History Project, ACM Archives
AS-ACM—Anacostia Story: 1680–1930, exhibition records, ACM Archives
CA—Colored American
CDP-ACM—Community Documentation Project, ACM Archives
DP-ACM—Dale-Patterson family collection, ACM Archives
EC-ACM—Evolution of a Community, Exhibition Records, ACM Archives
EP—Evening Post (Washington, D.C.)
ES—Evening Star (Washington, D.C.)
ET—Evening Times (Washington, D.C.)
HABS—Historic American Buildings Survey
HSWDC—Historical Society of Washington, D.C.
JNE—Journal of Negro Education
JNH—Journal of Negro History
LOC—Library of Congress
NAACP—National Association for the Advancement of Colored People
NARA—National Archives and Records Administration
NCHA—National Capital Housing Authority
NCPPC—National Capital Park and Planning Commission
NSOHC—Neighborhood Survey Oral History Collection, HSWDC

NYT—New York Times
PC—Pittsburgh Courier
RCHS—Records of the Columbian Historical Society
RG—Record Group
RTTC—A Right to the City Oral History Collection, ACM
UC-ACM—ACM Unprocessed Collection, ACM Archives
WAA—Washington Afro-American
WDN—Washington Daily News
WH—Washington Herald
WH–HSWDC—Washington History
WP—Washington Post
WT—Washington Times
WTH—Washington Times Herald

Chapter 1

1. James, "Most Pleasant and Healthful Place," 19–23. For a discussion on the etymology of the name Anacostia, see John R. Wennersten, *Anacostia: The Death and Life of an American River* (Baltimore, MD: Chesapeake Book Company, 2008), 8.
2. Edward D. Neill, *The Founders of Maryland as Portrayed in Manuscripts, Provincial Records and Early Documents* (Middletown, DE: Leopold Classic Library, 2016), 27.
3. William H. Whitmore Jr., "St. Elizabeth's Tract, St. Thomas Bay, Charles County, Maryland, 1663—St. Elizabeths Hospital, Washington. D.C., Founded 1852," n.d., unpublished manuscript; list of deeds related to St. Elizabeths Tract from November 20, 1799, to October 20, 1837, AS-ACM.
4. Allen C. Clark, "Captain James Barry," *RCHS* 42 (1940–41), 1–2, 15; Hutchinson, *Anacostia Story*, 28.
5. Clark, "Captain James Barry," 9, 11; Madison Davis, "The Navy Yard Section during the Life of the Rev. William Ryland," *RCHS* 4 (1901), 212–13; Whitmore, "St. Elizabeths Tract."
6. James D. Barry and Juliana Coombe, married April 16, 1811, Washington D.C. Marriages, 1801–25; James D. Barry, 1840 U.S. Federal Census, Slave Schedules; James David Barry, U.S. Find a Grave Index, 1600s–current; J. Barry, 1850, U.S. Federal Census, Slave Schedules; Juliana

Barry, April 30, 1862, Washington, D.C., Slave Emancipation Records, 1851–63, ancestry.com.

7. Johnson to Howard, December 17, 1867, District of Columbia Freedmen's Bureau Field Offices, 1863–72, familysearch.org.

8. "An Act to Change the Name of Barry Farm or Potomac to Hillsdale, Legislative Assembly of the District of Columbia, 3rd Session, approved June 5, 1873," UC-ACM, Box 83; "An Act to Change the Name of Barry Farm or Potomac to Hillsdale," *Daily National Republican*, July 14, 1873; Louise Daniel Hutchinson, "Barry's Farm: The Anacostia Experiment," unpublished manuscript, EC-ACM. There is a new initiative attempting to revive the name Hillsdale that is being spearheaded by local organizations. See Discover Hillsdale, http://www.discoverhillsdale.org.

Chapter 2

1. Keith E. Melder and Melinda Young Stuart, *City of Magnificent Intentions: A History of Washington District of Columbia* (Washington, D.C.: Intac, 1988), 137.

2. "Runaway Slaves Arrested by Northern Soldiers," *ES*, June 1, 1861; *Frank Leslie's Illustrated Newspaper*, December 1861.

3. O.O. Howard, *Autobiography of Oliver Otis Howard, Major General, United States Army* (New York: Baker & Taylor Company, 1907), 416–17.

4. Ibid., 420.

5. *ES*, April 26, 1867; Howard, *Autobiography*, 420–21.

6. "Who Was Nichols? And What Happened to His Street?" *WP*, August 20, 2011; Robinson and Associates Inc., "Martin Luther King Jr., Avenue Determination of Eligibility," April 16, 2010, http://assets.stelizabethsdevelopment.com/documents/document_center/MPAmendMOAExhibit_9_MLK_DOE_20120430081008.PDF?CFTREEITEMKEY=D1293.

7. Receipt no. 1, signed by General O.O. Howard to "apply for payment for Lot No. 5 Section No. 2 'Barry Farm,'" District of Columbia Freedmen's Bureau Field Offices, 1863–72, familysearch.org; entries for Richard A. Hall, 1870 Washington City Directory; 1870 U.S. Federal Census and 1880 Atlanta, Fulton, Georgia, U.S. Federal Census, ancestry.com; Metropolitan African Methodist Episcopal Church, "The History of Metropolitan African Methodist Episcopal Church," https://metropolitaname.org/history.

8. Howard, *Autobiography*, 420.

9. *Centennial Encyclopaedia of the African Methodist Episcopal Church,* "Hunter, William Hammett" (Philadelphia: Book Concern of the AME Church, 1916), 122; Horace Talbert, *The Sons of Allen* (Xenia, OH: Aldine Press, 1906), 59.

10. *Centennial Encyclopaedia of the African Methodist Episcopal Church,* "Hunter, William Hammett," 122; Edwin S. Redkey, "Black Chaplains in the Union Army," *Civil War History* 33 (December 1987): 350; William H. Hunter, "Compiled Military Service Records of Volunteer Union Soldiers Who Served with the United States Colored Troops, 2nd through 7th Colored Infantry Including 3rd Tennessee Volunteers (African Descent), 6th Louisiana Infantry (African Descent) and 7th Louisiana Infantry (African Descent)," Fold3.com.

11. Eric Gardner, *Black Print Unbound: The Christian Recorder, African American Literature, and Periodical Literature* (New York: Oxford University Press, 2015), 131–32; Edwin S. Redkey, "Henry McNeal Turner: Black Chaplain in the Union Army," in *Black Soldiers in Blue: African American Troops in the Civil War Era,* ed. John David Smith (Chapel Hill: University of North Carolina Press, 2002), 338; Talbert, *Sons of Allen,* 59–60; William H. Hunter, 1880 U.S. Federal Census; 1900 U.S. Federal Census; entries for William H. Hunter and Henrietta Hunter, in U.S. National Cemetery Interment Control Forms, 1928–62, ancestry.com; "Negro Army Chaplain Dead," *ES,* October 18, 1908.

12. Johnson to Eldridge, November 27, 1867, letter authorizing the sale of lumber to William Alexander, owner of lot 5, section 1, and Brown to Sleigh, Superintendent, Barry Farm, October 13, 1868, District of Columbia Freedmen's Bureau Field Offices, 1863–72, familysearch. org; Wade H. Carter, ed., Hillsdale Civic Association, Affiliated with Federation of Civic Associations Washington, D.C., AS-ACM, Box 3, Folder 18 (hereafter Carter, Hillsdale Civic Association).

13. Carter, Hillsdale Civic Association, 7; Clark to Johnson, June 20, 1867; Howard to Johnson, October 9, 1867, Barry Farm, District of Columbia Freedmen's Bureau Field Offices, 1863–72, familysearch.org.

14. Howard, *Autobiography,* 421.

15. Ella Pearis, AOHP; survey maps of the area showed that the original lot 20, section 4 of Barry Farm–Hillsdale had already been subdivided into six lots by 1903, with two structures facing Elvans and one facing Sheridan. The 1913 survey showed six structures built on the property, three each facing both streets. *Baist's Real Estate Atlas of Surveys of Washington, District of Columbia,* 1903, plate 36, and 1919, plate 22.

16. John G. Warner, AOHP; *U.S. Register of Civil, Military, and Naval Service, 1863–1959*; entries for Henrietta Holliday and Frank Luckett, U.S. 1880 Census; Henrietta Luckett, widow of Frank Luckett, Washington, D.C., City Directory, 1922, ancestry.com; Thomas Taylor, AOHP.
17. Johnson to Howard, November 30, 1867, District of Columbia Freedmen's Bureau Field Offices, 1863–72, familysearch.org.

Chapter 3

1. Katherine M. Franke, "Becoming a Citizen: Reconstruction Era Regulation of African American Marriages," *Yale Journal of Law & the Humanities* 11, no. 2 (2013): 252, 277; "An Act to Protect All Persons in the United States in Their Civil Rights, and Furnish the Means of Their Vindication," Library of Congress, https://www.loc.gov/law/help/statutes-at-large/39th-congress/session-1/c39s1ch31.pdf. The act is colloquially known as the Civil Rights Act of 1866.
2. Reginald Washington, "Sealing the Sacred Bonds of Holy Matrimony Freedmen's Bureau Marriage Records," *Prologue* 37 (Spring 2005), https://www.archives.gov/publications/prologue/2005/spring/freedman-marriage-recs.html; "An Act Legalizing Marriages and for Other Purposes in the District of Columbia," ch. 240, 14 Stat. 236 (1866). We found information about the legalization of the unions of first settlers Abraham Scott and Ann Jackson, John Newton and Margaret Pendleton, Randall Johnson and Bettye (Elizabeth) Baylor, Isaac Diggs and Letty Smith, Osborne Holland and Henrietta Dixon, Clement Smith and Ann Finekum and Armsted (also spelled as Armstead) Taylor and Jemina Harris, Register of Marriages, District of Columbia, Freedmen's Bureau Field Office, 1863–72, familysearch.org.
3. "First Settlers of Barry's Farm. Listings for Howard Town from Records of Washington County, First District," Tax Book (1871), Louise D. Hutchinson, comp., June 1981, AS-ACM, Box 226 (hereafter "First Settlers"); Register of Marriage of Abraham Scott and Ann Jackson, April 1867, Register of Marriages, District of Columbia, Freedmen's Bureau Field Office, 1863–72, familysearch.org; Abraham Scott, U.S. 1870 Census and 1880 Census, and John W. Scott, U.S. 1880 Census and 1920 Census, ancestry.com.
4. Edgar Banks to Freedmen's Bureau, November 9, 1867, District of Columbia, Freedmen's Bureau Field Office, 1863–72 (hereafter Banks

to Freedmen's Bureau), familysearch.org; "First Settlers"; Edgar Banks, 1870 U.S. Federal Census, ancestry.com.

5. Banks to Freedmen's Bureau; John Thomas Seay, Graves Company, Kentucky, 1860 U.S. Federal Census; Edgar Banks, U.S. 1870 Census, ancestry.com.

6. Winnefred [*sic*] Lawrence, Rhode Island State Census, 1885, Jeremiah Laurence [*sic*], Rhode Island State Census, 1885; Winifred Laurence [*sic*] death certificate, September 1, 1895, Providence Rhode Island, espouse Jeremiah Laurence, parents Edward [*sic*] and Malvina [*sic*] Banks; familysearch.org; "Suburban News. Anacostia," *ES*, September 5, 1895.

7. "First Settlers"; Caroline Chase, 1840, 1850 and 1860 U.S. Federal Census, ancestry.com.

8. Caroline Chase, 1870 U.S. Federal Census, ancestry.com; order to sell lumber to Elizabeth Chase, June 2, 1868, District of Columbia, Freedmen's Field Office Records, 1863–72; Elizabeth Chase, record no. 15371, April 1, 1873, United States, Freedmen's Bank Records, 1865–74, familysearch. org; Washington, D.C., City Directory, 1874, 1884 and 1887, ancestry.com.

9. "Petition from Woman Suffrage," Petitions and Memorials, Resolutions of State Legislatures and Related Documents Which Were Referred to the Committee on the Judiciary during the 45th Congress, 1877–79, Record Group (RG) 233, Records of the U.S. House of Representatives, File Code HR45A-H11.7, Folder 14, Tray 4489, NARA; Anne Firor Scott and Andrew MacKay Scott, *One Half of the People: The Fight for Woman Suffrage* (Urbana: University of Illinois Press, 1982), 20.

10. "Fire in the Suburbs," *ET*, September 5, 1895; "Corbbetts of Unsound Mind," *ES*, June 25, 1904; Elizabeth Chase death certificate, June 14, 1904, file no. 222880, Office of Public Records, D.C. Archives; Elizabeth Chase death notice, *ES*, April 10, 1915.

11. "The Rev. John M. Shippen, Jr.," AS-ACM, Box 7, Folder 2 (hereafter "Rev. John M. Shippen, Jr."); "First Settlers"; Eliza Spottswood, 1870 U.S. Federal Census, ancestry.com.

12. Return of a Marriage for John M. Shippen and Eliza F. Spottswood, September 30, 1874, AS-ACM, Box 3, Folder 57; "Rev. John M. Shippen, Jr."

13. "Rev. John M. Shippen, Jr."

14. Ibid.; Pierre McKinley Taylor, AOHP.

15. "Rev. John M. Shippen, Jr."; Paul Donnelley, "The First Black Golfer to Play the US Open," *Firsts, Lasts and Onlys of Golf: Presenting the Most Amazing Golf Facts from the Last 600 Years* (London: Hamlyn, 2010).

16. "Hillsdale News," October 1898, and "Negro Probably Murdered," *EP*, December 26, 1901; "With Throat Cut," *Marion Star*, December 26, 1901; "District of Columbia," *Baltimore Sun*, December 27, 1901; "Preacher Cuts His Throat," *WP*, December 27, 1901; "Rev. John M. Shippen, Jr."; Eliza Shippen, 1900 U.S. Federal Census, ancestry.com.

Chapter 4

1. John Alvord, *Freedmen's Schools and Textbooks* (New York: AMS Press, 1980), 10.
2. Carter, Hillsdale Civic Association, 9; Hutchinson, "Barry's Farm"; "Report of Persons Hired at Barry Farm, D.C. Employed in School Construction Oct.–Dec. 1867," AS-ACM, Box 9, Folder 15; Major Eldridge to Freedmen's Bureau, December 1, 1867, reprinted in Hutchinson, *Anacostia Story*, 80; U.S. Office of Education, *Special Report of the Commissioner of Education on the Condition and Improvement of Public School in the District of Columbia, Submitted to the Senate June 1866, and to the House with Additions June 13, 1870* (Washington, D.C.: Government Printing Office, 1871), 279.
3. For the history of Frances Eliza Hall, see Amos and Savage, "Frances Eliza Hall"; "Data on the Teachers Who Worked among the Freed People of the District of Columbia between 1861 and 1876," June 15, 2014, unpublished manuscript, History of Place research files.
4. U.S. Office of Education, *Special Report of the Commissioner of Education*, 279; "Teacher's Monthly School Report, April, 1868, Miss F.E. Hall," AS-ACM, Box 227, Folder Howard School, 1868–69.
5. "Teacher's Monthly School Report, November 1868, Flora A. Leland," AS-ACM, Box 227, Folder Howard School, 1868–69.
6. "Teacher's Monthly School Report, Frances E. Hall, May, June, July, 1868, and June 1869," AS-ACM, Box 227, Folder Howard School, 1868–69; U.S. Office of Education, *Special Report of the Commissioner of Education*, 279.
7. Hutchinson, *Anacostia Story*, 86; Hillsdale School, District of Columbia School Records, Vertical Files, Charles Sumner School Museum and Archives, Washington, D.C. (hereafter Vertical Files, Sumner Museum); Ethel Green and Raymond Bumbry, AOHP.
8. Hutchinson, *Anacostia Story*, 86; "Hillsdale Wants Another School," *ET*, February 10, 1897.
9. "School Examination at Barry Farm," *New National Era*, June 6, 1872, 2; "Hillsdale Citizens," *ES*, December 15, 1889, 16; "A Historical Sketch of the Barry's Farm Community and Its Early Educational Institutions," unpublished

manuscript, AS-ACM, Box 2, Folder 14; "Nichols Avenue Elementary School: 2427 Martin Luther King Avenue, Southeast, Washington, D.C."; Birney School lot acquired from Mary A. Henson, June 10, 1889, $1,200, Birney School, Vertical Files, Sumner Museum; "Hillsdale Wants Another School," *ET*, February 10, 1897; "Suburban News. Anacostia," *ES*, May 18, 1895; "Hillsdale's Public Schools," *ET*, March 27, 1897.

10. "Birney School Opened," *WP*, October 20, 1901, 7; "Building History, School: Birney, James G.," and F[lorence] S. McClendon, "A History of Birney School," Birney School, Vertical Files, Sumner Museum.

11. "Birney School, use of, Patrons to hold entertainment for a stereopticon, 5/16/17," Birney School, Vertical Files, Sumner Museum.

12. James, "Most Pleasant and Healthful Place," 38–39; Carter, Hillsdale Civic Association, 4–5.

13. Carter, Hillsdale Civic Association, 9–10; "History of St. John Christian Methodist Episcopal Church (CME) 1875–2002," CDP-ACM.

14. Marguerite Duckett, "History of Macedonia Baptist Church, Anacostia D.C.," undated manuscript, AS-ACM, Box 10, Folder 15; *Map of the Division of the North Tract of Land Called St. Elizabeth*, 1867, Geography and Map Division, LOC; "First Settlers." John W. Cromwell gives another version of the creation of Macedonia Baptist Church. According to him, the church was created in 1867 by Sandy Alexander of the First West Washington Church. John W. Cromwell, "The First Negro Churches in the District of Columbia," *JNH* 7 (1922), 97.

15. "Anacostia and Vicinity: Special Services Held at Macedonia Baptist Church Yesterday," *ES*, November 27, 1905.

16. "Purpose Driven Parish," unpublished leaflet published at the time of the 125th anniversary of St. Teresa de Avila Parish in 2005, CDP-ACM.

17. Interview with Reverend Carl F. Dianda, November 2, 2009, CDP-ACM; Elizabeth Crawford, NSOHC.

18. "Our Lady of Perpetual Help Church," CDP-ACM; "Our Lady of Perpetual Help Parish," AS-ACM, Box 11, Folder 9; "The Dedication of the New Church of Our Lady of Perpetual Help," Sunday, September 12, 1976, DP-ACM, Box 11, Folder 10.

19. "Our Lady of Perpetual Help Church"; Kenneth Chapman, DP-ACM. Mr. Chapman's grandfather Arthur Chapman was one of those who participated in the building of the church. "The Dedication of the New Church of Our Lady of Perpetual Help."

Chapter 5

1. John Dale and Ethel G. Greene, AOHP.
2. Information contained in the previous paragraphs, unless otherwise noted, was compiled by reviewing the 1880 U.S. Census, Seventh Enumeration District of the County of Washington, ancestry.com. Health statistics were taken from District of Columbia Health Department, "Chart Showing the Distribution of Mortality with Reference to Population. Count East of Anacostia River," *Report of the Health Officer, 1889* (Washington, D.C.: Government Printing Office).
3. Carolyn Taylor Crocker, Ella Pearis, Anita E. Blake, Irene Donnelly and John G. Warner, AOHP.
4. Edith P. Green and Margueritte and James Johnson, AOHP. In 1943, the W6 and W8 bus lines went up Morris Road, turned into Stanton Road and connected with Alabama Avenue in Congress Heights. The A2, A4 and A6 bus lines served Nichols Avenue. *Guide Map: Capital Transit Street Car and Bus Lines*, October 1, 1943, Washington, D.C.
5. Hutchinson, *Anacostia Story*, 100; LeRoy O. King Jr., *100 Years of Capital Traction: The Story of Streetcars in the Nation's Capital* (Dallas, TX: Taylor Publishing Company, 1972), 13; John DeFerrari, *Capital Streetcars: Early Mass Transit in Washington, D.C.* (Charleston, SC: The History Press, 2015), 78–79; John Muller and Jason Levinn, "H.A. Griswold and Anacostia's Streetcar Story," Greater Greater Washington, https://ggwash.org/view/30275/h-a-griswold-and-anacostias-streetcar-story; "The Anacostia Railway Company," *ES*, July 3, 1876.
6. "Roadside Sketches," *ES*, December 5, 1891; Ethel G. Greene, "Things I Remember About Anacostia (That Have Not Already Been Mentioned)," AS-ACM, Box 12, Folder 12.
7. Earl Shipley, AOHP; Hutchinson, "Barry's Farm"; David Simpson, 1870 Census and 1880 Census, Washington, District of Columbia, ancestry.com.
8. David Simpson, 1870 Census and 1880 Census, Washington, District of Columbia, ancestry.com; "Georgiana R. Simpson," *JNH* 29 (1944): 245–47; Black Past, "Simpson, Georgiana (1866–1944)," www.blackpast.org/aah/simpson-georgiana-1866-1944; News from the Division of the Humanities, "Special Collections Exhibit Tells the Stories of Georgiana Simpson, African American Students," https://lucian.uchicago.edu/blogs/news/2009/02/16/special-collections-exhibit-tells-stories-of-georgiana-simpson-african-american-students. Georgiana Simpson received her degree on June 14, 1921, and Sadie Tanner Mossell Alexander received her

degree from the University of Pennsylvania the next day. Eva Beatrice Dykes received her PhD on June 22, 1921, but she had completed her work before both Simpson and Alexander did. So technically Simpson is considered the second African American woman to receive a PhD. Electronic message from Dr. DeWitt Williams to author on August 28, 2018.

9. For information on this historical episode, see John H. Painter, "The Fugitives of the Pearl," *JNH* 1 (1916): 243–64; John H. Paynter, *Fugitives of the Pearl* (New York: AMS Press, 1971); Josephine F. Pacheco, *The Pearl: A Failed Slave Escape on the Potomac* (Chapel Hill: University of North Carolina Press, 2005); Winifred Conkling, *Passenger of the Pearl: The True Story of Emily Edmonson's Flight from Slavery* (Chapel Hill, NC: Algonquin Young Readers, 2015).

10. Pacheco, *Pearl*, 239–41; Larkin Johnson, 1850 Census, Arundel County, Maryland. Johnson was married to Lucy, and they had four children; marriage of Larkin Johnson and Emily Fisher, April 5, 1860, D.C. Marriages, 1811–1950, familysearch.org. Emily had been married for a short period to a man named Fisher, but we have no information about this relationship.

11. Larkin Johnson, 1870 Census, Montgomery County, Maryland. Larkin Johnson's record at the U.S. Freedman's Records Bank Records, 1865–71, was dated April 24, 1874, and lists his address as Hillsdale. Larkin Johnson's 1880 Census entry includes, besides his family, a man named Marcellus Williams, who was identified as a servant. Perhaps this was the carriage driver, ancestry.com; Anita B. Blake and Irene Donnelly, AOHP. They were the grandchildren of Larkin and Emily Johnson.

12. Death of Larkin Johnson, February 26, 1885, D.C. Deaths, 1874–1961; "Suburban News. Anacostia," *ES*, September 17, 1895; Anita B. Blake and Irene Donnelly, AOHP.

13. On at least one occasion, he gave the date of his birth as February 14, 1832. "Solomon G. Brown," undated manuscript, AS-ACM, Box 3, Folder 2; William J. Simmons, *Men of Mark: Eminent, Progressive and Rising* (New York: Arno Press, 1968), 302; Louise Daniel Hutchinson and Gail Sylvia Lowe, "Kind Regards of S.G. Brown," *Selected Poems of Solomon G. Brown* (Washington, D.C.: Anacostia Museum of the Smithsonian Institution, Smithsonian Press, 1983), 3.

14. Black Past, "Solomon G. Brown (1829–1906)," https://www.blackpast.org/african-american-history/brown-solomon-g-1829-1906.

15. Hutchinson and Lowe, "Kind Regards," 3–4; marriage of Solomon G. Brown and Lucinda Adams, Marriage Records of the District of

Columbia, 1810–1953; S.G. Brown, 1870 U.S. Federal Census; Solimon [*sic*] G. Brown, 1880 U.S. Federal Census, ancestry.com; copy of probate of personal estate of Solomon G. Brown, August 17, 1906, AS-ACM, Box 18, Folder 12, lists a "Library 3 chairs 1 Divan About 300 books 2 Bookcases 1 Stand"; "Career of S.G. Brown," *AA*, July 7, 1906.

16. "The death of John A Moss…," *The Crisis* 25 (January 1923): 127; Cultural Tourism DC, "John A. Moss Residence Site, African American Heritage Trail," http://www.culturaltourismdc.org/portal/web/portal%20/303; "John A. Moss Dead; Formerly a Slave," *WP*, May 6, 1921; Howard University, "Law Department Graduates—1873," *Annual Report*, June 14, 1874, 21.

17. Undated newspaper article from AS-ACM, Box 7, Folder 4; "Case of John A. Moss," *ES*, May 4, 1904; "John A. Moss, Esq.," *WB*, August 1, 1896; Pierre McKinley Taylor, AOHP.

18. John A. Moss marriage to Ellen Abel, District of Columbia, December 11, 1875, Compiled Marriage Index, 1830–1921, ancestry.com; "John A. Moss Dead; Formerly a Slave," *WP*, May 6, 1921; "Former Slave Who Became Lawyer, Dies," *WH*, May 6, 1921; "John A. Moss," *WT*, May 6, 1921; "Praise Given Attorney John A. Moss," *Washington Bee*, May 14, 1921.

19. "First Settlers"; "Roster of Freedmen Employed at Barry Farm"; Fredk [Frederick] Smith, 1870 Census; Harriet Smith, 1880 Census; 1900, 1910, 1920, 1930 and 1940 Census, ancestry.com. These census entries also include several members of the Smith family who resided in the house over the decades.

20. "Program of Exercises. Testimonial to Miss Emma V. Smith, Teacher in the James G. Birney School, Anacostia for 48 Years, Upon Her Retirement from Service in the Public Schools, Washington, D.C., by the City of Anacostia, D.C. Friday Evening, April 19, 1929," AS-ACM, Box 7, Folder 1 (hereafter "Program of Exercises").

21. "Program of Exercises"; information on St. Philip the Evangelist Episcopal Church, CDP-ACM; John Dale and Carolyn Taylor Crocker, AOHP.

22. [Florence] McClendon, Almore Dale, John Dale, Norman E. Dale, Ethel G. Greene, A.G. Scott, Ella Pearis, Carolyn Taylor Crocker, Henry Sayles Jr. and Dr. Charles Qualls, AOHP.

23. Nancy J. Kessner, paper presented at the Historical Studies Conference Martin Luther King Jr. Library, February 27–28, 1987, Barry Farms [*sic*] Vertical File, Martin Luther King Jr. Library, Washington, D.C. See also the Louis Berger & Associates Inc. Cultural Resource Group, *Archeological*,

Architectural, and Historical Investigations at the Howard Road Historic District (Washington, D.C.), 1 (1986): 316–33.

24. George Trivers and Thomas Taylor, AOHP.

25. Edith P. Green, Norman E. Dale and John G. Warner, AOHP.

26. "Suburban News. Anacostia," *ES*, March 29, 1895.

27. Anita E. Blake, AOHP.

28. Hutchinson, *Anacostia Story*, 132; W.E. Burghardt Du Bois, *Efforts for the Social Betterment Among Negro Americans* (Atlanta: Atlanta University Press, 1909), 44.

29. Hutchinson, *Anacostia Story*, 132; Du Bois, *Efforts*, 44; "National Sewing Council," *ES*, August 1, 1903; "Home Coming Dinner," invitation, AS-ACM, Box 11, Folder 5.

Chapter 6

1. George W. Butler, 1900 U.S. Census, ancestry.com. Mr. Butler was a widower in 1900 and worked for the U.S. government as a messenger; John R. Tertrault, "A History of Black Commercial Enterprise in Barry Farms 1867–1915," unpublished manuscript, September 20, 1974, AS-ACM, Box 2, Folder 13; A.G. Scott and Frances Mason Jones, AOHP.

2. ONE DC, "Black Workers Center," https://www.onedconline.org/blackworkerscenter.

3. "The Pioneer Sabbath School Association Met at Douglass Hall, Hillsdale, Last Night," *ES*, November 13, 1879; "A Surprise to Marshall Frederick Douglass," *ES*, April 7, 1879; "Douglass Hall," *ES*, September 5, 1889; "Buildings Burned," *ES*, April 12, 1897; "Bad Blaze in Hillsdale," *WT*, April 12, 1897; "A Big Blaze in Hillsdale," *WP*, April 12, 1897.

4. "Douglass Hall," panel 30, exhibit script, AS-ACM, Box 1, Folder 6; Earl Shipley, Martha Ellis, Mary A. Cooke and Henry Sayles Jr., AOHP; "Hillsdale Notes," January 13, 1900.

5. "William E. Gales, druggist, Hillsdale," Washington, D.C., City Directory, 1896; William E. Gales, 1900 U.S. Census; "William E. Gales, druggist clerk, NW," Washington, D.C., City Directory, 1892, ancestry.com; "Anacostia and Vicinity," *ES*, May 3, 1902; "Anacostia," *ES*, October 5, 1910.

6. "Marriage of William E. Gales and Frances Dyson," D.C. Compiled Marriages Index, 1830–1921; William E. Gales, 1910 U.S. Census; "William E. Gales, druggist, 5238 G NE," Washington, D.C., City

Directory, 1913; "William E. Gales, death date July 5, 1913," District of Columbia, Select Deaths and Burials Index, 1769–1960, ancestry.com.

7. Louise Sayles Ball, NSOHP; photograph of Henry Sayles letterhead, 1910s, Hutchinson, *Anacostia Story*, 118; "Douglass Hall," panel 30, exhibit script, AS-ACM, Box 1, Folder 6; Andrew F. Hilyer, *The Twentieth Century Union League Directory: A Compilation of the Efforts of the Colored People of Washington* (Washington, D.C.: Union League of the District of Columbia, 1901), 101.

8. Anita E. Blake, AOHP; Howard University Medical Department, *A Historical, Biographical and Statistical Souvenir* (Washington, D.C.: Beresford, 1900), 215, 248–49; "Wedding Bells," *CA*, December 28, 1901; "Town Topics," *CA*, October 27, 1900; R. Henry Shipley, 1880 U.S. Census, Howard County, Maryland, ancestry.com; "Commencement Exercises: Medical, Dental, and Pharmaceutical Graduates, Howard University," *ES*, May 9, 1899; Rezin Shipley, 1910 U.S. Census, ancestry.com.

9. 1915 Washington, D.C., City Directory, 1822–1995, ancestry.com; "A Postoffice [*sic*] Contract Station Has Been Established at Nichols Avenue and Howard Road," *WT*, October 13, 1913; "Oneida Community Silverspoons [*sic*]," *WH*, March 7, 1915; "Here's Where You Can Buy Your War Savings and Thrift Stamps…," *WH*, February 11, 1918.

10. "Read All the News of Interest in Your Neighborhood in This Page," *WH*, October 16, 1922; "Colored Druggists Incorporate," *WH*, June 25, 1919; death of Rezin H. Shipley, December 22, 1924, District of Columbia, Select Deaths and Burials Index, 1769–1960, ancestry.com; Earl Shipley, AOHP.

11. Rezin Shipley, 1920 U.S. Census; Fannie J. Shipley, 1930 U.S. Census, ancestry.com; "Home Literary Circle Entertained," *ES*, January 28, 1904; Earl Shipley, AOHP.

12. Edith P. Green, John G. Warner, Raymond Bumbry, William Butler, Anita E. Blake, Irene Donnelly and Earl Shipley, AOHP.

13. Tertrault, "History of Black Commercial Enterprise."

14. "First Settlers"; Mack McKenzie, 1880, U.S. Census, ancestry.com; Tertrault, "History of Black Commercial Enterprise."

15. "Walter Singleton McKenzie, 1876–1970 and Family," AS-ACM, Box 11, Folder 6; Smithsonian American Art Museum, "Edward C. Messer," http://americanart.si.edu/collections; Edward C. Messer, 1900 U.S. Census, ancestry.com.

16. Raymond McKenzie, interview May 21, 1974, AS-ACM, Box 11, Folder 7.

17. Hutchinson, *Anacostia Story*, 121, 125; "Ourisman Chevrolet," *WT*, September 28, 2007; Mandell Chevrolet Company Inc. ad in Greater Southeast Washington, Eighth Annual Parade and Crab Apple Blossom Festival, Anacostia Park, April 18, 1953, UC-ACM, Box 36, Mack Taylor Folder; Thomas Taylor and Henry Sayles Jr., AOHP; Everett McKenzie, DP-ACM; Stanley Anderson, NSOHC.
18. Stanley Anderson and Erma Simon, NSOHC; James Chester Jennings Jr., DP-ACM.
19. Raymond McKenzie, interview May 21, 1974, AS-ACM, Box 11, Folder 7; R.L. Haycock, Superintendent of Schools, to Committee of Buildings, Grounds and Equipment, December 5, 1944; F.S. McLendon, "The History of Birney School," Charles Sumner School Museum and Archives.
20. Thelma Dale Perkins, DP-ACM.
21. Maurice Berger, circa 1930–40; Benjamin Bronstein (Blonstein), circa 1930–40; Max Catzva, circa 1910–20; Solomon Chotin, circa 1930–44; Irvin Furman, circa 1940; Solomon Iskow, circa 1953; Isadore and Israel Lublin, circa 1923–25; Louis and Nathan Miller, circa 1914–1950s; Nathan Miskin, 1916–59; Jacob Rubin, 1951–58; Edward Schrier, 1951–58; Jacob Steppa, circa 1930.
22. Louis Miller in 1914, 1915, 1916, 1922 and 1927 District of Columbia City Directory; Louis Miller in 1910, 1920, 1930 and 1940 U.S. Census, ancestry.com; Jonathan Penn, NSOHC; Everett McKenzie, DP-ACM; Louis Miller obituary, *WP*, September 3, 1961; Cantwell, "Anacostia Strength in Adversity," 359. In 1975, an interviewee remembered that Miller's Cash Market had changed into a DGS (District Grocery Store). It is not clear when that change happened. Marvin Moon, NSOHC. For information on DGS, see John Kelly, "At Peak, District Grocery Stores Collective Comprised 300 Mom-and-Pop Stores," *WP*, October 2, 2010, and "Half a Day on Sunday: Jewish-Owned Mom and Pop Grocery Stores," https://www.jhsgw.org/exhibitions/online/momandpop/database.
23. "Nathan Miskin, Grocery Owner," *ES*, December 11, 1973; "Southeast Family Returns to Build Hillcrest House," *ES*, June 5, 1964; Nathan Miskin in "Half a Day on Sunday."
24. Solomon Chotin, World War II draft registration card, 1942; Solomon Chotin, 1920, 1930 and 1940 U.S. Census, 1935 D.C., City Directory, ancestry.com.
25. Dale, *Village that Shaped Us*, 9, 242–44.

26. "First Settlers"; Spencer Coleman, 1880 U.S. Census, ancestry.com.

27. Isaac B. Ray, 1910, 1920 and 1930 U.S. Census, ancestry.com; Henrietta Myers and Robert Penn, 1940 U.S. Census, ancestry.com; Stanley Anderson and Jonathan Penn, NSOHC.

28. "1875–1939, Dedication Program—St. John C.M.E. Church," AS-ACM, Box 11, Folder 24; "Negro Businesses in Anacostia," *Birney School Life* 2 (November, 1950): 21–22, DP-ACM, Box 11, Folder 9.

29. Patsy Mose Fletcher, *Historically African American Leisure Destinations Around Washington, D.C.* (Charleston, SC: The History Press, 2015), 18; Pierre McKinley Taylor, AOHP.

30. John G. Warner, Raymond Bumbry, William Butler, Anita E. Blake and Irene Donnelly, AOHP; "Sixth Annual Picnic of the Congregational Sunday School of St. Luke's Church…," *CA*, June 16, 1900; "Sunday School Picnic of Berean Baptist Church," *CA*, May 23, 1903; "Noisy Demonstration Marked the Fourth of July in Anacostia…," *ES*, July 4, 1902; Fletcher, *Historically African American Leisure Destinations*, 21.

31. "Anacostia to Form Home Defense Unit," *WT*, March 29, 1917; "Meeting at Hillsdale. Association Installs New President and Transacts Business," *ES*, April 10, 1908; "Refuse Eureka Park Amusement License," *WH*, May 8, 1918; "License Is Refused for Eureka Park," *WT*, May 8, 1918; District of Columbia, Department of Playgrounds, *Annual Report*, 1926, 5, 6.

32. "Established 1890. Green Willow Park," *WP*, May 9, 1915; Fletcher, *Historically African American Leisure Destinations*, 22–24; "Shriners Give Picnic," *WP*, June 8, 1913; "Odd Fellows Outing," *WT*, July 2, 1912; "True Reformers Busy," *ES*, September 3, 1907; "Big Crowd at Barbecue," *ES*, July 26, 1907.

33. "Mothers Are Shown on How to Save Babies," *WH*, July 22, 1915; "Colored Fat Men Will Race at Church Benefit," *WT*, September 15, 1916.

34. Fletcher, *Historically African American Leisure Destinations*, 24; District of Columbia, Department of Playgrounds, *Annual Report*, 6.

35. "Florence Stokes Mathews. Statement by the Family, April 26, 1955," AS-ACM, Box 7, Folder 29; "In Tribute to Mrs. Florence S. Matthews," UC-ACM, Box 2; District of Columbia, Department of Playgrounds, *Annual Report*, 5; "Recreation Official Dies Here at 64," *WP*, April 24, 1955.

36. District of Columbia, Department of Playgrounds, *Annual Report*, 1929, 18, 6; "Pencil Sketches Win First Prize for Playground," *AA*, September 5, 1936.

37. Mildred Raby and Erma Simon, NSOHC.

38. Percy Battle, NSOHC.

39. "Roving Leaders…neutralize, and control hostile behavior in youth and youth groups through the development of positive relationships between teens/youth and outreach workers. Roving Leaders utilize recreation and leisure time activities as the intervening vehicles for redirecting antisocial and aggressive behaviors." D.C. Department of Parks and Recreation, "DPR Roving Leaders," https://dpr.dc.gov/service/dpr-roving-leaders; "Stanley Anderson Dies," *WP*, November 8, 1998.

40. Stanley Anderson, NSOHC.

41. George Trivers, AOHP; Paul J. Kocin et al., *Northeast Snowstorms* (Boston: American Meteorological Society, 2004), Table 2-3, 22; Almore Dale, AOHP; James Chester Jennings Jr., DP-ACM.

42. Carolyn Taylor Crocker, AOHP.

43. Robert Simon Jr., DP-ACM.

44. Oscar Tyler, NSOHC; *Oral History Project Interview with Ella B. Howard Pearis, Member Anacostia Historical Society. Interview 1* (City of Washington, D.C.: Archives and Special Collections of the Smithsonian Institution, 1986), 4.

45. Ethel K. Green and [Florence] McClendon, AOHP; Norman E. Dale, Stanley Anderson, NSOHC.

46. Ethel K. Green, AOHP; "Death of Union Veteran," *ES*, January 29, 1904.

47. Erma Simon, NSOHC.

Chapter 7

1. Althea Richardson Smith, DP-ACM.

2. Paul Dickson and Thomas B. Allen, *The Bonus Army: An American Epic* (New York: Walker and Company, 2005), 1–2, 96, 115.

3. Althea Richardson, 1930 U.S. Census, ancestry.com; Althea Richardson Smith, DP-ACM; Charles P. Greene interview, May 2, 2002, Bonus Army Research Collection, MS 0738, Container 7, HSWDC.

4. Dickson and Allen, *Bonus Army*, 118; James G. Banks interview, April 30, 2002, Bonus Army Research Collection, MS 0738, Container 7, HSWDC.

5. Roy Wilkins, "The Bonuseers [*sic*] Ban Jim Crow," *The Crisis* (October 1932): 316.

6. Dickson and Allen, *Bonus Army*, 120.

7. Ibid., 153–57, 164–80.

8. Joseph C. Harsch, *At the Hinge of History: A Reporter's Story* (Athens: University of Georgia Press, 1993), 13.

9. "Eyewitness Account of Bonus March Incident Including the Burning of the Camp at Anacostia, 1932," Papers of Mrs. Elbridge C. Purdy, RG 15, Materials Donated by the General Public, MacArthur Memorial Archives, Norfolk, Virginia.

10. "A Neglected Section," AS-ACM, Box 1.

11. "Suburban News. Anacostia," *ES*, April 23, 1895; "Hillsdale Wants Free Delivery," *WP*, May 3, 1895; "A Postoffice [*sic*] Contract Station Has Been Established."

12. "Typhoid Menaces Hillsdale Colony," *WH*, February 20, 1911; Raymond Bumbry, 1910 U.S. Census, ancestry.com; Raymond Bumbry, NSOHC.

13. Pierre McKinley Taylor, AOHP.

14. "Typhoid Menaces Hillsdale Colony."

15. *Sanborn Fire Insurance Maps, District of Columbia*, vol. 3 (New York: Sanborn Map Company, 1916), Plate 382; John Dale and Thomas Taylor, AOHP; paper on Anacostia history presented by Thomas Cantwell at the Columbia Historical Society, 1973, 21, AS-ACM, Box 2, Folder 15.

16. "Study of the Barry Farm Area. Prepared in Cooperation with National Capital Housing Authority, November 14, 1944," RG 328, Records of the National Capital Planning Commission General Records/Planning Files, 1924–67, Barry Farms Dec. Code 545-45-30, NARA; Ethel G. Greene, "My Community—'Barry Farms,'" AS-ACM.

17. "A Fatal Storm," *WP*, July 2, 1884. The 1880 Census has an entry for Elizabeth J. Blue, fifty-six years old, living with her son Benjamin F. Blue, a grocer, and a granddaughter named Laura G. Arnold at Sheridan Avenue. It is possible that this is the victim of the flooding, ancestry.com.

18. "Rainfall at End," *ES*, August 28, 1906; "Hillsdale Association," *ES*, September 12, 1906; "Saves Life by Leap," *WP*, September 24, 1907.

19. Vivian H. Tibbs, 1920 U.S. Census, ancestry.com; Maurice C. Hill, AOHP.

20. "2 Drowned in Flood after Rain Storm; Scores Are Rescued," *ES*, April 29, 1923; "Two Die in Flood after Cloudburst," *Pittsburgh Post-Gazette*, April 30, 1923; Edith P. Green, AOHP.

21. "Flood Shows Need of Construction," *ES*, April 30, 1923; "District May Get Million Increase in Budget Amount," *ES*, October 17, 1923.

22. Merriam-Webster, "Eminent Domain," https://www.merriam-webster.com/dictionary/eminent%20domain.

23. John R. Browning, "The History and Construction of the Alexandria Branch of the Baltimore and Ohio Railroad," paper presented for admission to the Tau Beta Pi Honorary Fraternity, University of Maryland, December 18, 1936, unpublished manuscript; *Baist's Real Estate Atlas of Surveys of Washington, District of Columbia, 1919–1921*, Plate 22; "Senate Street Act Held Inadequate," *WH*, May 14, 1921.

24. "Suit to Condemn Land," *WP*, November 28, 1903; "Report of Appraisers," *ES*, April 26, 1904; "Land Appraised for Sewer," *WP*, April 27, 1904.

25. "Anacostia," *WP*, February 21, 1889; "Free Fight in Hillsdale," *WP*, December 26, 1893; "Six Dealers Caught: A General Midnight Raid on Unlicensed Liquor Dealers," *WP*, November 19, 1894; "Midnight Stir in Hillsdale," *WP*, July 12, 1896; John Patterson, AOHP; "Woman Cut to Death: Brutal Christmas Eve Murder at Hillsdale," *ES*, December 25, 1902.

26. Melder and Stuart, *City of Magnificent Intentions*, 71; Mathew B. Gilmore and Michael R. Harrison, "A Catalog of Suburban Subdivisions of the District of Columbia, 1854–1902," *WH-HSWDC* 14 (Fall/Winter 2002–3): 40–41; Charles R. Burr, "A Brief History of Anacostia, Its Name, Origin and Progress," *RCHS* 23 (1920), 170; Henry Sayles, Carolyn Taylor Crocker and Almore Dale, AOHP; James Chester Jennings Jr., DP-ACM; Herbert Hunter, RTTC. It is interesting to note that White residents of Anacostia also seemed to keenly feel the isolation of their community from the rest of Washington, D.C. A White resident stated in the early 1970s that the residents of Anacostia were "distant cousins of the city," according to Carl Smuck, AOHP.

27. Thelma Dianne Dale interview, D.C. Public Libraries Special Collections, OHP 26, U Street Oral History Project, 2014; "Anacostia's Anathema: It Falls on Those Who Are Mixing Her Up with Hillsdale," *Sunday Herald*, May 11, 1890.

28. Carolyn Taylor Crocker, AOHP. In 1974, Ethel Graham Greene had a different recollection; in a letter to a local journalist, she stated, "Both Negroes and White persons were welcomed at the soda fountain of this establishment [Bury's Drug Store] many years before desegregation was the law." Letter from Ethel Graham Greene to Jacqueline Trescott, January 28, 1974, UC-ACM, Box 37, Ethel Graham Greene folder.

29. Norman E. Dale, NSOHC.

30. George Patterson, AOHP; George Patterson, 1920, U.S. Census, ancestry.com.
31. Almore Dale, AOHP.
32. John Dale, AOHP.
33. "Whites in Far SE Bitter, Estranged," *WP*, August 4, 1970.
34. James Chester Jennings Jr., DP-ACM.
35. "Remembering Anacostia as It Was," *WP*, July 10, 1986; "Anita F. Allen, Former President of D.C. School Board, Dies at 87," *WP*, February 12, 2013.

Chapter 8

1. The information in the previous paragraphs comes from analyzing the 1940 U.S. Federal Census for Barry Farm–Hillsdale in ancestry.com.
2. Erma Simon, NSOHC.
3. World War II draft registration cards for Ulysses Jesse Banks and Nathan Joseph Bronstein, World War II Draft Registration Cards, Fold3.
4. Roland W. Dale [Sr.], U.S. Federal Census 1920, 1930 and 1940, ancestry. com.
5. Roland Winfoot Dale, World War II draft registration card, Fold3; Roland W. Dale Jr., U.S. World War II army enlistment record, familysearch.org; Roland Winfoot Dale Jr. death certificate, Virginia Death Records, 1912–2014; Roland W. Dale Jr., interment control form, Arlington Cemetery, U.S. National Cemetery Interment Control Forms, 1928–62, ancestry. com.
6. Milton Wright, U.S. Federal Census 1920 and 1940, ancestry.com; U.S. World War II Army Enlistment Records, 1938–46, familysearch.org; U.S. National Cemetery Interment Control Forms, 1928–62, ancestry.com.
7. George D. Graham, Civil War Soldiers: Union Colored Troops; Civil War Pension Index, Fold3.
8. "Flyer Given Oak Leaf After Death," *Journal & Guide*, December 11, 1943; "Charles Irvin Cassell (1924–)," in *African American Architects: A Biographical Dictionary, 1865–1945*, ed. Dreck Spurlock Wilson (New York: Routledge, 2004), 95–96.
9. "Their Son Killed in Sicily: AFRO Brought First News of Pilot's Death in Sicily," *AA*, September 18, 1943; Harry Mitchell, U.S. Federal Census, 1940, ancestry.com.

NOTES TO PAGES 93–97

10. Daniel L. Haulman, "Tuskegee Airmen Chronology," Organizational History Branch, Air Force Historical Research Agency, Maxwell AFB, Montgomery, Alabama, 36112-6424, November 25, 2015, https://media.defense.gov/2010/Dec/22/2001330157/-1/-1/0/AFD-101222-041.pdf.

11. "Things Popping in N. Africa, Says Flyer. Boys in 99th Write D.C. Parents They Are 'in the Midst of It,'" *AA*, July 10, 1943.

12. Haulman, "Tuskegee Airmen"; "Flyer Given Oak Leaf."

13. "Their Son Killed in Sicily"; "9 Members of the 99th Squadron Promoted," *AA*, September 4, 1943; "The Air Medal," *Journal & Guide*, January 8, 1944; "Mitchell Village at Tuskegee Honors Fallen Airman of 99th," *Journal & Guide*, February 19, 1944.

14. "Washington Air-Raid Wardens, Defense Committeemen Listed," *WP*, December 10, 1941; Certificate Citizens Defense Corps Metropolitan Area District of Columbia, Food and Housing Warden Louise C. Dale, DP-ACM, Box 2, Folder 7; "Barry Farms," *WP*, October 13, 1942.

15. "Public Housing in the United States, 1933–1949," National Register of Historic Places, 2004, https://www.nps.gov/nr/publications/guidance/Public%20Housing%20in%20the%20United%20States%20MPS.pdf, E53 and Appendix 4:3.

16. "The Local Housing Situation for National Capital Housing Authority Meeting August 3, 1943," John Ihlder Papers, Box 17, Franklin D. Roosevelt Library, Hyde Park, New York; "Public Housing in the United States, 1933–1949," Appendix 4:3.

17. National Capital Housing Authority, *Report of the National Capital Housing Authority for the Ten-Year Period, 1934–1944* (Washington, D.C., 1944), 55 (hereafter *Report of the National Capital Housing Authority*); "Southeastern Group Opposes NCHA Housing on New Sites," *WP*, November 5, 1943; Kenesaw M. Landis and National Committee on Segregation in the Nation's Capital, *Segregation in Washington: A Report of the National Committee on Segregation in the Nation's Capital, November, 1948* (Chicago: The Committee, 1948), 41.

18. *Baist's Real Estate Atlas and Surveys of Washington, District of Columbia: Complete in Four Volumes* (Philadelphia: G. Wm. Baist's Sons, 1931 [1936].

19. George Trivers, AOHP; Erma Simon, NSOHC; Kenton D. Hamaker, "Concrete Masonry War Homes Near Washington, D.C. Designed for Economy, Dignity and Color Interest," *Concrete Builder* 17 (Autumn–Winter 1943).

20. Kenneth Chapman, DP-ACM; birth certificate for [Cora West] Green, daughter of John Alfred Green and Mary Dunmore Green, ancestry.com; "First Settlers"; Ethel G. Greene, AOHP.

21. Richard Wilkinson, U.S. Federal Census, 1900, marriage of Richard W [Ulysses] Wilkinson, 24, and Cora W [West] Green, 22, June 26, 1901, Richard Wilkinson, U.S. Federal Census, 1910, ancestry.com; "Interest in Kindergarten Work," *ES*, October 5, 1906; Carolyn Taylor Crocker, AOHP; Ethel Graham Greene, "Things I Remember About Anacostia," AS-ACM, Box 12, Folder 12; Cora W. Wilkinson, U.S. Federal Census, 1940, ancestry.com.

22. *Report of the National Capital Housing Authority*, 56–57.

23. Ibid., 58.

24. Ibid., 58, 119; "Investigation of the Program of the National Capital Housing Authority," Hearings before the Subcommittee of the Committee on the District of Columbia, United States, 78th Congress, 2nd Session, Part 1, 1,072; James G. Banks and Peter S. Banks, *The Unintended Consequences: Family and Community, the Victims of Isolated Poverty* (Dallas, TX: University Press of America Inc., 2004), 33.

25. James C. Jennings, U.S. Federal Census, 1940, ancestry.com; Luberta Jennings, NSOHC; James Chester Jennings Jr., DP-ACM.

26. Banks and Banks, *Unintended Consequences*, xi, 33.

27. Lugene Lee Russell, NSOHC.

28. Louise Daniel Hutchinson, "Barry's Farm, a Changing Community," August 1976, UC-ACM, Box 121.

29. "Land Purchase Section, Thursday & Friday, July 29–30, 1937," 25–26, vol. 12, Transcripts of the Proceedings and Minutes of Meetings, 1926–76, RG 328, Records of the National Capital Planning Commission, General Records, U.S. Department of the Interior (hereafter RG 328, Records of the NCPPC); National Park Service, National Register of Historic Places, Registration Form "Suitland Parkway," continuation sheet, page 1, https://mht.maryland.gov/secure/medusa/PDF/NR_PDFs/NR-1175.pdf; Jeffers to Nolen, February 27, 1942, RG 328, Records of the NCPPC, General Records Planning Files, 1924–67, File 545-100, Suitland Parkway, Folder 1 (hereafter RG 328, Records of NCPPC, File 545-100).

30. Extract from Minutes of the 175th meeting of the NCPPC held on August 13–14, 1942 (hereafter Extract Minutes NCPPC); Secretary of War to Harold D. Smith, Director of the Budget; Roosevelt to Secretary of War, August 25, 1942, RG 328, Records of NCPPC, File 545-100, Folder 1.

31. Demaray to Grant, July 21, 1943, RG 328, Records of NCPPC, File 545-100, Folder 1.

32. "Status of Dwellings within Taking Lines of Camp Springs Freeway DC," April 14, 1943, and "600 Face Eviction September 10," *WP*, September 4, 1943; "600 More Made Homeless in D.C. for Road Project," *AA*, September 18, 1943. There is conflicting information about the number of houses destroyed for the building of the road. In testimony to the Senate in 1944, Franklin Thorne, an African American man who was housing manager for the NCHA, declared that 112 houses were destroyed. "Investigation of the Program of the National Capital Housing Authority," 1,074.

33. "It's Headline News: The Passing of Old Anacostia," *Pulse* (October 1943): 24.

34. Henrietta Myers and Robert Penn, 1940 U.S. Federal Census, ancestry. com; Stanley Anderson and Jonathan Penn, NSOHC; "Legal Notices," *Washington Law Reporter* 71, 859–60; "These Homes Must Make Way for Military Highway; Families in Quandary," *AA*, September 18, 1943.

35. Kenneth Chapman, DP-ACM; Arthur Chapman, Piscataway, Maryland; Maude A. Morse, Washington, D.C., U.S. Federal Census, 1880; Arthur N. Chapman, U.S. Federal Census, 1900; marriage record of Arthur N. Chapman and Maud[e] E. Morse, District of Columbia, June 6, 1895, ancestry.com.

36. Kenneth Chapman, DP-ACM. The census for 1940 listed the families of Mathew Chapman and Evelyn [Chapman] Saunders at 1024 Sumner Road, Ruth [Chapman] Brooks and family at 1022 Sumner Road and George M. Chapman and family at 1026 Sumner Road. They were the children of patriarch Nathan Chapman. U.S. Federal Census, 1940, ancestry.com. By 1948, George Chapman was living in another area of Southeast, and Mathew Chapman had moved to Northwest. We found no information for the other two families. 1948 City Directory for Washington, D.C., ancestry.com.

37. Marriage certificate of Wilbur Leslie Gray and Doris Churchill Elmore, District of Columbia, November 5, 1936, D.C., Marriage Records, 1810–1953, ancestry.com; "Mortgage Firm's Real Estate Tax Unpaid 5 Years," *WP*, January 14, 1977; Brown to Nolen, April 22, 1942, RG 328, Records of NCPPC, File 545-100, Folder 1.

38. *Baist's*, 1931; Project Ownership Maps for Suitland Parkway Reservation, RG 79, Records of the National Park Service, Folder "Numbered Drawings," NARA, College Park, Maryland; Arthur R. Bradley, Sadie Reed and Adelena Stanley, U.S. Federal Census, 1910, ancestry.com.

39. Deed between Adelena M. Howard and Sadie B. Reed and Doris Churchill Gray, selling lot 949 in square 5868, old lot 8, section 7, Barry Farm, for $150 on April 20, 1943, Office of the Recorder of Deeds, Washington, D.C.; Brown to Nolen, April 22, 1942, RG 328, Records of NCPPC, File 545-100, Folder 1.
40. Memo, April 30, 1943, RG 328, Records of NCPPC, File 545-100, Folder 1.
41. Paul E. Sluby Sr., "Macedonia Cemetery Barry Farm Washington, D.C.: A Disinterred Black Burial Ground Formerly Located in the Southeast Section of the City," April 26, 2013, unpublished manuscript, History of Place research files; "Thirty Minutes to Chesapeake Bay: Super-Speed Road to Open Maryland," *WTH*, December 11, 1944.
42. Letter from Mrs. Lucille Dale to Sergeant N[orman] E. Dale, October 25, 1945, DP-ACM, Box 2, Folder 17; funeral program for Norman E. Dale, July 3, 1991, Campbell AME Church, DP-ACM, Box 4, Folder 9.

Chapter 9

1. "Barry Farms Subdivision," Extract from Minutes of the 162nd meeting of the National Capital Park and Planning Commission, held on June 26–27, 1941; Ihlder to Nolan, October 23, 1941, RG 328, Records of the NCPPC, General Records Planning Files, 1924–67, File 545-45-30, NARA.
2. "Suggests Moving Capital Negros 'Across River,'" *Atlanta Daily World*, April 4, 1942.
3. U.S. Congress, House Committee on the District of Columbia, *Elimination of Alley Dwellings, Hearings before the Subcommittee on the District of Columbia… on H.R. 4819, 4847, 4850…May 23–September 1, 1944* (Washington, D.C.: Government Printing Office, 1944), 356.
4. U.S. Congress, Senate Committee on the District of Columbia, *Investigation of the Program of the National Capital Housing Authority, Hearings before a Subcommittee of the Committee on the District of Columbia, United States Senate, 78th Congress, Second Session, on S. Res. 184, a Resolution Authorizing an Investigation of the Program of the National Capital Housing Authority…* (Washington, D.C.: Government Printing Office, 1944), 1,236.
5. U.S. Congress, *Investigation of the Program of the National Capital Housing Authority*, 1,238; obituary of James C. Mason, *WP*, February 20, 1987.
6. "Study of the Barry Farm Area. Prepared in Cooperation with National Capital Housing Authority, November 14, 1944," RG 328, Records of

NCPPC, Transcripts of Proceedings and Minutes of Meetings, 1924–99, Thursday, November 18, 1944, Box 48 (hereafter "Study of the Barry Farm Area," RG 328, Box 48).

7. Ibid.

8. Library of Congress, "District of Columbia Redevelopment Act of 1945," https://www.loc.gov/law/help/statutes-at-large/79th-congress/session-2/c79s2ch736.pdf.

9. "3 Slum Areas Selected for Elimination," *WP*, December 5, 1946; "Suggests Moving Capital Negros 'Across River'"; "D.C. Funds to Clear Slum Areas," *WP*, January 31, 1948; Constance McLaughlin Green, *The Secret City: A History of Race Relations in the Nation's Capital* (Princeton, NJ: Princeton University Press, 1967), 279.

10. "Marshall Heights Settlers Recall the Birth of Their Neighborhood," *WP*, December 15, 1977; "Marshall Heights Braves Realities of Urban Living," *WP*, February 18, 1995.

11. Resolution from the Barry Farm Civic Association, January 14, 1947, RG 328, Records of NCPPC, File 545-45-30.

12. Howard to Grant, December 7, 1946, RG 328, Records of NCPPC, File 545-45-30.

13. "Urban Redevelopment Proposals Affecting Barry Farms [*sic*] and Marshall Heights Areas," RG 328, Records of NCPPC, File 545-45-30. There was definitely a division between the Hillsdale and Barry Farm sections of the community. Mrs. Pearis, in an interview in 1974, stated this in response to a question of whether she considered the other side of Nichols Avenue as part of Barry Farm: "That was Hillsdale. They formed a different association. There was a division, then, between Hillsdale & Barry Farms [*sic*]. When it started I couldn't tell you." Ella Pearis, AOHP. Around the same time, Mr. Raymond Bumbry, responding to a question about civic organizations, stated, "The civic organization isn't doing anything over there. There were two over here, Barry Farms [*sic*] and Hillsdale and they never would merge and it looks like to me now that both of them died." Raymond Bumbry, AOHP.

14. "Howard Dilworth Woodson (1876–1962)," in *African American Architects*, 459–61; U.S. Senate, 80th Congress, 2nd Session, *Hearings Before the Subcommittee of the Committee of Appropriations on H.R. 5214, a Bill Making Appropriations for the Executive Office and Sundry Independent and Executive Bureaus, Boards, Commissions, and Offices for the Fiscal Year Ending June 30, 1949, and Other Purposes* (Washington, D.C.: Government Printing Office, 1948), 343.

15. U.S. Senate, *Hearings before the Subcommittee of the Committee of Appropriations on H.R. 5214*, 344–46.

16. "DC Funds to Clear Slum Areas: House Committee Rejects Request after Objections by Negro Groups," *WP*, January 31, 1948; "Redevelopment of Barry Farms [*sic*]: Summary of Housing Appraisal Survey by Bureau of Public Health Engineering, D.C. Department of Health," Blackwell to Nolen, March 17, 1948, RG 328, Records of NCPPC, Office Files of John Nolen Jr., 1926–58, Box 19, Barry Farms [*sic*], Housing Appraisal Survey, 1948.

17. "Residents Fear Loss of Homes," *PC*, March 6, 1948; Howard, *Autobiography*, 420.

18. U.S. House of Representatives, 81ˢᵗ Congress, 1ˢᵗ Session, Independent Offices Appropriation Bill for 1950, *Hearings before the Subcommittee on Appropriations* (Washington, D.C.: Government Printing Office, 1949), 1,472.

19. Ibid., 1,058.

20. U.S. Congress, House Committee on Appropriations, Third Deficiency appropriations bill for 1949, *Hearings before a Subcommittee of the Committee on Appropriations, House of Representatives, 81ˢᵗ Congress, First Session, on the Third Deficiency Appropriation Bill for 1949* (Washington, D.C.: Government Printing Office, 1949), 532.

21. National Capital Park and Planning Commission, *Housing and Redevelopment: A Portion of the Comprehensive Plan for the National Capital and Its Environs* (Washington, D.C.: Government Printing Office, 1950), 33.

22. "D.C. Heads Asked to Spur Barry Farm Redevelopment," *WP*, October 7, 1953; "Barry Farms Slum Study Is Proposed," *WTH*, October 7, 1953; "Barry Farms Referred to New Committee for Slum Study," *ES*, October 7, 1953; "Slum Areas Listed by 5 Civic Groups," *WP*, October 21, 1953.

23. "Way Opened to Develop 2 D.C. Sites," *WP*, May 25, 1954; "Barry Farms Residents Like Their Homes as They Are," *WDN*, June 11, 1954; "2 Redevelopment Plans Axed by Hill Conferees," *WP*, July 10, 1954.

24. James W. Rouse and Nathaniel S. Keith, *No Slums in Ten Years: A Workable Program for Urban Renewal: Report to the Commissioners of the District of Columbia* (Washington, D.C.: Government Printing Office, 1955), 47–48.

25. Ella Pearis, AOHP.

Chapter 10

1. Dale, *Village that Shaped Us*, 231; "The Oral History Interview of Dianne Dale by Sandi Wetzel," April 20, 2002, DP-ACM, Box 1, Folder 16; Groceteria, "Washington DC Chain Grocery/Supermarket Locations, 1925–1975," https://www.groceteria.com/place/washington-dc/chain-supermarkets-in-washington-dc-1925-1975.

2. Ben Bradlee, *A Good Life: Newspapering and Other Adventures* (New York: Simon and Schuster, 1995), 124–26.

3. *Park Improvement Papers: A Series of Seventeen Papers Related to the Improvement of the Park System of the District of Columbia; Printed for the Use of the Senate Committee on the District of Columbia* (Washington, D.C.: Government Printing Office, 1901–2), 16.

4. Anacostia Waterfront Trust, "Anacostia in History."

5. Robert Simon Jr. and Kenneth Chapman, DP-ACM; Stanley Anderson, NSOHC.

6. Everett McKenzie, DP-ACM; Everett McKenzie, U.S. Federal Census 1940, ancestry.com; E.B. Henderson, "Negro Swimmers," *WP*, July 5, 1949.

7. Victoria W. Wolcott, *Race, Riots, and Roller Coasters: The Struggle over Segregated Recreation in America* (Philadelphia: University of Pennsylvania Press, 2012), 81; "Anacostia Pool Closed 3 Hours as Guards Quit Over Non-Segregation," *ES*, June 26, 1949; "Six Negroes Booed Out of Anacostia Pool," *WP*, June 27, 1949.

8. Bradlee, *Good Life*, 125–26.

9. "Anacostia Swimming Pool Ordered Closed Indefinitely," *WP*, June 30, 1949; "Close Pool After Riot," *AA*, July 9, 1949; electronic message from Donna Hunter, director of Registration and Records, West Virginia State University, December 19, 2017; Everett McKenzie and James Chester Jennings Jr., DP-ACM.

10. Everett McKenzie, DP-ACM; "Pool Row Puts off Trial for Assault," *AA*, July 1, 1949.

11. "Krug, Commissioners to Meet Tomorrow on 'Recreation Problems,'" *ES*, June 30, 1949.

12. "Anacostia Swimming Pool Ordered Closed Indefinitely"; "Close Pool after Riot"; "Groups Seek to Open Pool to All Races," *AA*, July 26, 1949.

13. "SE Residents Ask Swimming Pool Opening," *AA*, July 30, 1949; "Krug, Commissioners to Meet Tomorrow on 'Recreation Problems.'"

14. "25 Mothers Ask Krug to Reopen Pool to All Races," *WP*, August 16, 1949; "Adventures in Race Relations," *Chicago Defender*, August 20, 1949.

15. "Capital Pools Open to All," *AA*, March 18, 1950; "No Incidents as Pools Open," *AA*, June 17, 1950; "Interracial Swimming Pools' Results Held Success, Failure," *AA*, October 21, 1950; "Attendance at Six Pools Off One Third," *WP*, September 6, 1950.
16. "Report Urges Improved D.C. Playgrounds: Anacostia Center Bid Dropped," *WTH*, December 10, 1952.
17. Donald D. Brewer, "Integration: A Challenge to Community Agencies and Institutions," in *Civil Rights in the Nation's Capital: A Report on a Decade of Progress*, ed. Ben D. Segal, William Korey and Charles N. Mason Jr. (New York: National Association of Intergroup Relations Officials, 1959), 10–11.

Chapter 11

1. For the history of the Dale family of Barry Farm–Hillsdale, see Dale, *Village that Shaped Us*; "3000 Persons Attend Barry Farms Festival," *WP*, June 7, 1956; John Dale, AOHP.
2. "Greater Southeast Washington, Eight Annual Parade and Crab Apple Blossom Festival. Anacostia Park, April 18, 1953," UC-ACM, Box 36, Mack Taylor Folder. A list of participants with their respective schools appears in the first page of the leaflet. "S.E. Plans Crab Apple Celebration," *WP*, April 18, 1952; "4000 View Crab Apple Parade in Anacostia," *WP*, April 25, 1954.
3. *Brown v. Board of Education*, 347 U.S. 483, 74 S. Ct. 686 (1954); *Bolling v. Sharpe*, 347 U.S. 497, 74 S. Ct. 693 (1954).
4. District of Columbia Board of Education, *Compilation of Laws Affecting Schools of the District of Columbia, 1804–1929* (Washington, D.C.: Government Printing Office, 1929), 147–48, 150.
5. Ibid., 149.
6. "Minutes of the Seventeenth (Stated) Meeting of the Board of Education, May 21, 1947," Minutes of the Board of Education of the District of Columbia, April 16, 1947, to July 1, 1947, 9, Sumner Museum; Richard Kluger, *Simple Justice: The History of Brown v. Board of Education and Black America's Struggle for Equality* (New York: Knopf, 1976), 511.
7. Mary A. Morton, "The Education of Negroes in the District of Columbia," *JNE* 16 (Summer 1947): 325–31.
8. Ibid., 332.
9. George S. Strayer, *The Report of a Survey of the Public Schools of the District of Columbia* (Washington, D.C.: Government Printing Office, 1949), 337.

10. Carl F. Hansen, *Danger in Washington: The Story of My Twenty Years in the Public Schools in the Nation's Capital* (West Nyack, NY: Parker Publishing Company Inc., 1968), vii.

11. "Minutes of the Seventeenth (Stated) Meeting of the Board of Education, May 21, 1947," 21.

12. "Colored Pupil Barred from White School," *ES*, February 3, 1944; Morton, "Education of Negroes," 334; "Capital Confetti," *PC*, June 21, 1947.

13. Martha Strayer, *Reliable Sources: The National Press Club in the American Century* (Paducah, KY: Turner Publishing Company, 1997), 177; Strayer to Eleanor Roosevelt [January 22, 1944], Folder "Strayer, Martha 1944," Series: Personal Letters, Eleanor Roosevelt Papers, Franklin D. Roosevelt Library, Hyde Park, New York.

14. Morton, "Education of Negroes," 335; "School Board, in Answer to Suit, Denies Responsibility," *AA*, July 24, 1944; "Capital Confetti"; Chris Myers and George Derek Musgrove, *Chocolate City: A History of Race and Democracy in the Nation's Capital* (Chapel Hill: University of North Carolina Press, 2017), 306. The Mary McLeod Bethune Public Charter School occupies the space today.

15. "Court Backs White School Ban on Negro," *WP*, May 17, 1944.

16. Mary Gibson Hundley, *The Dunbar Story (1870–1955)* (New York: Vantage Press, 1965), 39, 42, 44.

17. Francis Wilkinson, free colored, Charleston Neck, Charleston, South Carolina, U.S. Census, 1840, owner of one female slave; J.F. Wilkinson, mulatto, butcher, St. Michael and St. Phillip Parish, Charleston, U.S. Census, 1850; Francis L. Wilkinson [*sic*], mulatto, butcher, $6,000 in assets, Ward 6, Charleston, U.S. Census, 1860, ancestry.com. The discrepancies in the names were common at the time. For more information about the "brown" elite of Charleston before the Civil War, see Michael P. Johnson and James L. Roark, eds., *No Chariot Let Down: Charleston's Free People of Color on the Eve of the Civil War* (Chapel Hill: University of North Carolina Press, 1984).

18. Garnet Crummell Wilkinson, U.S. World War I draft registration card; King-Farley-Holmes Family Tree, ancestry.com; James W. Wilkinson, U.S. Freedman's Bank Records, 1865–71; entries for A.M. Wilkinson and Paul H. Wilkinson, St. Paul's Parish, Colleton County, South Carolina, $7,000 in assets, owned eighty-five enslaved persons, U.S. Census, 1850, and Slave Schedule for St. Paul's Parish, Colleton County, South Carolina, ancestry.com.

NOTES TO PAGES 128–131

19. James W. Wilkinson, Washington, D.C., City Directory, 1889–1916; King-Farley-Holmes Family Tree, ancestry.com; "Deaths Reported: James W. Wilkinson, 74 Years, 1439 Morris Road, Southeast," *ES*, September 26, 1916.

20. "Alumni News," *Oberlin Alumni Magazine* 9 (May 1913): 264.

21. "Along the Color Line," *The Crisis* 5 (December 1912): 61; "Alumni News," *Oberlin Alumni Magazine* 13 (April 1917): 206. For a brief history of the famous M Street High School and the opening of Dunbar High School in 1916, see J.C. Wright, "The New Dunbar High School, Washington, D.C.," *The Crisis* 13 (March 1917): 220–22.

22. "School Board Fixes Tuition of Non Resident Children...," *ES*, September 16, 1921; "Anacostia News," *Washington Bee* (September 24, 1921); "The Horizon," *The Crisis* 23 (February 1922): 151; Tikia K. Hamilton, "The Cost of Integration: The Contentious Career of Garnet Wilkinson," *WH-HSWDC* 30 (Spring 2018): 54–55.

23. Hamilton, "Cost of Integration," 52.

24. W.E. Burghardt Du Bois, "Does the Negro Need Separate Schools," *JNE* 4 (July 1935), 328, 330.

25. "Schools to Open with Shortage of 30 Teachers," *ES*, September 16, 1946.

26. Ibid.

27. "Meyer, Agnes Elizabeth Ernst, Jan. 2, 1887–Sept. 1, 1970," in *Notable American Women: The Modern Period: A Biographical Dictionary*, ed. Barbara Sicherman and Carol Hurd Green (Cambridge, MA: Belknap Press of Harvard University Press), 471–73; "'Modern' Browne Junior High Far Behind White Schools," *WP*, March 9, 1947; "Our Dual School System: One Question Now Is Whether District Meets Judicial Requirement of Equal If Segregated Facilities," *ES*, October 14, 1947.

28. Maya Annette McQuirter, "'Our Cause Is Marching On': Activism, Browne Junior High School, and the Multiple Meanings of Equality in Post-War Washington," *WH-HSWDC* 16 (Fall/Winter, 2004–5): 72; "School Strike Ultimatum Laid Down by Parents," *WP*, December 15, 1947; "Transfer of 5 White Schools for Negroes' Use Protested," *WP*, November 13, 1947.

29. Strayer, *Report of a Survey*, 345.

30. In fact, Ms. Carr's name is spelled Margurite, but because the name is spelled as Marguerite in all the legal documentation, that is how we will spell it in this text. See Rachel Devlin, *A Girl Stands at the Door: The Generation of Young Women Who Desegregated America's Schools* (New York: Basic Books,

2018), 285, n.1; Amy Crawford, "The Defiant Ones," *Smithsonian Magazine* (June 2018), https://www.smithsonianmag.com/history/defiant-ones-school-desegregation-180969011.

31. *Carr v. Corning*, 192 F.2d 14 (D.C. Circ. 1950).

32. "Interview of Richard Kluger with Mr. Gardner L. Bishop, August 22, 1974, Washington, D.C.," Brown v. Board of Education Collection, MS 759, Series I, Box 1, Folder 5, "Bishop, Gardner," Yale University Library, Manuscripts and Archives, Yale University, New Haven, Connecticut (hereafter Kluger/Bishop interview); Kluger, *Simple Justice*, 513.

33. Kluger/Bishop interview; Kluger, *Simple Justice*, 515. The possibility of retaliation was real. According to Marguerite Carr, her father was fired from his job at the Pentagon as the head of a maintenance crew that ran the boilers because of his participation in the suit against the board of education. Devlin, *Girl Stands at the Door*, 78.

34. "Five Students Attend Classes as Parents Strike Second Day," *WP*, December 5, 1947.

35. Kluger/Bishop interview; "School Board Head to Attend Strikers' Meeting," *WDN*, December 16, 1947; "Parents Will End Strike on Own Terms," *WDN*, December 12, 1947.

36. "Pupils Return to Browne as Strike Ends," *WP*, February 3, 1948.

37. "Constitution of the Consolidated Parent Group," Series A, Box 19-1, Consolidated Parent Group Inc. Papers, Moorland-Spingarn Research Center, Howard University (hereafter Consolidated Parent Group Inc. Papers); Genna Rae McNeil, "Community Initiative in the Desegregation of District of Columbia Schools, 1947–1954: A Brief Historical Overview of Consolidated Parent Group Inc. Activities from *Bishop to Bolling*," *Howard Law Journal* 23 (1980): 31.

38. "Anacostia Schools Past and Present," August 16, 1974, UC-ACM, Box 121, Folder Anacostia Schools; "Historic Site Study. Nichols Avenue Elementary School," Sumner Museum.

39. "D.C. Parent Was Sure of Decision," *AA*, May 18, 1954; Luberta Jennings, NSOHC; Kenneth Chapman, DP-ACM.

40. "The Year Was 1950," *WP*, May 16, 1979; Strayer, *Report of a Survey*, 346; "13 Million Junior High Replaces 'Shameful' Shaw," *WP*, September 5, 1977.

41. "Staff of Over-Crowded Kramer Awaits Transfer of 400 Students to New Sousa," *WP*, February 27, 1950; "Sousa Junior High. District's Latest, Ready to Open…," *WP*, March 6, 1950; "Classes Open at Sousa as Workmen Finish Their Jobs…," *WP*, March 7, 1950; Peter Irons, *Jim*

Crow's Children: The Broken Promise of the Brown Decision (New York: Penguin Books, 2002), 101–3.

42. The text of the letter erroneously states "September, 1951," but it is clear from the context that it meant September 1950. Althea V. Howard to Board of Education, July 20, 1950, AS-ACM, Box 12, Folder 33.

43. Luberta Jennings stated that the group met at Campbell AME "once a week or once a month or something like that." Luberta Jennings, NSOHC; a photograph in the *Afro-American* of September 16, 1950, shows Gardner Bishop with a group of Barry Farm–Hillsdale residents meeting at Campbell AME. "People Can Never Lose When They're United," *AA*, September 16, 1950.

44. "Group Assails Junior High Segregation," *WP*, June 24, 1950.

45. Bishop to Watkins, August 30, 1950; Sharpe to Bishop, August 31, 1950; telegram from Bishop to Sharpe, September 2, 1950; Minutes of the Board of Education Meetings, Sumner Museum.

46. Bishop to Board of Education, September 6, 1950; "Anacostia Parents Continue to Oppose 'Makeshift' Junior Hi at Old Birney," *PC*, undated clipping; letters from pastors from St. John's CME, Mathew Memorial Baptist, Campbell AME, St. Philips Episcopal Church, Allen-Garfield AME and Emmanuel Baptist; petition signed by 396 persons, most of them residents of Barry Farm Dwellings, Minutes of the Board of Education, Sumner Museum.

47. Minutes of the Board of Education, October 4, 1950, 119, Sumner Museum; petition presented to the board of education on September 6, 1950, Consolidated Parent Group Inc. Papers; "PTA Threatens Law Suit over Crowded N.E. School," *WP*, October 5, 1950. The headline of the article was incorrect; the story was about what was happening in Southeast.

48. We have identified the names of nine children who were connected with the movement for the desegregation of schools in Washington, D.C., and whose names appeared in the two cases filed after their attempt to attend Sousa Junior High School was denied. They must have been part of the attempt to integrate Sousa Junior High School on September 11, 1950: Spotswood Thomas and Wanamaker Von Bolling; Sarah Louise Briscoe; Adrienne and Barbara Jennings; Valerie Cogdell; Wallace Morris; Felecia Brown; and Lauretia Parker. Copy of *Bolling v. Sharpe* filing in the U.S. District Court for the District of Columbia, Series M, Box 19-2, Consolidated Parent Group Inc. Papers; "Parents Open Big Guns on DC School Jimcrow," *New York Amsterdam News*, October 6, 1951.

49. Frances Mason Jones, AOHP; "The Fading Line," *TIME*, 62 (December 21, 1953): 17; McNeil, "Community Initiative," 36; "Parents Will Sue Over Anacostia School Bias," unidentified newspaper clipping in Consolidated Parent Group Inc. Papers; Kluger, *Simple Justice*, 521.

50. "Parent Drop Pupil 'Strike,' Plan to Sue," *WDN*, September 11, 1950.

51. "James Nabrit Jr. Dies at 97; Led Howard University," *NYT*, December 30, 1997; "George Hayes, 74, a Rights Lawyer Argued School Segregation Case Before High Court," *NYT*, December 21, 1968.

52. James M. Nabrit Jr., "Resort to the Courts as a Means of Eliminating 'Legalized' Segregation," *JNE* 20 (Summer 1951), 467–68.

53. Frances Mason Jones, AOHP; Kluger/Bishop interview; "Civil Rights 'Money Tree,'" *WAA*, January 27, 1950; "Parents Outline Funds Campaign," *PC*, April 14, 1951; McNeil, "Community Initiative," 34, 40–41.

54. McNeil, "Community Initiative," 37–38; copy of *Bolling v. Sharpe* filing in the U.S. District Court for the District of Columbia, Series M, Box 19-2, Consolidated Parent Group Inc. Papers.

55. Devlin, *Girl Stands at the Door*, xii; Carl and Lillian Cogdell, 1259 Stevens Road SE, 1954 Directory for Washington, D.C., U.S. City Directories, 1822–1995, ancestry.com. Mrs. Cogdell and Mrs. Morris were among the residents of Barry Farm Dwellings who signed the petition to the board of education in September 1950. Gardner Bishop to Board of Education, September 6, 1950; petition signed by 396 persons, most of them residents of Barry Farm Dwellings; Minutes of the Board of Education Meeting, September 6, 1950, 170–73, Sumner Museum; Emerson Brown, 1940 Census for District of Columbia, ancestry.com; program for a reception honoring the counsels for the Supreme Court cases on March 15, 1953— the program lists the names of the parents of the plaintiffs of the two cases, Consolidated Parent Group Inc. Papers.

56. Copy of *Bolling v. Sharpe* filing in the U.S. District Court for the District of Columbia, Series M, Box 19-2, Consolidated Parent Group Inc. Papers.

57. Richard A. Primus, "Bolling Alone," *Columbia Law Review* 104 (May 2004): 976.

58. Kluger, *Simple Justice*, 522–23.

59. Ibid., 539; McNeil, "Community Initiative," 37–38; "Herbert O. Reid Sr., 75, Lawyer Who Taught Many Black Leaders," *NYT*, June 16, 1991; "Dorsey E. Lane Dies," *WP*, July 24, 1996; "James A. Washington, Jr., 83, Judge and Dean of Law School," *NYT*, September 2, 1998; "George Johnson, 87, Dies," *WP*, August 14, 1987.

60. "Overcrowding Reported in 34 District Schools," *ES*, October 16, 1952; "Corning Hopes to Hold Down Teacher Firing," *ES*, August 29, 1952; "School Board Asks Views on Integration," *WP*, December 18, 1952; Kluger, *Simple Justice*, 540; Minutes of the Board of Education, December 17, 1952, A-30-A-34, Sumner Museum.
61. Kluger, *Simple Justice*, 578–80.
62. Ibid., 702–7.
63. Ibid., 708.
64. Ibid.; "Ethel Meets Boy Made Immortal by U.S. Supreme Court Decision," *Chicago Defender*, May 29, 1954.
65. "D.C. Group Opened Case in Fall of '47," *AA*, May 18, 1954; "4 Years of Legal Work End in Victory for Two Colored Lawyers," *ES*, May 18, 1954.
66. "Ethel Meets Boy"; "D.C. Boy Helps Make History: 'We'll Get Better Schools Now,'" *WDN*, May 18, 1954.
67. "D.C. Parent Was Sure of Decision," *WAA*, May 18, 1954.
68. "Text of Dr. Corning's Proposal for Desegregation of D.C. Schools," *WP*, May 26, 1954.
69. "Corning's Step-by-Step Integration Voted, 5–1," *WP*, June 24, 1954; "Federation Asks Ban on Integration," *WP*, September 8, 1954; "Judge Refuses to Halt School Desegregation," *ES*, September 9, 1954.
70. Bell Clement, "The White Community's Dissent from 'Bolling,'" *WHHSWDC* 16 (Fall/Winter 2004–5): 100.
71. "Most D.C. Schools Have Integrated Classes," *WP*, September 16, 1954.
72. "Capital's Schools Begin Racial Integration Smoothly," *NYT*, September 14, 1954.
73. "District of Columbia," *Southern School News* (November 4, 1954): 4.
74. Ibid., 4–5; "Two Way Ultimatum Given to Pupils," *WP*, October 7, 1954; "Students' Return Pick Up Momentum," *WP*, October 8, 1954.
75. Gerald B. Boyd Sr., DP-ACM.
76. Dale, *Village that Shaped Us*, 43–44.
77. Oral history interview with Sheila Eileen Cogan, August 22, 2007, East of the River Continuity and Change Exhibit Collection, ACM.
78. Ibid.
79. Merriam-Webster Dictionary's definition of *white flight* is "the departure of whites from places (such as urban neighborhoods or schools) increasingly or predominantly populated by minorities," https://www.merriam-webster.com/dictionary/white%20flight; Myers and Musgrove, *Chocolate City*, 316; Wolters, *Burden of Brown*, 16; "Pupil

Desegregation Here Is 'Complete' Corning Announces," *WP*, October 31, 1957.

80. Gerald B. Boyd Sr., DP-ACM.

81. "Separate and Unequal: The State of the District of Columbia Public Schools Fifty Years After *Brown* and *Bolling*," a Parents for the D.C. Public Schools Civic Leader Advisory Committee Report, March 2005, unpublished report; Gerald B. Boyd Sr., DP-ACM.

Chapter 12

1. Program for twentieth-anniversary celebration of the Anacostia Business and Professional Association Inc., Sunday, November 16, 1969, DP-ACM, Box 3, Folder 16; "Hillsdale News," December 1951, DP-ACM, Box 16, Folder 19.

2. The Coordinating Committee of Anacostia and Vicinity honored yearly outstanding District of Columbia residents such as F. Joseph Donahue, commissioner of the District of Columbia, who was honored in 1952, AS-ACM, Box 18, Folder 4; "Charles Qualls, Civic Leader in SE, Dies at 72," *WP*, June 28, 1984. It is necessary to point out that already in the 1930s, a sport team organized in Barry Farm–Hillsdale was named the Anacostia ACs. Dale, *Village that Shaped Us*, 60, 64, 99.

3. Zora Martin-Felton and Gail S. Lowe, *A Different Drummer: John Kinard and the Anacostia Museum, 1967–1989* (Washington, D.C.: Anacostia Museum, 1993), 19–21.

4. "This Is Anacostia," *WP*, May 8, 1966.

5. District of Columbia, Communal Renewal Program, *Washington's Far Southeast 70: A Report to the Honorable Mayor Walter E. Washington, District of Columbia* (Washington, D.C., 1970), 1–4, plate 3.

6. Ibid., 23–28.

7. Ibid., 37; Arthur Morrissette, AOHP; "Arthur Morrissette, 82, Dies," *WP*, April 26, 1996.

8. "Statement of Community Problems," EC-ACM, Southeast Neighborhood House and Southeast Neighborhood Development Program, September 1968, Box 287.

9. William Raspberry, "Anacostia: Housing's 'City Dump,'" *WP*, June 19, 1968.

10. Table 8, Data on Elementary Schools in Far Southeast, 1969, and Table for Enrollment for Area 9 in *Washington's Far Southeast 70*.

11. Ethel G. Greene, AOHP; Almore Dale, AOHP; Historic American Buildings Survey (HABS), *Southwest Washington Urban Renewal Area*, HABS DC-856 (Washington, D.C.: Historic American Buildings Survey, National Park Service, U.S. Department of the Interior, 2004), 2, 116.

12. For details on the beginnings of Southeast House in Capitol Hill in the late 1920s until its opening in 1930, see Stephanie Ivette Felix, "African American Women in Social Reform, Welfare, and Activism: Southeast Settlement House, Washington, D.C., 1950–1970," MA thesis, University of Wisconsin, Madison, 1992, 27–33, and Anne M. Valk, "Separatism and Sisterhood: Race, Sex and Women's Activism in Washington, D.C., 1963–1980," PhD diss., Duke University, 1996, 109–10. Also informative is the oral interview of the founder of Southeast House, given in 1979 and published in 1991: "Interview with Dorothy Boulding Ferebee: December 28 and 31, 1979," in *The Black Women Oral History Project: From the Arthur and Elizabeth Schlesinger Library on the History of Women in America, Radcliffe College* 3, ed. Ruth Edmonds Hill (Westport, London: Meckler Publishing, 1991), 433–79.

13. Fertig, *Passion for Justice*, 111; Felix, "African American Women," 48.

14. "Relief Aides Sweetened for Work," *WP*, February 11, 1965. The first ten neighborhood organizers at the Southeast Settlement House were Bob Jackson, Alberta Johnson, Theresa Jones, Mary Kidd, Mary Manning, Otis Morgan, James Murphy, Bernice Rivers, Lois Wilson and William Wilson. John Kinard, Jerry Lowenstein and Eurie Purvis were hired as education aides. "First Anti-Poverty Workers Graduate at Southeast House," *WAA*, March 6, 1965.

15. "I Speak the Language of the Poor," *WAA*, June 11, 1966; "First Anti-Poverty Workers Graduate at Southeast House"; Felix, "African American Women," 55–56.

16. Mary Kidd, AOHP.

17. Valk, "Separatism and Sisterhood," 115; Joy G. Kinard, *The Man, the Movement, the Museum: The Journey of John R. Kinard as the First African American Director of a Smithsonian Institution Museum* (Washington, D.C.: A.P. Foundation Press, 2017).

18. "Proposed Guidelines for Direct Action for the Neighborhood Organizers in the Southeast Neighborhood Development Program, July 14, 1966," Ralph Fertig Papers, Box 2, University of Southern California Libraries, Specialized Research Collections, Los Angeles, California; Pharnal Longus, "Change in a Public Housing Development: A Case Study, Barry Farms," unpublished manuscript, 1978, 3–5, Dorothy Burlage

Papers, ACM (hereafter Burlage Papers, ACM); Valk, "Separatism and Sisterhood," 116–17.

19. *Washington's Far Southeast 70*, 90; U.S. Congress, Senate Committee on Banking and Currency, *FHA Investigation. Report of the Senate Committee on Banking and Currency, Eighty-fourth Congress, First Session, pursuant to S. Re. 229* (Washington, D.C.: Government Printing Office, 1955), 121. Melvin Schlosberg's name appears misspelled as "Flossburg"; Gwendolyn Wright, *Building the Dream: A Social History of Housing in America* (New York: Pantheon Books, 1981), 246.

20. *FHA Investigation*, 121; Wright, *Building the Dream*, 247; "The Loan Scandals," *TIME* (April 26, 1954), 22.

21. "Vandalism Closes 78 Apartments in Project," *ES*, May 27, 1967; "Tenant Co-op under Study," *ES*, July 17, 1967; "Parkchester Tenants Plan Low-Income Cooperative," *Southeast News*, September 1967; "Work Can Be Down Payment on Home," *ES*, October 9, 1967; "Builder's Report: Low-Income Co-op Set in Southeast," *ES*, October 13, 1967; "Anacostia Co-Op May Be a Model," *WP*, December 25, 1967; "Anacostia Apartments Taking on New Look," *ES*, April 15, 1968; Dorothy Burlage, "Community Organization and Social Change in Anacostia: 1966–1968," January 1972, Burlage Papers, ACM; *Washington's Far Southeast 70*, 90.

22. David Riley, "Report on the Howard Road Tenant Council," October 6, 1966, unpublished manuscript, Burlage Papers, ACM.

23. "Road Sketches: Hillsdale," *ES*, December 5, 1891; Riley, "Report on the Howard Road Tenant Council," 1–2.

24. Riley, "Report on the Howard Road Tenant Council," 1–2.

25. Felix, "African American Women," 59–60; U.S. Congress, Senate Committee on Government Operations, Subcommittee on Executive Reorganization, *Federal Role in Urban Affairs* (Washington, D.C.: Government Printing Office, 1967), 2,621 (hereafter *Federal Role in Urban Affairs*); Carol Williams, "Cleaning Up Washington Forgotten Backyard," *Communities in Action* 2 (1967): 4.

26. *Federal Role in Urban Affairs*, 2,623.

27. Riley, "Report on the Howard Road Tenant Council," 6.

28. Ibid., 17–19, 22–25.

29. "Irate Tenants Stage Sit-In to Get Gas Heat Instead of Coal Stoves," *WP*, October 25, 1966; "SE Tenants Resume War Over Heat," *WP*, October 29, 1966. On November 29, the owners of the Howard Road buildings advertised one-bedroom apartments with "automatic gas heat" for $69.50 per month, while apartments with "coal heat" were being

offered for $62.50, signaling a partial victory for the tenants; Williams, "Cleaning Up Washington Forgotten Backyard," 4–5.

30. *Federal Role in Urban Affairs*, 2,623.

31. "He Got Help, Now Gives It," *ES*, October 6, 1965; Longus, "Change in a Public Housing," 49.

32. Longus, "Change in a Public Housing," 6.

33. Ibid., 6; Burlage, "Community Organization and Social Change," 7, 16–18.

34. Longus, "Change in a Public Housing," 31–38.

35. The name of the women's group was probably taken from *Band of Angels*, a 1957 film starring Clark Gable, Yvonne de Carlo and Sidney Poitier. IMDb, *Band of Angels*, https://www.imdb.com/title/tt0050166.

36. In June 1966, Lillian Wright became a SEH neighborhood worker at Barry Farm Dwellings and Parkchester Cooperative. Felix, "African American Women," 60–61; "'Angels' from Barry Farms War on Public Housing Unit," *WP*, February 27, 1966; "Band of Angels, Rebels with a Cause, Give Housing Chief Tough Afternoon," *WP*, February 28, 1966; "Project Tenants Discuss Repair," *ES*, March 1, 1966; "Barry Farm Tenants Ask 'Say' About Money Spent on Homes," *WP*, March 1, 1966; Longus, "Change in a Public Housing," 43. Members of the group besides Lillian Wright, who lived on Stevens Road, included Rachel Lawrence, unit 1120; Mary Taylor, unit 1121; and Hattie Patterson, unit 1227.

37. Etta Mae Welch, U.S. Census 1930, Charlotte, Mecklenburg Company, North Carolina; Etta Mae Welch [Etta Mae Horn, Etta Prather], U.S. Social Security Applications and Claims Index, 1936–2007; marriage record of Etta Mae Welch with Joseph Xavier Horne, July 10, 1949, D.C. Marriage Records, 1810–1953, ancestry.com; Etta Horn interview with Mary Kotz, November 20, 1974, Tape 143, Nick Kotz Papers, Collection 1304A, State Historical Society of Wisconsin, Madison, Wisconsin; Anne M. Valk, *Radical Sisters: Second-Wave Feminism and Black Liberation in Washington, D.C.* (Urbana: University of Illinois Press, 2008), 38–39.

38. Horn interview, November 20, 1974; Felix, "African American Women," 61.

39. Valk, "Separatism and Sisterhood," 123.

40. IMDb, *Rebel without a Cause*, 1955, https://www.imdb.com/title/tt0048545; Fertig, *Passion for Justice*, 136; Burlage, "Community Organization and Social Change," 15; U.S. Congress, House Education and Labor Committee, *The Juvenile Delinquency Prevention Act of 1967, Hearings before the General Subcommittee on Education* (Washington, D.C.), 563.

41. "Barry Farm's 'Rebels with a Cause' Organize to Get Help for Project," *WP*, February 23, 1966; "'Rebels' Pledged Help for Their Cause," *WP*, February 26, 1966.

42. Fertig, *Passion for Justice*, 136; "Eartha Fascinates D.C. Youngsters," *WAA*, March 19, 1966.

43. Fertig, *Passion for Justice*, 136–37; Eartha Kitt, *Alone with Me* (Chicago: Henry Regnery Company, 1975), 238–39.

44. "'Rebels' Fight for Teen Role at Front in Poverty War," *ES*, March 18, 1966.

45. Valk, "Separatism and Sisterhood," 120, 135; *Juvenile Delinquency Prevention Act of 1967*, 560, 555.

46. "Neighborhood Development Youth Program—A Proposal for Youth Economic and Political Viability," unpublished and undated report, History of Place research files.

47. Gail Lowe, "Congress Heights: A Many-Layered Past," in *Washington at Home: An Illustrated History of Neighborhoods in the Nation's Capital*, ed. Kathryn Schneider Smith (Baltimore, MD: Johns Hopkins University Press, 2010): 338–39; Eddie Dean, "A Brief History of White People in Southeast: No Part of the District Was Hit Harder by White Flight than Southeast. But Some Whites Never Left," *Washington City Paper*, October 16, 1998, https://www.washingtoncitypaper.com/news/article/13016398/a-brief-history-of-white-people-in-southeast.

48. "Young Adults Pelt Stores with Rocks," *WP*, August 16, 1966; Our Redneck Past, "The Riot at the 1023 Club," http://ourredneckpast.blogspot.com/2011/02/riot-at-1023-club.html.

49. "Teen Gangs Attack Anacostia Police, Stone Cars, Buses," *ES*, August 16, 1966; "300 Rampage in SE," *WDN*, August 16, 1966; "Report of the Citizens Committee on 11th Precinct of District of Columbia Police Department," *U.S. Congressional Record*, 89th Congress, 2nd Session, v. 112, pt. 21, October 20, 1966, to October 22, 1966, 28,049 (hereafter "Report of Citizens Committee").

50. "Teen Gangs"; "300 Rampage"; "Probe Is Set to Violence in Anacostia," *WP*, August 17, 1966; "Report of Citizens Committee," 28,049–50.

51. "Report of Citizens Committee," 28,050; "'Police Dog' Is Now Negroes' Bad Word," *WP*, August 21, 1966.

52. "Report of Citizens Committee," 28,051–52.

53. "11th Precinct Gets Negro Captain," *ES*, August 22, 1966; "Top Negro Captain Is Put in Command in Tense Anacostia," *WP*, August 23, 1966; "Anacostia Wins Help from D.C. Officials; UPO Role Queried," *WP*, August

19, 1966; "Tobriner Sets 36-Member Committee to Investigate Monday's Disturbance," *WP*, August 19, 1966; "Report of Citizens Committee," 28,048; "Henry K. Willard, II (Age 92)," *WP*, December 30, 2018, https://www.legacy.com/obituaries/washingtonpost/obituary.aspx?n=henry-willard&pid=191119759; "Sterling Tucker, Civil Rights Leader and Pioneering D.C. Politician, Dies at 95," *WP*, July 17, 2019, https://www.washingtonpost.com/local/obituaries/Sterling-Tucker-civil-rights-leader-and-pioneering-D-C-politician-dies-at-95/2019/07/17/26d23342-a8bc-11e9-9214-246e594de5d5_story.html.

54. "Police and Demonstrators," *WP*, October 4, 1966; "Report of Citizens Committee," 28,053–54.

55. Mary Kidd, AOHP.

56. "Racist Carvings Adorn SE Stationhouse Benches," *WP*, January 25, 1967; Mary Kidd, AOHP.

57. "Racist Carvings"; "Cartoons, Epithets Reported Removed," *WP*, January 25, 1967. Max Robinson's documentary was awarded a Regional Emmy in 1967. We Buy Black, "Daily Dose of History: Max Robinson—News Anchor," https://webuyblack.com/blog/daily-dose-history-max-robinson-news-anchor.

58. "SNCC Leader Gives 'Black Power' Talk (by Dan Morgan)," U.S. Congress, *Congressional Record*, Proceedings of the 89th Congress, House, July 28, 1966, 17,538.

59. "SNCC Leader"; Stokely Carmichael with Ekweme Michael Thelwell, *Ready for Revolution: The Life and Struggles of Stokely Carmichael (Kwame Ture)* (New York: Scribner, 2003), 507.

60. Frederick Saunders, DP-ACM.

61. "Successor to Banks Risks Reputation," *WP*, May 19, 1967; Pharnal Longus, "Outline of a Study-Action Project in the Anacostia Area of Washington, D.C., September, 1966 to September, 1967," unpublished manuscript, History of Place research files.

62. "UPO Facing Major Challenges as Antipoverty Dreams Fade," *WP*, October 31, 1967; "D.C. Youth Corps Faces Slash in Jobs," *WP*, January 19, 1968; "Promise of '60s Faded: The Man Called Lamb Recalls Glory of Brief Period that Had a Future," *WP*, June 3, 1979.

63. "Chronological Report of Events Relating to Disorders within the Eleventh Precinct Beginning Thursday, April 4, 1968, Problems Encountered, Solutions Utilized and Recommendations," D.C. Public Library, Special Collections; Nancy Ciatti's father's store on Good Hope Road survived the initial disturbances on April 5 because somebody wrote

"Soul Brother" on its front window. But the business was burglarized a few weeks later. Nancy Ciatti, interview with Mara Cherkasky, May 22, 2012, cited by permission; Human Rights 2, FG 216, Situation Reports, U.S. Secret Service, April 5–9, 1968, White House Central Files, Lyndon B. Johnson Library and Museum, University of Texas–Austin; "Homegoing Service Celebrating the Life of Frances Mason Jones, February 10, 1916–March 8, 2002," DP-ACM, Box 16, Folder 6.
64. "A Comparison of Some Street Names in Anacostia (or Uniontown) D.C. as of 1887 and 1970," Box 7, Folder 24, AS-ACM; "Nichols Yields to King," *ES*, January 15, 1971.

Conclusion

1. The oral history project interviewed at least fifty-two people and covered the period from 1886 to 1975. "Center for Anacostia Studies: Changing an Image," *WP*, October 23, 1975; "The Center for Anacostia Studies of the Anacostia Neighborhood Museum Progress Report," UC-ACM, Box 128, Folder Research Department.

Selected Bibliography

Oral History Collections

Anacostia Oral History Project, ACM (AOHP).
Community Documentation Project, ACM.
Dale-Patterson Collection Oral Histories, ACM (DP-ACM).
Neighborhood Survey Oral History Collection, HSWDC (NSOHC).

Published Works

Amos, Alcione M., and Patricia Brown Savage. "Frances Eliza Hall: Postbellum Teacher in Washington, D.C." *WH-HSWDC* (Spring 2017): 43–54.

Anacostia Waterfront Trust. "The Anacostia in History." October 15, 2015. https://www.anacostiatrust.org/anacostia-trust/2015/10/15/the-anacostia-in-history.

Cantwell, Thomas J. "Anacostia Strength in Adversity." *RCHS* 49 (1973–74): 330–70.

Dale, Dianne. *The Village that Shaped Us*. Lanham, MD: Dale Publishing, 2011.

Fertig, Ralph D. *A Passion for Justice: One Man's Dedication to Civil Rights*. Pittsburgh, PA: Dorrance Publishing Company, 2018.

Hutchinson, Louise Daniel. *The Anacostia Story: 1608–1930*. Washington, D.C.: Smithsonian Press, 1977.

James, Portia. "The Most Pleasant and Healthful Place in All the Country." In *East of the River: Continuity and Change.* Edited by Gail S. Lowe. Washington, D.C.: Anacostia Community Museum, Smithsonian Institution, 2010.

Index

About the Author

Alcione M. Amos, currently a museum curator at the Smithsonian Institution Anacostia Community Museum in Washington, D.C., is originally from Brazil and has lived and worked in the United States for almost five decades. She received an MSLS from Catholic University in Washington, D.C. Ms. Amos worked as a researcher and librarian at the World Bank, Washington, D.C., for more than two decades while at the same time maintaining a career as an independent scholar. Her fields of interest include post-slavery societies such as those of the Black Seminoles and African Americans in Washington, D.C., after the Civil War, as well as Afro-Brazilians who moved to West Africa in the nineteenth century. She also has studied the Gullah communities of coastal Georgia and South Carolina. Ms. Amos has published in Africa, Brazil, the United States and Europe. Among other works, she has published two books: *The Black Seminoles: History of a Freedom Seeking People* and *Os Que Voltaram: A História dos Retornados Afro-Brasileiros na África Ocidental no Século XIX* (*Those Who Returned: The History of the Afro-Brazilian Returnees in West Africa in the 19ᵗʰ Century*). She has also curated two exhibits, "World Shout Song" (2010–11) and "How the Civil War Changed Washington" (2015), at the Smithsonian Institution Anacostia Community Museum. Her exhibit "Gullah Bahia África" (Portuguese version of "World Shout Song") was shown in Salvador, Bahia, and São Paulo, Brazil, in 2015.

Visit us at
www.historypress.com